THE FORGOTTEN AGE OF JUDAH

THE FORGOTTEN AGE OF JUDAH

The Untold Story of Grace
In the Second Temple Period

By

Dr. Douglas Hamp

Chris Winters Steinle

Foreword by John Haller

2026

The Forgotten Age of Judah
The Untold Story of Grace in the Second Temple Period
By Dr. Douglas Hamp and Chris Winters Steinle

Ordering Information:
Special discounts are available on quantity purchases by corporations, associations, educators, and others. Contact the publisher or distributor for details.

info@commonwealthofisrael.org

Commonwealth of Israel Foundation
P.O. Box 31007
Phoenix, AZ 85046

U.S. trade bookstores and wholesalers: Please contact the distributor.

"treacherous sister" was not, because "THE SCEPTER SHALL NOT DEPART FROM JUDAH" (Gen. 49:10; Num. 24:17; Psa. 2:6; 60:7; 72:8; 108:8; Isa. 42:1, 4) . . . but now a New Covenant, made in blood, has been made!

The peculiar commentary concerning Genesis 49:9-10 befuddles many who would dare exegete and/or commentate on this rich morsel of the Word of the Almighty . . . so, Moses would prophesy:

"9 Judah is a young lion—my son, you return from the prey. Like a lion, he crouches and lies down; like a lioness, who dares to rouse him? 10 The scepter will not depart from Judah, nor the staff from between his feet, until Shiloh comes and the allegiance of the nations is his.

The House of Ephraim (Acts 15:16-17; Amos 9:11-12) were once accorded to be the "Lord's helmet" . . . but the Scepter was in the hand in Judah--the Kingship, King David - the United Kingdom or Tabernacle of David. But what is this "Scepter will not depart from Judah . . . until Shiloh comes and the allegiance of the nations is his"?

May I suggest, commensurate with the splendid exegesis and commentary afforded to us by authors Hamp and Steinle that the ambiguous name of Shiloh (the closest meaning appears to be "tranquility" or "peace") finds its initial placement of the ark of the covenant and of the "Tabernacle in the Wilderness" - this "Tent of Meeting" to be found in Ephraim's Shiloh under Joshua's advisement/allocation--for he was of the Tribe of Ephraim and dwelt in his inheritance of the same tribal name with the Tent of Meeting--there for nigh 396 years. So the Lion of Judah (Gen. 49) finds an interesting connection "until Shiloh comes" and the "allegiance of the nations is His."

Indeed, the "Prince of Peace" - our Shiloh abides now in Ephraim--He has come . . . yet He wields His Scepter in the hand of the Lion of the Tribe of Judah. What you are about to both understand and become spiritually aware of is this mysterious connection between Shiloh and the Scepter - between Ephraim and Judah. This writing is a major theological blockbuster of the first order--if this doesn't excite us all UNTIL SHILOH COME . . . and the allegiance of the nations is His, then I'm not sure what else will! **—Doug Krieger**: Chair, Commonwealth of Israel Foundation; Editor-in-Chief, *Tribnet Publications.*

An oft-repeated claim in Christianity is that before Jesus died on the cross there was an Age of Law; and since the time of His resurrection, we have been in the Age of Grace. Authors such as Scofield and others claim that during the Age of Law, the Jews were doing their best to keep the Law, and in essence, to earn God's favor. However, what is grossly overlooked is that, according to Scripture, the nation of Judah already had God's favor.

During the first-temple era, the southern kingdom of Judah had a series of bad kings, starting with Solomon, who went after the Ba'alim and Ashtaroth. They were caught up in the heinous sin of sacrificing their children to the false gods and were committing spiritual adultery. In many respects, the problems of Judah at that time prefigured a pattern that is being repeated among the *ecclesia* of today. For Judah's sins, God sent Nebuchadnezzar who razed Jerusalem to the ground, destroyed the Temple, and carried many Jews to Babylon. For seventy years, they remained in exile until God's appointed time, when a remnant returned with God's full blessing and favor.

For roughly the next five centuries, the restored people of Judah (Jews), lived and prospered in their land. While there were many ups and downs politically, spiritually, and economically, they were zealous for God's laws. Indeed, the feast of Hanukkah is a celebration of the Maccabee's victory against the Seleucids (the Greeks) who under Antiochus IV outlawed the keeping of the Sabbath, circumcision of their children, and eating biblically clean food. The Jews of that age were so zealous for God that they would sooner be hacked into pieces than to forsake God's ways. Sadly, many suffered such a fate as recorded in the book of Maccabees.

It was during this era that a pronounced sense of Messianic hope took root like never before. The coming of the Promised One had always been in the pages of the Bible. But only in the second-temple era did it come into focus. Writings like the book of Enoch, the Testament of the Twelve Patriarchs, Jubilees, and more became popular, describing the Son of Man who would destroy the works of darkness.

Even more indicative of their Messianic zeal, in Sanhedrin 97 and other rabbinic texts some of the Rabbis deduced the approximate time when Messiah should appear. However, when the Messiah did appear, the leadership in Jerusalem failed to acknowledge and welcome Him; and repeatedly missed the signs right in front of them. Jesus said, "If I had not done among them the works which no one else did, they would have no sin; but now they have seen and also hated both Me and My Father" (John 15:24). To be clear, it was only after the leadership in Jerusalem, who held the national authority, officially rejected Jesus that Judah's Age of Grace came to an end.

In the *Forgotten Age of Judah: The Untold Story of Grace in the Second Temple Period,* Chris and Doug demonstrate the good standing that Judah enjoyed with God. Instead of the idea that the Jews were slavishly trying to keep the Law in order to obtain God's favor, the authors show that Judah already had that favor. This book will give you new insight into the covenantal standing of the Jews prior to Jesus' advent and how God intends to put things right once more at the end of the Age.

—John Haller, Esq., host of *John Haller's Prophecy Update.*

Preface

A person with a rare disease may go through extensive tests including x-rays, CAT scans, blood work, etc. to try to determine what is wrong. Only after the disease has been correctly diagnosed can the doctors prescribe the treatment. When we look at the history between Jews and the Church, there is obviously a debilitating disease at work. While early on there was some persecution of Christians at the hands of the Jews, the vast majority of this history has been marked with pogroms, the inquisition, and the holocaust. How could people who claimed to believe in the God of the Jews and follow a Jewish Messiah have such hatred toward the Jews themselves? The disease that we are speaking of does not show up in x-rays; and cannot be cured by using a scalpel. Rather, this disease is genetic; it is in the nucleus of much of our Christian theology.

Historical Christianity has, by and large, been built on the belief that the Jews were in bad standing with God before the coming of Jesus. For Replacement theology (Supersessionism), the time of Jesus' teaching and sacrifice was the point at which God broke off his relationship with the house of Judah (the Jews) and replaced this relationship with the Church, God's new Elect. Whereas for Dispensational theology, this was the point at which God put His relationship with the house of Judah on hold and started a new relationship with the Church during the "Age of Grace" (church age). In both theological systems, the Jews were stripped of their covenantal standing with God either permanently or for an indefinite period. The misidentification of Judah and its chosen status has led to aberrant theologies such as Calvinism (predestination) and its other extreme of Arminianism.

So, what is the diagnosis of the disease that has led to misunderstanding, distrust, and hatred? In a nutshell, mainstream Christianity has overlooked the covenantal good standing of Judah at the time of Christ because it has chosen to ignore God's dealing with the two houses of Israel. There is a forgotten age of Judah; and there is an untold story of grace in the second temple period that will provide the needed diagnosis, which will allow us to begin treatment. The treatment we are seeking will bring us to a fuller and deeper appreciation of God's love for His people; the meaning of the Old Covenant; the need for a new covenant, and what God had to do to heal the fractured relationship between Judah, Israel, and Himself.

CONTENTS

INTRODUCTION

"Father, forgive them, for they do not know what they do."
—Luke 23:34
"... But he who does not believe is condemned already, because
he has not believed in the name of the only begotten Son of God."
—John 3:18

How are these two proclamations to be reconciled? On the one hand, the Head of the Body (the Church) has forgiven His crucifiers. Dare, then, the Visible Church Militant oppose her sovereign? Yet, the Church has adamantly withheld the mercies of God from the Jews.

On the other hand, "He who has the Son has life; he who does not have the Son of God does not have life" (1 John 5:12). Aren't all those without the Son under condemnation?

The compatibility of these seemingly contradictory statements is found by discovering that the Bible speaks in both a national and individual context: One context concerning God's promises to National Israel, the other concerning the individual soul and eternal life.

Rightly dividing these precepts is not difficult, as will be demonstrated in the course of this volume. Nevertheless, Christian theologians from the second century forward have convoluted these distinctions so as to hold the Jews in constant contempt. The motives for this hostility toward the Jews by the Early Church will be addressed in the course of this book.

The challenge today is in overcoming the normalcy bias established by nearly 2,000 years of propaganda—supposedly based upon Scripture—that continues to pit Christian against Jew and Jew against Christian.

Figure 1. "My Wife and My Mother-in-Law"[1]

---

[1] My Wife and My Mother-in-Law"; Appears in Puck, v. 78, no. 2018 (1915 Nov. 6), p. 11.

https://commons.wikimedia.org/wiki/File:My_Wife_and_My_Mother-in-Law.jpg

Optic illusions are a good means by which to demonstrate the persistence of one's own perception. Perhaps the most famous illusion is the merged illustration of the young and old woman above. The viewer will fixate on the first impression that registers in the mind's eye. It then becomes difficult to notice a secondary image at all. When, in fact, two images can be clearly detected, as shown below.

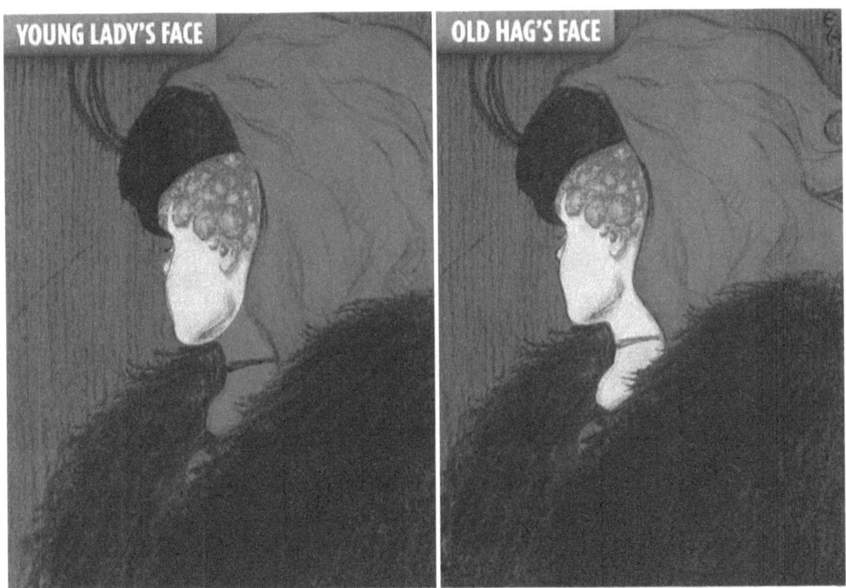

Figure 2. Courtesy, TheSun.UK:
https://www.thesun.co.uk/news/7307450/optical-illusion-young-or-old-woman-depends-on-age

And so it is with long held views on philosophy, politics, and our immediate focus—religion. Even though a more biblical comprehension of God's love for the House of Judah might be adequately outlined by the authors, time and personal study will likely be required for the reader to embrace an altogether new way to look at the Jews. This will take time; perhaps several years of reading through the Bible on one's own.

Figure 3 Obi-Wan-Kenobi

To quote an appropriate profundity uttered by the Star Wars character, Obi-Wan-Kenobi: "Luke, you are going to find that many of the truths we cling to depend greatly on our own point of view...The truth is often what we make of it..." Unfortunately, "the truth" regarding God's promises and relationship to the Jews has been, until now, what the rulers of empires have made of it. This accusation will be supported in subsequent chapters.

THE COVENANTAL STATUS OF JUDAH

What's so important about the House of Judah's covenant relationship with God? It is important because God used covenants to establish who, of all people on earth, would be His chosen people, His "Elect." And the integrity—the standing—of God's people within His covenants is what determines who remains chosen, and who is, in effect, cut off. In Hosea, God used the terminology, "My people," and "not My people." Understanding who is chosen becomes paramount when it comes to interpreting Bible prophecies about Israel. This issue of covenantal status is what separates Christians who believe the Church has taken the place of Israel (Supersessionists), and Christians who believe that God takes turns dealing with Gentiles and Jews (Dispensationalists). (For simplicity, we have used "Israel" and "Jews" interchangeably, but we will be more precise in the future.)

Both "Replacement" Theology and Dispensation Theology make the assumption that at the time of the cross, or shortly thereafter, God discontinued His relationship with the Jews and "favored" the Church instead. Not only does the Bible fail to support this assumption, the reader will discover that the Scriptures speak to the contrary. Although the errors of mainstream Christian thought are too complex to unpack in this introduction, the main fallacies about God's relationship with Judah stem from the following:

1. Ignoring the difference between the House of Israel and the House of Judah.
2. Applying verses about God's rejection of the Northern Kingdom (Israel) to the Jews.
3. Assuming that "all Israel" was cut off, rather than restored, by the New Covenant.
4. Assuming that Messiah's mission had to do with choosing/favoring a new group of people and forsaking those whom He foreknew.

In the body of this book, it will be handily demonstrated from Scripture that the House of Judah was in good covenantal standing during the Second Temple period because of the Davidic Covenant. Presuming, at this point in our introduction, that Judah does indeed continue through the Second Temple period under covenant, consider how strange and mysterious the assertions of mainline Christianity really are:

Imagine that you are a first century Jew who keeps the Law and walks in fellowship with God—a Jew "inwardly" as Paul says: "of the heart, in the Spirit, not in the letter; whose praise is not from men but from God" (Rom. 2:29). Imagine also that you—as the men of Ephesus (Acts 19) some 20-30 years after the fact—had only heard about John the Baptist and had no knowledge of Jesus' ministry or of His crucifixion. Now, just because the Jewish leaders had rejected Christ, would the godly Jew in our example suddenly, at the time of the cross, sense that fellowship with God had ceased? That his obedience had become irrelevant? That he was no longer pleasing to God? That he was no longer chosen? As if some remote switch had been turned off on God's end? Yet this is the very scenario presented by both Replacement and Dispensation theologies—that God's election was either permanently terminated, or put on hold until after the "Church Age," regardless of God's covenants and promises.

This apropos illustration does in fact frame the eschatology and Israelology of both Catholic/Orthodox/Reformed, and Dispensation/Evangelical theologies. It is all about their assumptions regarding the place and the future—if any—of the Jews. In order to begin to correct this erroneous doctrine in the mind of the reader it is necessary to address some common Bible interpretation errors. These will be explained in more detail throughout the book. **Disregarding the Bible's robust saga of the two houses of Israel is by far the greatest failing in the study of Israelology.** The average Christian reader may not even recognize the terminology: the "House of Israel" and the "House of Judah." Why is it important to distinguish between the two houses—the Northern Kingdom called "Israel" and Southern Kingdom called "Judah?" Because the covenantal status of each house is unique; and any hope of understanding God's relationship with the Jewish House is obscured without paying close attention to what God had to say about the two kingdoms.

For the reader who is new to Commonwealth Theology, an overview of the two houses of Israel is provided in this book. Moreover, the purpose of this writing is not to fit an examination of the Jewish House into the context of Commonwealth Theology; but rather, to address the spiritual status of the Jews and the shortcomings of mainline Christian assumptions about the place of the Jews within God's plan for the Age.

The reader who has been following the research and literature of the Commonwealth of Israel Foundation has already been well educated regarding the plight and redemption of the House of Israel—the scattered Northern Kingdom of Israel. The House of Israel is central to Commonwealth Theology in that it explains God's making "a people who were not a people," and is germane to the inclusion of "the rest of mankind" in repairing David's fallen tent according to Acts Ch. 15.

Dr. Hamp will provide a more complete study of the two houses in his chapter, "Recognizing the Two Houses of Israel." At this juncture, mention must be made that the Northern Kingdom—aka Ephraim, Jezreel, or simply "Israel"—has also been the object of its own theological inversion. The common modern-day assumption is that the House of Israel rejoined and fused with the Jews sometime before Judah's Babylonian captivity. This, however, is not the reality according Early Judaic and Christian sources.

According to the *Epistula ad Africanum,* whose authorship has been ascribed to Origin but which nevertheless dates to the second or first century, B.C.:

"... the Romans only take account of **two tribes**, while at that time **besides Judah there were the ten tribes of Israel**. Probably the Assyrians contented themselves with holding them in subjection..."[2]

This quote shows that the House of Israel was assumed to have remained under the control of their Assyrian captors at least until the immediate centuries before Christ. The Romans, who had established a peace treaty with Judea in the time of the Maccabees, could only account for the two tribes, Judah and Benjamin—the House of Judah. The House of Israel could not be accounted for at that time, and only a conjecture could be made as to their whereabouts. The book of 4 Ezra/2 Esdras, commonly dated to the first century A.D., expresses the early Jewish understanding of the unlocated (lost) of the Ten Tribes:

"These are the **ten tribes** that were taken captive from their land in the days of King Hoshea, whom King Shalmaneser of the Assyrians took across the river as a captive. They were taken into another land, but they made this plan for themselves: They

---

[2] Origin, *Epistula ad Africanum*, Sec. 14. jewishencyclopedia.com
https://jewishencyclopedia.com/articles/14126-susanna-the-history-ofOne.

would leave the **multitude of the nations** and go into a more remote region, where the human race had never lived… They made a long journey through that region for a year and a half... They lived there until the last time, and now they begin again to return" (Excerpts 4 Ezra 13:40-48 CEV).

Two things must be noted about this Ezra quotation: First, although the passage is only describing a vision, such an account of the Ten Tribes would never have been proposed if any true location of the House of Israel had been known at the time the vision was composed. Secondly, the "gathering" from the multitude of the nations (an allusion to Gen 48:19), mentioned in the final verse, was not anticipated "until the last time,"—the end of the Age—, and, therefore, no officially recognized gathering of the Ten Tribes had previously occurred.

Consistent with the above sources, the Bible and other early writings convey the fact that the Ten Tribes were indeed swallowed up by the Nations. Emil Schürer, in his five-volume work, *A History of the Jewish People at the Time of Christ*, states: **"The 'ten tribes' never returned at all from captivity**, and **even in the times of Akiba there were disputes**[3] **as to whether they would ever do so."**[4] Correcting the popular narrative regarding the House of Israel remains a primary objective of the Commonwealth Theology community. This book, however, turns its attention to the House of Judah and its continuation under the Davidic promises: "Yet I will have mercy on the house of Judah" (Hosea 1:7).

Our study will reinforce the biblical record: that the Jewish House—after 70 years of chastening under Babylonian captivity—was forgiven and returned to the Land with God's full blessing. This age of national "good graces" (Zech. 4:7) prevailed through the onset of the Messianic Age. Thus, the appropriateness of Jesus' pronouncement:

"If I had not come and spoken to them, **they would have no sin…**" (John 15:22, Emphasis added). This recognition of absolution only conforms to Christian doctrine when it is applied on the national level,

---

[3] Sanhedrin X. 3, fin. : "The ten tribes never return, for it is said of them (Deut. xxix. 27) : He will cast them into another land, as it is this day. As then this day departs and never returns, so too are they to depart and never return. As the day becomes dark and then again light, so will it one day be light again to the ten tribes with whom it was dark."

[4] Schürer, Div. 2, Vol. 2, p. 223. See also Josephus. *Antt.* xi. 5. 2. 4

as will be further expounded. As previously stated, mainstream Christianity has overlooked the covenantal good standing of Judah at the time of Christ because it has chosen to ignore God's dealing with the two houses of Israel. Theologians have conflated Bible passages regarding the divorce of the Northern Kingdom (e.g., Hos. 1:6; 2:2; Jer. 3:1, 8) with passages speaking of God's continued relationship with Judah. These homogenous interpretations have superimposed the picture of the House of Israel's estrangement, overshadowing God's affirmations of the Promises to the Fathers extended toward Judah.

This confusion has been compounded by Bible expositors who have used the names, "Israel" and "Jews," interchangeably. To be fair, in modern day vernacular Israel is assumed to be the nation-state of the Jews. And in a broader sense, because the House of Israel's identity was lost when the people of the Northern Kingdom were assimilated into foreign lands, "Israel" was, and continues to be, used to denote *what is left*, that can be easily identified, of both houses; that being the House of Judah—the Jews. But often the Bible is specific when referring to "Israel"—those belonging to the House of Israel and to "Jews"—those belonging to the House of Judah. Mainline theologians have disregarded these distinctions because the two houses don't factor into their doctrinal narratives.

Recognizing the true national standing of Judah during the Second Temple Period helps in understanding the readiness of the God-fearing Jews of the first century to embrace the good news of the gospel. Devout Jews at the time of Christ were already "holding on to faith and a good conscience" (1 Tim. 1:19). Many were wholly open to—even anticipating—the arrival of their Messiah. It was first to such Jews in good standing to whom the gospel was preached, "then to the Gentile." The House of Judah was by far the largest contingency of the early first-century Congregation of Christ—familiarly translated, "Church."

The fact that it was the members of the House of Judah, which were "in good graces" with God, who were finding redemption through the cross, eventually invoked the question as to whether anyone belonging to the rejected House of Israel—now mixed with the Nations—could possibly be saved! This was the very question under consideration by the first, informal, council at Jerusalem, wherein Peter defended his successful outreach to the God-fearers among the Gentiles. Only through the miracles of the appearance of an angel and the outpouring of the gift of tongues were the Apostles convinced: "Then God has also granted to the Gentiles (Nations) repentance to life." Until then, Jesus' Jewish Congregation did not believe that God had chosen *any* Gentiles to be "His people."

However, did the reality of Judah's favor become inverted, so that today it seems most natural for non-Jews to find salvation in Christ? Whereas, the Jews are perceived by believers from the Nations to be under condemnation and alienated from God—and somehow, to a greater extent than the non-Jew? (Thus, the optic illusion presented in Figure 1 above.) Furthermore, this false perception is starkly incompatible with Commonwealth Theology and with the Scriptures themselves, which insists it was the Gentiles—rather than the Jews— who were "aliens from the commonwealth of Israel and strangers from the covenants of promise, having no hope and without God in the world" (Eph. 2:12).

In light of this acknowledgment—this rediscovery—of Judah's covenant relationship, it is equally important to recognize that the Jews' knowledge of God and individual righteousness could not be made complete apart from Christ. As stated in the opening verses of the letter, "To the Hebrews," God revealed Himself through the Prophets, but the full revelation of the Godhead was not available until the incarnation of the Son of God. Likewise, the Law could not perfect the soul. Neither, could it generate a "new creation," nor give birth through the Spirit to an eternal life.

It is needful in this introduction to stress the distinction between national covenantal standing and the salvation found through the New Covenant in Yeshua's blood. Antagonists to the authors' assertion of Judah's good standing will undoubtedly bring an accusation of "Dual Covenant Theology." So, let's set the facts in order. There is only one New Covenant that concerns both the House of Israel and the House of Judah (Jer. 31:31). This new covenant, we solemnly believe and teach, is the same new covenant proclaimed in the Upper Room and memorialized in the book of Hebrews; and is, therefore, also God's covenant by which the Nations are saved.

The covenant of primary importance in discussing the difference between the standing (election) of Judah and the standing of Israel is, "the covenant that I made with their fathers in the day that I took them by the hand to lead them out of the land of Egypt, My covenant which they broke…" (Jer. 31:32). This covenant, often referred to as the Sinaitic Covenant, is the covenant of interest. Why? Not because God made two covenants—a dual covenant—, that is, one with ten tribes (who would become the tribes of the north), and the other with Judah (Benjamin and some Levites included). But rather because **God determined to treat the offenses of the two houses differently**. God pronounced the House of Israel, "not My people." And "though I was a husband to them," God divorced the Northern Kingdom. Yet God, responding specifically to His oath to perpetuate the kingdom and throne of David; and, because of His love for Jerusalem—where He had established His name—, God extended His mercy and grace to the House of Judah. Not because of anything they had done, not by works; but because of His sovereign will: "I will have mercy on whomever I will have mercy, and I will have compassion on whomever I will have compassion" (Rom. 9:15).

While affirming the surpassing grace bestowed through Messiah, **this book seeks to encourage a long overdue epiphany by recognizing—rather than denying—the "richness of the olive tree" through which the Nations have become partakers (Rom. 11:17).** Invoking this epiphany will require drawing the reader's mind's eye away from the broadly accepted image of Judah's impaired spiritual condition, then refocusing on the biblical record of Judah's divine relationship up through the Second Temple Period—a covenant relationship with National Judah that was fully intact at Christ's first appearing.

A forensic investigation of Judah's covenantal standing is demanded at what appears (to many) to be the close of this Age, in order to right the wrong theological assumptions that have for too long undergirded prejudice, hostility, and despicable acts. The hope is that hostility and ostracism might finally cease and give way to Messiah's finished workmanship: "For He Himself is our peace, who has made both one, and has broken down the middle wall of separation, having abolished in His flesh the enmity, that is, the law of commandments contained in ordinances, so as to create in Himself one new man from the two, thus making peace" (Eph. 2:14-15).

The nuances of this peace among the constituents of the Commonwealth are beyond the scope of this book, but such interrelationships are discussed in detail in *Commonwealth Theology*

Essentials. Ultimately, peace and unity is the destiny of the two houses. For we see that both houses exist and are brought together under one head in Ezekiel's prophecy of the Two Sticks. Note: in the passage that follows, the "tribes of Israel" are distinct from Judah and therefore represent the Ten Tribes of the House of Israel, and Judah represents the House of Judah:

Again, the word of the Lord came to me, saying, "As for you, son of man, take a stick for yourself and write on it: 'For Judah and for the children of Israel, his companions.' Then take another stick and write on it, 'For **Joseph, the stick of Ephraim, and for all the house of Israel**, his companions.' Then **join them one to another** for yourself into one stick, and they will become one in your hand.

"And when the children of your people speak to you, saying, 'Will you not show us what you mean by these?'—say to them, 'Thus says the Lord God: "Surely I will take the stick of Joseph, which is in the hand of Ephraim, and the **tribes of Israel**, his companions; and I will join them with it, with the **stick of Judah**, and make them one stick, and they will be one in My hand." ' And the sticks on which you write will be in your hand before their eyes.

"Then say to them, 'Thus says the Lord God: "Surely I will take the children of Israel from among the nations, wherever they have gone, and will gather them from every side and bring them into their own land; and I will make them one nation in the land, on the mountains of Israel; and one king shall be king over them all; **they shall no longer be two nations**, nor shall they ever be divided into two kingdoms again. They shall not defile themselves anymore with their idols, nor with their detestable things, nor with any of their transgressions; but I will deliver them from all their dwelling places in which they have sinned, and will cleanse them. Then they shall be My people, and I will be their God.

"David My servant shall be king over them, and they shall all have one shepherd; they shall also walk in My judgments and observe My statutes, and do them. Then they shall dwell in the land that I have given to Jacob My servant, where your fathers dwelt; and they shall dwell there, they, their children, and their children's children, forever; and My servant David shall be their prince forever. Moreover, I will make a covenant of peace with them, and it shall be an everlasting covenant with them; I will establish them and multiply them, and I will set My sanctuary in their midst forevermore. My tabernacle also shall be with them; indeed, I will be their God, and they shall be My people. The nations also will know that I, the Lord, sanctify Israel, when My sanctuary is in their midst forevermore" (Ezek. 37:15-28, Emphasis added).

Now consider that the unifying work of Yeshua, the son of David, involves the same entities in Ephesians 2 and Ezekiel 37. Certainly, those from the resurrected House of Israel will be in that number, as well as those who have been grafted in (Rom. 11:24)—addressed in Ephesians as "you Gentiles," those "far off" in distant nations. And Judah is expressly named in both passages and further alluded to in Ephesians as those "near." Daniel employed this same language in his great petitionary prayer

> "O Lord, righteousness belongs to You, but to us shame of face, as it is this day–to the **men of Judah,** to the inhabitants of Jerusalem and all Israel, those **near** and those **far off** in all the countries to which You have driven them, because of the unfaithfulness which they have committed against You (Dan. 9:7).

MAINSTREAM CHRISTIANITY'S VIEW OF JUDAH

Knowing, then, God's ultimate plan for the Commonwealth, it becomes evident that neither Replacement Theology (RT) nor Dispensation Theology (DT) can accommodate God's simultaneous embrace of these discrete members: RT recognizing but one surviving entity; and, DT contending that God has determined to deal with only one party at a time.

Commonwealth Theology, on the other hand, recognizes God's Ultimate Ekklesia. The Commonwealth of Israel Foundation, moreover, anticipates God's peace plan; and strives for the portended unity between Christians and Jews. It is the hope among a growing band of likeminded brethren—having the prophesied United Kingdom of David in view—that the future perfect peace between Christians and Jews might be approximated now, not waiting for a supernatural change of heart at the climax of the Age. The normative Christian view—the delusion up until now—has embodied the antithesis of such hope, even falling fathoms short of the admonition of loving and praying for one's perceived enemies.

Although the balance of this book is based on the historical record preceding and throughout the time of the Second Temple, the motivation for our study is made crystal clear by observing the conclusions of mainline theologies. The two main camps of Christianity, which we will group under the banners of "Catholicism" and "Protestantism," both harbor anti-Semitic elements. The former—along with Reformed Protestants—bears a history of blatant anti-Semitism; the latter, especially Dispensationalists, manage to segregate the Jews from the Church by more subtle means.

JUDAH WITHIN REPLACEMENT THEOLOGY

The attitude of the Catholics toward the Jews is well represented by the following entry under "Church" in the 1913 Catholic Encyclopedia:

> "When it is asked what is this kingdom of which Christ spoke, there can be but one answer. It is His Church . . . He organizes it and appoints rulers over it, establishes rites and ceremonies in it, **transfers** to it the name which had hitherto designated the **Jewish** Church, and solemnly warns the Jews **that the kingdom was no longer theirs, but had been taken from them and given to another people.**"[5]

This encyclopedic entry captures the essence of Supersessionism, in which it is supposed that the Church has replaced Ancient Israel; and, as the entry implies, this doctrine is aptly called "Replacement Theology." Although the above citation is not an official pronouncement by the Catholic Church, its sentiment and conclusion are far from being a theological outlier. For hundreds of years—dated by artifacts as far back as 870 A.D.[6]—Europe has celebrated the triumph over, and humiliation of, the Jews. The European churches merely carry the torch of the anti-Semitic attitude memorialized by the Romans in the Arch of Titus.

---

[5] *The Catholic Encyclopedia*, Charles George Herbermann, Gilmary Society, 1913 "Church"; Vol.3, p. 746.

[6] See: Ivory relief panels for book covers of the Crucifixion. Nina Rowe, *The Jew, the Cathedral and the Medieval City: Synagoga and Ecclesia in the Thirteenth Century*, 2011, Cambridge University Press, pp. 52, 57-59.

Figure 4 The Arch of Titus. Built on Rome's Via Sacra, the "Sacred Road," around 82 CE, the Arch of Titus features sculptural reliefs depicting Titus's triumphal procession into the Eternal City in July, 71 CE. Painfully for Jews, the sacred vessels of the Jerusalem Temple are shown being carried into Rome by victorious Roman soldiers. At the center of the representation of the Spoils of Jerusalem is the seven-branched golden menorah, which, since 1949, has been used as the emblem of the State of Israel.[7]

---

[7] Center for Jewish History: The Arch of Titus.
https://www.cjh.org/visit/exhibitions/the-arch-of-titus

Figure 5 Ecclesia and Synagoga from the portal of Strasbourg Cathedral, now in the museum and replaced by replicas.[8]

Images and statues of the two women, Ekklesia and Synagoga, representing the Christian Church and the Jewish Synagogue, have been featured on cathedrals and literature throughout Europe for more than a millennium. As in Figure 5 (above), Ecclesia typically faces forward and wears a crown. She usually holds a chalice and a staff with a cross. Synagoga is blindfolded and looks downward. She carries a broken lance, thought possibly to symbolize the lance used to pierce Jesus' side. The tablets of the Law appear to be slipping from her hand.[9] Sometimes Synagoga carries a sheep or goat or just its head, which signifies the sacrifices of the Old Testament.[10]

Figure 6 Cathédrale de Chartres, Canon of the Mass : Te igitur Initial T: Ecclesia and Synagoga

---

[9] Michael, Robert, A History of Catholic Antisemitism: The Dark Side of the Church, 2008, Macmillan, p. 42.

[10] Schiller, Gertud, Iconography of Christian Art, (English trans from German), Lund Humphries, London, Vol. II, 1971, p. 112.

In the Canon of the Mass: Te igitur Initial T. Ecclesia and Synagoga (Figure 6), Synagoga, unusually placed on the left, stands with bowed head, holding a broken lance. She is blindfolded and her crown is being removed by Ecclesia, who is crowned and carries a chalice.[11]

It is said that history repeats itself; so, here we must note the haunting historical fact that it was not the Romans who first ransacked Jerusalem and claimed victory over the Jews:

> "So Joash king of Israel went out; and he and Amaziah king of Judah faced one another at Beth Shemesh, which belongs to Judah. And Judah was defeated by Israel, and every man fled to his tent. Then Joash the king of Israel captured Amaziah king of Judah, the son of Joash, the son of Jehoahaz, at Beth Shemesh; and he brought him to Jerusalem, and broke down the wall of Jerusalem from the Gate of Ephraim to the Corner Gate—four hundred cubits. And he took all the gold and silver, all the articles that were found in the house of God with Obed-Edom, the treasures of the king's house, and hostages, and returned to Samaria" (2 Chron. 25:21-24).

How horrific it is to find the Church—representative of the House of Israel among the Nations—celebrating the conquest over the Jewish House: that house which, for the sake of David's lineage, God had sworn unrelentingly to preserve. Now, as it were, reenacting the House of Israel's conquest of Judah, the Church has not hesitated to "touch God's anointed."

---

[11] Cathédrale de Chartres, Canon of the Mass : Te igitur Initial T: Ecclesia and Synagoga; early 13th c. Identifier FCMO144F71V1. Ecclesia and Synagoga are also shown at Chartres Cathedral in the Passion Typological Window (Delaporte no. 59, Deremble-Manhes no. 37) and there may have been statues of them on the jambs of north transept east portal.

Figure 7 "Synagoga and Ecclesia in Our Time" by Joshua Koffman.[12]

In 2015, Pope Francis gave his blessing over the statue (above) produced by Saint Joseph's University in honor of the 50th anniversary of the Second Vatican Council declaration, Nostra Aetate (Latin for "In Our Time"). That 1965 statement repudiated centuries of Christian claims that Jews were blind enemies of God whose spiritual life was obsolete. The document called instead for friendship and dialogue between Catholics and Jews. Shortly after, what was then Saint Joseph's College became the first American Catholic college to respond to this appeal by establishing the Institute for Jewish-Catholic Relations.[13] Below is a statement made by Pope Francis prior to the creation of the statue:

---

[12] https://commons.wikimedia.org/wiki/File:Synagoga_and_Ecclesia_in_Our_Time.jpg
[13] https://www.sju.edu/news/sju-announces-details-sculpture-mark-50-years-new-catholic-jewish-relationship.

"We hold the Jewish people in special regard because their covenant with God has never been revoked, for "the gifts and the call of God are irrevocable" (Rom. 11:29). … Dialogue and friendship with the children of Israel are part of the life of Jesus' disciples. The friendship which has grown between us makes us bitterly and sincerely regret the terrible persecutions which they have endured, and continue to endure, especially those that have involved Christians. God continues to work among the people of the Old Covenant and to bring forth treasures of wisdom which flow from their encounter with his word. For this reason, the Church also is enriched when she receives the values of Judaism"—Pope Francis, Evangelii Gaudium, §247-249.

There are, nevertheless, a few deficiencies in the pope's statement:

1. This reconciliation was born out of regret rather than from love.
2. It was a response to a worldwide movement, which continues today, to end social injustice.
3. The statement provokes the notion of a Dual Covenant in regards to salvation.
4. It does nothing to explain how the Church and the Jews became divided and hostile to one another—their history.

Thus, the value of *The Forgotten Age of Judah*, which touches upon the history of this contention; and, most thoroughly details the biblical theology explaining exactly why there should not only be peace, but love between Christians and Jews.

JUDAH WITHIN DISPENSATION THEOLOGY

Much credit must be given to Dispensation Theology, in general, for affecting a radical change in Christian attitude toward the Jews. Shortly after the Reformation, some Protestant Christians embraced the notion that the Second Coming of Christ could be ushered in by the conversion of the Jews to the Christian faith. This movement for the conversion of the Jews was perhaps based on the *Restoration* spoken of by St. Peter in Acts 3:19-21; *"Repent therefore and be converted, that your sins may be blotted out, so that times of refreshing may come from the presence of the Lord, and that He may send Jesus Christ, who was preached to you before, whom heaven must receive until the times of restoration of all things, which God has spoken by the mouth of all His holy prophets since the world began."*

The hope was that if the Jews could be persuaded to return to the Holy Land, the Spirit of God would surely fall on them; and, consequently, they would *"look upon Him whom they pierced"* unto repentance and place faith in Jesus as their Messiah. Thus, the "Jewish Restorationists" drew a connection between the salvation of the Jews and the *"restoration of all things."*

In 1809, the *London Society for Promoting Christianity Amongst the Jews* was established and even set up a ministry in Jerusalem. A similar society was established by the churches in Scotland, which sponsored an expedition to inquire of the condition of the Palestinian Jews and their readiness to receive the gospel. There they found a few thousand Jews who had mostly struggled in poverty under the rule of the Ottomans (and later the Egyptians). Some had lived in the Land for several generations, but many had traveled there in their old age to die and to be buried in their sacred soil.

Upon returning from Palestine, the Scottish explorers, led by the Reverends Robert McCheyne and Andrew Bonar, published their findings in the *Narrative of a Visit to the Holy Land and Mission of Inquiry to the Jews*. Shortly after the Scottish expedition, the Zionist Movement in England, led by Anthony Ashley-Cooper (7th Earl of Shaftesbury), became so influential that the following article was published in-full on the front page of the *Colonial Times*.

Colonial Times, Feb. 23, 1841

The following is a transcription of the full article. We added emphasis to help point out some of the key points.

COLONIAL TIMES [Vol. 29] Tuesday, February 23, 1841

Memorandum,

To the Protestant Powers of the North of Europe and America, - Victoria by the grace of God, Queen of Great Britain and Ireland, Frederick, (William) III, King of Prussia; William (Frederick) (Frederich), King of the Netherlands; Charles (John) XIV, King of Sweden and Norway: Frederick VI., King of Denmark; Ernest Augustus, King of Hanover; William, King of Württemberg; the Sovereign Princes and Electors of Germany; the Cantons of the Swiss Confederation professing the Reformed Religion; and the States of North America, zealous for the glory of God; grace, mercy, and peace from God the Father, and the Lord Jesus Christ,

High and Mighty Ones,

The Most High God, who reigns in the kingdoms of men (Dan. iv, 32), by whom kings reign and princes decree justice (Prov. viii. 15), having in these days granted a season of repose to his witnessing church (Acts ix. 31, Rev. xii. 16), planted in the lands whereof ye are kings and governors (Isaiah xlix. 23); the vine of his planting among the **Gentiles** (Acts xxviii. 28) hath extended her boughs unto the seas and her branches unto the rivers (Isaiah xlix. 6), that now in nearly all the world the gospel of the kingdom is being lifted up as a witness unto all nations (Matt. xxiv. 14), and in the **isles afar off.** The days are drawing near (Rev. xxiii. 20) when the dominion, and the glory, and the kingdom, with all people, nations and languages, shall serve Him who cometh in the clouds of heaven (Dan. vii. 14, Rev. i. 7), whose dominion is an everlasting dominion, and kingdom that which shall not be destroyed (Psalm xlv. 6), Blessed be He! He hath given him waiting people to hear the sound of His approaching footstep, and to mark the signs of His drawing near (1 Thess. v. 4). The fig-tree putteth forth her leaves again (Matt. xxvi. 32). Israel's sons are asking the way to Zion, by which we know that the summer is at hand. Blessed are all they that wait (2 Thess. iii. 5) and hold fast (Rev. iii. 11), for quickly He cometh. Amen.

In the prospect of the Christian church, of the speedy appearing of her glorified head, the zeal of the Lord's servants hath been stirred up (Rev. iii. 2), when the Son of God, as a man taking a journey into a far country, bade his servants occupy until he returned again (Luke xix. 13). With other responsibilities, the circumstances of one peculiar people, whom the Most High hath separated (Gen. iii, 7, Exod. xxxiv. 7), and which covenant no act of theirs, however iniquitous and rebellious, can repeal or destroy (Mal. iii. 6) whom He hath scattered in all lands as witnesses of His unity and power (Isa. xliii. 19) connected with whom the welfare of mankind is bound up, and in the lifting up of whose head the most stupendous consequences are made to depend (Rom. xi. 15) are presented at this eleventh hour for the repentance and faith of Christendom, that the blood of our brethren of the circumcision which has been unjustly shed may be atoned for in the blood of the Lamb (Matt. iii. 8) in presenting the children of this people continually at the throne of grace (1 Pet. ii. 5., Ps. cxxii. 6) for the atoning sacrifice of Christ to cover them (Joel. ii. 17); and as the Almighty, in His providential appointments, shall make the way plain to present the children of Israel who may be willing to go up as an offering to the Lord of Hosts in Mount Zion (Isa. xviii. 7.)

For 300 years the testimony of the churches, planted in the lands over which Almighty God hath made you rulers, hath been lifted up against that apostasy which usurped the authority of the Lord Jesus Christ in the earth (Rev. xvii. 5, and Rev. xviii. 5) daring presumptuously to assert power over nations (Rev. xviii. 7) and over kingdoms, to root up and to pull down, to build, to plant, and to destroy (Dan. vii. 20, Rev. xiii. 2, 7). The millstone which shall sink the Great Babylon in the abyss of an unfathomable perdition (Rev. xviii. 21) when her hour arrives (and it is very near!), with the judgment under which she hath long lain, for being drunken with the blood of the saints and of the martyrs of Jesus (Rev. xvii., 6) shall include the avenging of the wrongs of God's ancient people (Isa. li. 22, 23) and a terrible account it is; and the issue shall be joy and gladness to the whole earth, for it is written, "Rejoice, O ye nations, with His people: for He avengeth the blood of His servant, and shall render vengeance unto His adversaries, and **will be merciful to His land, and His people.**" (Deut. xxxii. 43). "Happy art thou, O **Israel**; who is like unto thee, O people saved by the Lord, the shield of thy help and the sword of thy excellence; and thine enemies shall be found liars unto thee, and thou shalt tread on their high places." (Deut. xxxiii. 29.)

In the events on which the eyes of nations are fixed, taking place around, whilst the continuance and stability of your thrones and sway, O kings, is the earnest prayer of the Christian church (1 Tim. ii. 2) she cannot but uphold the witness that the days draw nigh, when, under the hallowed sway of Messiah the Prince, **the now despised nation of the Jews shall possess the kingdom** (Dan. vii. 27) and she directs, with reverential awe, your eye to that mighty empire in the east which is crumbling to the dust , and drying up in all her streams (Rev. xvi. 12) to make way for the event. Palestine hath been a burdensome stone (Zech. xii. 2) unto the followers of the false Prophet (Rev. xvi. 13) as it was to the ancestors of many of you, O Princes, when, under the banners of the Popish Antichrist, their mistaken zeal sought to recover the Holy City from the Saracen's grasp. But the fullness of the Gentiles is at hand (Rom. xi. 21) and unto Israel the dominion shall return. (Micah iv. 8.)

The apostate Julian sought to plant the children of this people in the seats of their fathers, in despite of that holy faith, one of the external evidences of whose truth was, that their house was left unto them desolate, until they should say, **"Blessed is he that cometh in the name of the Lord"** (Matt. xxiii., 38,39). But is it anywhere declared in the word of our God, that the children of Israel, scattered and pealed, humbled, and dispirited, impoverished and broken down, should not be presented as an offering in faith to Jehovah of Hosts in Mount Zion, that there their fathers (Isaiah xxv. 7) which is over their hearts (2 Cor. lii. 15) that there they may look on Him whom they have pierced? (Zech. xii. 10). Your attention, high and mighty ones, is directed to the recorded fact that such an offering is expected. And before that full and final gathering which follows the judgments poured out on all the earth (Isaiah lxiii. 15,16,20) a power, and that power a northern one, (Jer. iii. 12, xxxi.,6,9, xxiii., 7,8 - Isaiah xliii.,6, xlix., 12) shall be employed to lead a people wonderful from her beginning hitherto - a nation expecting and trampled underfoot - where land rivers have spoiled, unto the name of the Lord of Hosts in Mount Zion. (Isaiah xviii). These designs and purposes of the Lord God of Israel, King of Kings and Lord of Lords, are declared unto you, high and mighty ones, His servants (Dan. v. 23) that you may ponder them, and know His will, from the voice with which His is about to speak unto nations and unto men (Haggai ii, 6 - Isaiah 10) for the time is at hand (Rev. i. 7.)

Your wisdom hath been exercised to mark the boundaries of kingdoms, and to define the limits of empires; and has not the aggressor overleaped all barriers, and the strength of treaties snapped asunder as [low]? And why? Because when the Almighty awarded to the nations their inheritance, when He separated the sons of Adam, He set the bounds of the people according to number of the children of Israel (Deut. xxxii. 7, 8). **By an un-repealed covenant, the Lord God declared unto Abraham**, concerning the land of Palestine, "Unto thy seed have I given this land, from the river of Egypt to the great river, the river Euphrates" (Gen. xv. 18). This gift was ratified unto him for an everlasting possession, and to his seed after him, when the Almighty gave him His covenant, and changed his name to Abraham (Gen. xvii. 4, 8). For the purposes of infinite wisdom fast hastening to maturity, the Lord God hath scattered His inheritance to the four winds of heaven. But hear the word of the Lord, O ye nations, and declare it in the isles afar off. He that scattered Israel will gather him, and keep him as a shepherd doth his flock (Jer. xxxi. 10).

As the spirit of Cyrus, King of Persia, was stirred up to build the Lord's Temple, which was in Jerusalem (1 Chron. xxxvi. 22-23), who is there among you, high and mighty ones of all the nations, to fulfill the good pleasure of the holy will of the Lord of Heaven, saying to Jerusalem, "Thou shalt be built," and to the temple "Thy foundations shall be laid?" (Isaiah xliv. 28). The Lord God of Israel be with such. Great grace, mercy, and peace shall descend upon the people who offer themselves willingly; and the free offerings of their hearts and hands shall be those of a sweet-smelling savour unto Him who hath said, "I will bless them that bless thee (Gen. xii. 3), and contend with him who contendeth with thee" (Isa. xlix. 25).

The grace of our Lord Jesus Christ, and the love of God, and the communion of the Holy Ghost, be with you all. Amen.

Signed and sealed in London, 8th of January, in the year of our Lord 1839, in the name of the God of Abraham, of Isaac, and of Jacob, on behalf of many who wait for the redemption of Israel.

(Copy 1.)

London, January 22, 1890.

May it please your Majesty, - I have the high honor of laying at your Majesty's feet the accompanying memorandum relating to the present condition and future prospects of God's ancient people, the Jews. Your Majesty's pious feelings, I doubt not, will be excited to give the Scriptural hopes and expectations therein set forth your earnest attention, considering the high station which it hath pleased Almighty God to call this Protestant land to, as the great seat of the church.

According to the petitions of this peculiar people at the throne of grace, that in your Majesty's reign, **"Judah may be saved and Israel dwell safely,"** is the prayer of your Majesty's dutiful subject and servant.

> Her most Gracious Majesty Victoria,
> Queen of Great Britain and Ireland.

(Copy 2.)

My Lord, - I have the honor of transmitting through your Lordship a document which it is the desire of some of Her Majesty's subjects should be laid at Her Majesty's feet, relation to the Scriptural expectations of the church connected with **the restoration of the Jews to Palestine, the land of their fathers.**

I am induced to solicit your Lordship's good offices as being the medium of communicating this document to Her Majesty, as the substance of it relates to the present rights of an ally of this county - namely, the Sublime Porte. But I would respectfully press upon your Lordship's attention, that, in holding forth the Scriptural hopes of God's ancient people, those who emanate the accompanying document, never for one moment dream of political force to accomplish the end desired. When the hour comes of Israel's planting it, doubtless Almighty God will not fail to raise up chosen instruments, who, with willing hands and hearts, shall accomplish the good pleasure of His will. If we are wrong in the course we have taken to bring this memorandum before Her Majesty, we will be happy to be set right. Should your Lordship undertake the duty, desiring the glory of God in this matter to be furthered, the Lord God of Israel will not be slack to reward the labour of faith and love proceeding form a desire to honour His name.

I have the honour to be, &c.
The Rt. Hon. Lord Viscount Palmerston.

LORD PALMERSTON'S ANSWER.

(Copy, No. 3.)

Foreign-office, March 14, 1839.

I have to acknowledge your letter of the 13th of January, enclosing a letter and memorandum from some of Her Majesty's subjects, who feel deeply interested in the welfare and future prospects of the Jews, and I have to acquaint you, that I have laid those documents before the Queen, and that Her Majesty has been graciously pleased to receive the same.

I am, &c. PALMERSTON.

The Answer.
(Copy, No. 5.)
La Haye, le 13 Mai, 1939
Monsieur, - Le Roi, mon… Le Charge d'Affaires de Prusse, CONTE DE WESTPHALEN.
Monsieur -------, Londre.

Letters of similar tenor follow, addressed to the Kings of Sweden, Hanover, Denmark, the Netherlands, Wertemberg, and the President of the United States, to which no answers are appended.

TO THE EDITOR OF THE TIMES.

Sir, - Every right-minded person must feel gratified at the general expression of interest in the **Jewish nation** which has been elicited by the recent sufferings of their brethren at Damascus. It is to be hoped that the public feeling will not be allowed to evaporate in the mere expression of sympathy, but that some effectual measures may be adopted to prevent a recurrence of these atrocities, not merely in our own times, but in generations yet to come. We must not forget, when giving utterance to our indignation at the late transactions in the east, that but few centuries have passed since our country was the scene of similar enormities on a far larger scale. What reader of English history does not recall with shame and sorrow the wholesale tortures, executions, and massacres of the Jews who had sought shelter here, or who can estimate the amount of property seized and confiscated, or the number of hearts wrung by the endless repetition of cruelty and injustice? If in England they have till lately been thus treated, how can they look for more security elsewhere? Instead of wondering that they should become sordid and debased, the only cause for surprise is that any should rise to intelligence and respectability. Subject to the caprice and cruelty of any nation among whom they may dwell, fleeing from persecutions of one only to meet with like treatment from another, having no city of refuge where they can be in safeguard, on single spot to call their own, they are in a more pitiable condition than the Indian of the forest, or the Arab of the desert.

> "The wild bird hath her nest, the fox his cave,
> Mankind their country, Israel but the grave."

Is this state of things always to continue? They think not. Though many hundreds of years of hope deferred might have been enough to quench the anticipations of most sanguine, they still hope on, and turn with constant and earnest longing to the land of their forefathers. Their little children are taught to expect that they shall one day see Jerusalem. They purchase no landed property and hold themselves in readiness at a few hours' notice to revisit what they and we tacitly agree to call "their own land." It is theirs by a right which no other nation can boast, for God gave it to them, and though dispossessed of it for so many ages, it is still but partially people, and held with a loose hand and a disputed title by a hostile power, as if in readiness for their return.

There are political reasons arising from the present aspect of affairs in Russia, Turkey, and Egypt, which would make it to the interest not only of England but of other European nations, either by purchase or by treaty, to procure the restoration of Judea to its rightful claimants. About a year since, I heard it said by a German Jew, that a proposal had some time before been made by our (then) Government to the late Baron Rothschild, that he should enter into a negotiation for this purpose, and that he declined, assigning as a reason, "Judea is our own; we will not buy it, we wait till God shall restore it to us." The desirableness as well as the possibility of such a step seems daily to become more evident, but England has lately proved that she needs no selfish motives to induce her to discharge a debt of national honour and justice, or to perform an act of pure benevolence. The one now suggested would not, judging from appearances, cost 20,000,000 of money, or be unaccomplished after 50 years of exertion, or be so vast and so laborious an undertaking as the extinction of slavery throughout the world. It would be a noble thing for a Christian nation to restore these wanderers to their homes again. It would be a crowning point in the glory of England to bring about such an event. The special blessings promised in the Scriptures to those who befriend the Jews would rest upon her, and her sons and daughters would sit down with purer enjoyment to their domestic comforts when they thought that the persecuted outcasts of so many ages had, through their agency, been replaced in homes as happy and secure as theirs.

Hoping that some master mind may be led to take up this subject in all its bearings, and to form some tangible plan for its accomplishment, and that some Wilberforce may be raised up to plead for it by all the powerful and heart-stirring arguments of which it is capable,

I am, Sir, your obedient servant.

AN ENGLISH CHRISTIAN."—end transcription.

In contrast to the appalling ramifications of the Catholic/Reform presumptions regarding the Jews' demise, Dispensation Theology has had a positive social and political influence. However, in the arena of theology, DT may be farther away from recognizing Judah's right standing during the Second Temple Period than RT. Because adherents to Replacement Theology believe they have taken the place of "Israel"—whom they readily distinguish from the Jews—, they tend to attribute all good qualities to their spiritual ancestors.

The dispensational system, on the other hand, rigidly differentiates between the "Congregation in the wilderness" and the Congregation of Christ—the Church. Quite perplexingly, many Dispensationalists claim the Old Testament saints (OTS) had no knowledge of the Church Age that was to come; yet DT appropriates a substantial quantity of Old Testament passages as having application to the Church rather than to the saints of old. DT also recognizes a hard line—dispensation— between the Dispensation/Age of Law and the Dispensation/Age of Grace (commonly referred to as the Church Age). It has been deduced by followers of DT that the Law was a curse before Christ; and, that grace is the possession of the Church, unknown—or barely known— before Christ.

Then there is the matter of the Holy Spirit. Dispensationalists have good ammunition to support their position that the Holy Spirit was not given, sent, nor received before Christ (John 7:39; John 16:7; John

20:22). And certainly, the gifts of the Spirit were not "poured out" universally until "Christ ascended on high" (Acts 2:14-18; Eph. 4:8). But there is simply too much biblical evidence supporting the fact that the Spirit was involved in the everyday fellowship of the OTS. Take for instance David's plea: "Take not your Holy Spirit away from me" (Ps. 51:11). This topic will be discussed in greater detail in a later chapter.

JUDAH WITHIN COMMONWEALTH THEOLOGY

Therefore, *The Forgotten Age of Judah* unfolds to address the common shortsightedness of both theologies, namely, God's relationship with the Jews—and the Jews' relationship with God—before and at the onset of the Age of Messiah. The following chapters present the evidence from many angles, so as to reveal a picture clear enough to draw the reader's theological eye away from the mainstream model to a better, more biblical, paradigm. To see the paradigm, we need to properly understand the theological importance of the division of the United Kingdom of Israel into the House of Judah in the south and the House of Israel in the north.

Commonwealth Theology follows the distinction made within Scripture of the covenantal status of the northern and southern kingdoms. The details of the Bible show that the House of Judah remained, by God's mercy and grace, in good standing under the Sinaitic Covenant during the Second Temple period until the rejection of Jesus, which culminated in His crucifixion. The goal of this book is to guide the reader through the scriptural passages that have convinced the authors of the validity of this claim. Each chapter of this book is necessary to impart to the reader the underlying theological assumptions necessary to support our thesis. The chapters directly related to Judah's covenantal standing are interspersed at the appropriate locations in a way that this untold story gathers support as the book moves forward.

Chapter 1, which follows this introduction, will walk the reader through the biblical history of Israel's division. The reader will likely be surprised at how pervasive the topic of the two houses is in the Bible; and yet even people who have read the Bible many times tend to read these passages without pondering over them. This is because people see the breakup of Israel as dry and ancient history. But the division of Israel is far from the end of that particular conversation, as it continues to be mentioned even into the New Testament. Why? Because it is actually an important part of understand how the New Testament relates to the Old, which is essential in appreciating "the greatest story ever told."

Part of the theological disease affecting the relationship between the Jews and the church is that of improper nomenclature.

If you live here in America, you are part of one state but it does not mean your state is the sum total of all the states. Texans and New Yorkers are all Americans – we celebrate the same national holidays and hold to the same constitution. Nevertheless, it would be incorrect to say all Americans are New Yorkers. Texans are not New Yorkers, but they are all Americans. There is a clear distinction between states even though they are all part of the same bigger group.

Yet this very scenario happens in regard to the twelve tribes of Israel. In fact, there are many who commonly refer to Abraham, Isaac, and Jacob as Jewish, yet they were not. Before the break of the united monarchy, ca. 930 BC, there were technically no Jews. There were Hebrews who became the nation of Israel, which then split into the House of Judah and the House of Israel ca 722 BC. Despite this historical fact, most modern Jews use the term loosely to mean any descendant of Abraham, Isaac, and Jacob; and there are many who anachronistically refer to the Jews in Egypt and the Jews at Mt Sinai. So what? Not understanding this seemingly minor detail causes a lot of confusion about who is a Jew, who are gentiles, and even, what is the Church.

In this chapter, we will take a look at some scriptures to understand the distinction between the two houses of Israel, which is one of the missing keys in much of our biblical theology. We do not, for the most part, maintain the distinction between the House of Judah and the House of Israel. Now, why does this matter?

Figure 8 Map of the territories allotted to the "twelve tribes of Israel" according to the Book of Joshua, chapters 13–19.[14]

---

[14] commons.wikimedia.org/wiki/File:12_Tribes_of_Israel_Map.svg

TWO HOUSES CRITICAL TO BIBLE PROPHECY

It matters because we have many, many prophecies pointing to the fulfillment of these two houses coming together. And if we don't maintain the distinction early on, then when we try to bring them back together, we will be hard pressed to understand of whom we are speaking. By not understanding the identity of the House of Israel and the House of Judah, we run into two extremes. We run into the extreme theology called Dispensationalism, which claims the Jews and the Church are two completely different things and they have no real relationship to one another—even going so far as to imply there are two different sets of laws.

On the other extreme is Replacement Theology, which suggests that God has replaced Israel, and/or the Jews, with a new group of people. In this theology, it is all about the Church. Both of these views are extreme, in that they don't agree with the Bible. So let's look at some scriptures.

The question at hand is what happened to Ephraim (aka the House of Israel)? Hosea 13:12-14 says:

> The iniquity of Ephraim *is* bound up; his sin *is* stored up. The sorrows of a woman in childbirth shall come upon him. He *is* an unwise son, for he should not stay long where children are born. "I will ransom them from the power of the grave; I will redeem them from death. O Death, I will be your plagues! O Grave, I will be your destruction! Pity is hidden from My eyes" (Hos. 13:12-14).

This is a passage that, of course, is used in other places in Scripture, namely, in 1st Corinthians 15 where Paul says: "O Death, where *is* your sting? O Hades, where *is* your victory" (1 Cor. 15:55).

But he pairs this with Isaiah 25:

> He will **swallow up death forever**, And the Lord God will wipe away tears from all faces; The rebuke of His people He will take away from all the earth; For the LORD has spoken (Isa. 25:8). And it will be said in that day: "Behold, this *is* our God; we have waited for Him, and He will save us. This *is* the LORD;

we have waited for Him; we will be glad and rejoice in His salvation" (Isa. 25:9).

In 1st Corinthians Paul is pairing these two passages. In Hosea it is specifically speaking of Ephraim; not speaking of Judah. We know that the promise of resurrection is something that is given to all people who believe in Yeshua as their Savior. Thus, it is not a question of whether this is only speaking to Ephraim and not speaking to Judah. This particular passage is something that is being used to speak of Ephraim, and Paul is not glossing over that. What we need to understand is, "Who is Ephraim, and where did they go?" In the book of Hosea Chapter 14, it says:

> O Israel, return to the LORD your God, for you have stumbled because of your iniquity; take words with you, and return to the LORD. Say to Him, "Take away all iniquity; receive *us* graciously, for we will offer the sacrifices of our lips. Assyria shall not save us, we will not ride on horses, nor will we say anymore to the work of our hands, '*You are our gods,*' for in You the fatherless finds mercy. I will heal their backsliding, I will love them freely, for My anger has turned away from him. I will be like the dew to Israel; he shall grow like the lily, and lengthen his roots like Lebanon (Hos. 14:1-5).

Hosea Chapter 14 is talking again to the northern kingdom of Israel. This is very important because in Hosea 1:6-7 God says:

> For I will **no longer have mercy on the House of Israel**, yet I will have mercy on the house of Judah (Hos. 1:6, 7).

God makes a clear distinction between these two houses. He is telling Israel, that is, the northern kingdom, to return. Then continuing to speak of the northern kingdom, he says:

> "His branches shall spread; his beauty shall be like an olive tree, and his fragrance like Lebanon. Those who dwell under his shadow shall return; they shall be revived *like* grain, and grow like a vine. Their scent *shall be* like the wine of Lebanon. **Ephraim** *shall say*" (Hos. 14:6-8).

Hosea is not talking about Judah; but about Ephraim. This is very significant. Unfortunately, this is a topic that has been left out of the majority of theologies. The reason for this oversight is unclear. But the distinction between the two houses has simply not been taught. Once you see the Bible's narrative of the two houses, however, you cannot go back. It changes your understanding of the Scriptures, and certain pieces begin to fit together that were previously overlooked.

> **Ephraim** *shall say,* "What have I to do anymore with idols?" I have heard and observed him. I *am* like a green cypress tree; your fruit is found in Me (Hos. 14:8). Who *is* wise? Let him understand these things. *Who is* prudent? Let him know them. For the ways of the LORD *are* right; the righteous walk in them, but transgressors stumble in them (Hos. 14:9).

If we then go over to what Paul states, he quotes additional verses from Hosea:

> As He says also in Hosea: "I will call them My people, who **were not My people**, and her beloved, who was not beloved. And it shall come to pass in the place where it was said to them, 'You *are* not My people,' there they shall be called sons of the living God (Rom 9:25, 26)."

Isaiah also cries out concerning Israel: "Though the number of the children of Israel be as the sand of the sea, the remnant will be saved (Rom. 9:27)."

Here Paul is quoting specifically from Hosea, where God said to the northern kingdom of Israel, "You are not my people." He did not say "you are not my people" to Judah; God said it to Ephraim, the house of Israel. God made a plain distinction between the two houses: "I **will** have mercy on **Judah**, but I will **not** have mercy on the **House of Israel**." When we understand that God Himself makes a distinction between the two houses, and we maintain that distinction, then it is much easier for us when we come to passages such as Romans 9. Now we can understand exactly to whom he is speaking. He is not talking to all sons of Israel at large; he is speaking to Ephraim (the house of Israel).

Figure 9 Map of Israel and Judah in the 9th century BCE

Similar to our conclusion that Texans are not New Yorkers but all are Americans, so too Judeans (Jews) are not Ephraimites (House of Israel). It is misleading and confounding to suggest the ambiguous equivalence that "Jew" equals "Israel," and "Israel" equals "Jew." Rather, Judah is not Israel, and Israel (the House of Israel or Ephraim) is not Judah. This distinction has not been taught by mainline theologies though now at last, people around the world are awakening to the importance of the two houses in correctly interpreting the Bible.

Still, without understanding this truth, people continue to say, "Jew equals Israel," "Israel equals Jew." And reading the New Testament with that understanding causes further confusion and leads to aberrant theologies and sadly, even to anti-Semitism.

Notice again in Hosea 1:9:

> And the LORD said, "Name him Lo-ammi, because you **are not My people**, and I am not your God" (Hos. 1:9).

God in Jeremiah is referring to the northern kingdom of the house of Israel:

> "Behold, I will bring back the captivity of Jacob's tents, and have mercy on his dwelling places;" (Jer. 30:18) Their children also shall be as before, and their congregation shall be established before Me; (Jer. 30:20). '**You shall be My people**, and I will be your God'" (Jer. 30:22).

Peter tells us the same thing: "Who **once** *were* **not a people** but *are* now the people of God" (1 Pet. 2:10). Who were "not God's people"? Answer: the northern kingdom. To the 10 tribes, the Ephraimites in Hosea 1:9, He said, "You are not my people."

Was Peter's statement ever true of the House of Judah, the Jews? No, that was never true of them. God never said, "You are not my people" to the House of Judah. God chastised Judah when he sent them into Babylonian captivity for seventy years. But He never said to them, "You are not my people."

So we have on record both Paul, in Romans 9 and Peter in 1 Peter 2, stating that, "You were once not a people, but now you are God's people." Both were quoting specifically from Hosea Chapter 1 saying "This is the fulfillment."

However, still in the future:

> "Yet the number of the children of Israel shall be as the sand of the sea, which cannot be measured or numbered. And it shall come to pass in the place where it was said to them, 'You *are* not My people,' *there* it shall be said to them, '*You are* sons of the living God'" (Hos. 1:10).

Once again, all these things are fulfilled in Ephraim, not in Judah. But if we mingle those two, if we say that Ephraim is Judah and Judah is Ephraim, then we come to these New Testament passages, and we have nowhere to go other than saying, "The Jews no longer matter. God has quit on them and does not care about them. God has now transferred all of His promises to this thing called the Church." Obviously, that conclusion takes us off in a very wrong direction.

Paul goes on to say:

> For I do not desire, brethren, that you should be ignorant of this mystery, lest you should be wise in your own opinion, that blindness in part has happened to Israel until the fullness of the Gentiles has come in (Rom. 11:25).

Where does Paul get the phrase, "the fullness of the Gentiles" in Romans 11:25? He gets it specifically from Genesis 48:19. You may recall the story of when Jacob was blessing Joseph's sons, Manasseh and Ephraim. Manasseh was the older; Ephraim was the younger. Joseph carefully put Manasseh at Jacobs's right hand so that he could receive the blessing of the older son, but Jacob did a switch at the last second. He switched his hands and put his right hand on Ephraim and his left hand on Manasseh. Joseph said, "No, my father, don't do this." And Jacob said, "I know my son, I know. He also shall be a people and he also shall be great. But truly his younger brother [speaking of Ephraim] shall be greater than he and his descendants shall become a multitude of nations." If we look at that in the original Hebrew, it is M'lo HaGoyim, which is literally "the fullness of the nations." What we have in Romans Chapter 11, the fullness of the Gentiles or the nations, is the same exact word. The word *gen* is from Latin and is where we get the word "people." That is where we get the word Gentiles. It is the same thing. So Ephraim will be restored.

Notice there the parallel in Jeremiah 31:9: For I am a Father to Israel, And **Ephraim *is* My firstborn** (Jer. 31:9). God then goes on to say he will gather scattered Israel (not Judah):

> Hear the word of the LORD, O nations, and declare *it* in the isles afar off, and say, "He who scattered Israel will gather him, and keep him as a shepherd *does* his flock" (Jer. 31:10).

Keep in mind that in the days of Jeremiah, the Jews were not scattered all over. They were in fact, deported to the nation of Babylon, and a remnant of them would go back. Some of them remained in the area of Babylon; and then began to disperse throughout the Persian Empire. But they had the opportunity to go back as a unique people group. Even today, the Jews are still a unique genetic, ethnic people group.

So this is something that is very important to understand. And of course, the whole crux of the New Testament—the New Covenant—is built on this promise:

> "Behold, the days are coming," says the LORD, "when I will make a new covenant with the house of Israel and with the house of Judah" (Jer. 21:21).

We see this distinction between the two houses throughout the Bible. And of course, we see it incredibly clearly throughout the Hebrew Bible, or the Old Testament. If we look for it, we will see the "House of Israel" in the New Testament as well in Acts 2:36. In Matthew 15:24, the term "House of Israel" is used by Jesus.

The new covenant of Jeremiah Ch. 31 draws particular focus on the fact that the house of Israel was no longer His people, but would again be His people:

> "But this *is* the covenant that I will make with the house of Israel after those days," says the LORD: "I will put My law in their minds, and write it on their hearts; and I will be their God, and they shall be My people" (Jer. 31:33).

Here again we see the theme, "They shall be my people." They used to be His people; then, they were not His people. Yet He promised that they would be His people again. What we see is the restoration of Ephraim. It is the restoration of those two people groups. In other words, we have the House of Judah and the House of Israel. They will be restored.

THE TWO HOUSES WITHIN THE COMMONWEALTH

Paul makes it clear that it is the blood of Jesus that has made it possible for Ephraim, who was scattered and became wanderers among the Gentiles, to come back into a covenant relationship with God. Notice first of all from Hosea: "My God will cast them away, because they did not obey Him; and they shall be **wanderers among the nations**" (Hos. 9:17). This verse says they will become wanderers among the nations [*bagoim*]. And what does Paul then tell us? "Therefore remember that you, once Gentiles [*goyim*] (*ethnē* in the Greek [plural of *ethnos*]) in the flesh … " (Eph. 2:11).

"...that at that time you were without Christ, being aliens from the **commonwealth** of **Israel** and **strangers** from the covenants of promise, having no hope and without God in the world. But now in Christ Jesus you who once were **far off** have been brought near by the blood of Christ" (Eph. 2:12-13).

Paul goes on to say:

"...*thus* making peace, and that He might **reconcile them both** to God in one body through the cross, thereby putting to death the enmity" (Eph. 2:15-16). Paul is declaring the inception of the restoration of the two houses, which is clear when we look at Hosea again:

"Then the children of **Judah** and the children of **Israel** shall be **gathered** together" (Hos. 1:11).

What happens so often is that very well-meaning believers, many times even pastors, read the New Testament with the idea that it is all brand-new information; and they tend to neglect the Hebrew Bible— the Old Testament. The authors have been guilty of that in the past as well. But when Bible students ignore the Hebrew Bible (OT) and isolate the New Testament, then there is a lack of understanding which then leads to an inadvertent twisting of meaning. Paul was not writing about a brand-new, foreign concept. Rather, he was speaking of the restoration of the two houses which God had spoken of through his prophets for hundreds of years. It only takes a tiny bit of research; and then you see it!

Paul continues: "And He came and preached peace to you who were **afar off...**" (Eph. 2:17).

"Hear the word of the Lord, O nations, and declare it in the isles **afar off,** and say, 'He who scattered Israel will gather him, and keep him as a shepherd does his flock' for the Lord has redeemed Jacob" (Jer. 31:10,11).

The same language is used in Daniel's prayer:

"O Lord, righteousness belongs to You, but to us shame of face, as it is this day–to the men of Judah, to the inhabitants of Jerusalem and **all Israel, those near and those far off** in all the countries to which You have driven them, because of the unfaithfulness which they have committed against You. (Dan. 9:7)

There is the key to Eph. 2:17. They are afar off. They are in the isles. If you think of the words, "isle," "islands," or the "coastlands," the implication is that they are a long way away. So who is afar off? Ephraim, "all Israel" is "afar off." Paul gives a contrasting phrase within the same passage: "And those who are near…" To whom do those who are near refer? These are the House of Judah, who were not scattered abroad—not far away. He is speaking of the restoration of "all Israel" which includes the House of Israel and the House of Judah.

> "And He came and preached peace to you who were afar off and to those who were near for through Him we *both* have access by one Spirit to the Father" (Eph.2:17-18).

Notice that the two houses have access by one Spirit to the Father.

> "Now, therefore, you [Gentiles] are no longer strangers and foreigners, but fellow citizens with the saints and members of the household of God" (Eph. 2:19).

Paul is explaining how the gentiles, into which the house of Israel was scattered, can come back into a covenant relationship with God and be restored to Judah. It is not through the Old Covenant, but through a new covenant established through Jesus' blood.

EPHRAIM MIXED WITH THE NATIONS

"Ephraim mixes with the nations…" (Hos. 7:8).

When you examine charts or "family trees" on ancestry, great grandparents, and so forth, it is amazing how quickly the numbers go up. If you go back just 10 generations, you would have in your family tree 1,024 people. That is your eighth great grandparents. The number goes up very, very quickly. If you were to go back to just 40 generations ago, that would be your 38 great grandparents. You would have 1,099,511,627,776 people in your family tree. Now, of course, that is impossible because that would be more than the people on the planet who have lived throughout history, so far as we know.

What this shows is that over the course of time there is a lot of crossover, genetically speaking. You would have many people in your family tree and potentially—going back to the fourth generation—your family tree would touch upon everybody else's family tree.

The point is that when the northern 10 tribes of Israel were sent away, hundreds of thousands—perhaps millions—of people became wanderers among the nations / gentiles. They were swallowed up. They literally became part of the rest of the world. And this is what Scripture implies.

> Indeed He says, "It is too small a thing that You should be My Servant to raise up the tribes of Jacob, and to restore the preserved ones of Israel; I will also give You as a light to the **Gentiles**, that You should be My salvation to the ends of the earth" (Isa. 49:6).

What does Jesus say? "I was not sent except to the lost sheep of the House of Israel." And then again, in Isaiah 56: "The Lord GOD, who gathers the outcasts of Israel, says, 'Yet I will **gather to him** *others* besides those who are gathered to him'" (Isa. 56:8).

Once again, we get this image of others who are being gathered together. Jesus Himself seems to suggest that: "And other sheep I have which are not of this fold; them also I must bring, and they will hear My voice; and there will be one flock *and* one shepherd" (John 10:16).

Jesus was ministering in the land of Judea and talking with the Jews on a daily basis. But He said there were others He needed to bring in so that they would be one flock with one shepherd. The idea of gathering the two houses together is seen throughout Scripture. It is a shame that this teaching has been ignored. But God in His sovereignty is bringing an awareness of the two houses back to the forefront of theology.

We have yet another example in Isaiah 11:12-13:

> "He will set up a banner for the nations, and will assemble the **outcasts of Israel**, and gather together the **dispersed of Judah** from the four corners of the earth. Also the envy of **Ephraim** shall depart, and the adversaries of **Judah** shall be cut off; **Ephraim** shall not envy **Judah**, and Judah shall not harass **Ephraim**."

You might say, well, that is just parallelism. He is just saying Israel and Judah really means the same thing. But notice it says Ephraim shall not envy Judah and Judah shall not harass Ephraim. So they have to be two distinct people groups. This is not a parallelism. It is not just poetic language. He is talking about two specific people groups, and they will gathered together in the last days.

In Ezekiel we read:

> "I will bring you out from the peoples and gather you out of the countries where you are scattered…" (Ezek. 20:34). "And I will bring you into the wilderness of the peoples, and there I will plead My case with you face to face" (Ezek. 20:35). "I will make you pass under the rod, and I will bring you into the bond of the covenant" (Ezek. 20:37). "As for you, O **house of Israel**…" (Ezek. 20:39). "Then you shall know that I *am* the LORD, when I bring you into the land of Israel, into the country *for* which I raised My hand in an oath to give to your fathers" (Ezek. 20:42).

When God says, "House of Israel," it is not same as the House of Judah. There is a distinction that is brought out to clarify just who is being gathered: "I'm going to gather you. I'm going to bring you from the peoples and gather you out of the countries where you are scattered."

In the days of Ezekiel, Ezekiel was taken in the second wave of deportations over to Babylon. So Daniel went in the first wave, Ezekiel went in the second wave, and one would not want to be in the third wave because that was the worst. There were still Judeans living in Judea in those days. The House of Israel was living in Babylon. They had already been taken out by the king of Assyria and resettled in the land of Babylon. So they were not taken by King Nebuchadnezzar. They had already been there. They were there when Ezekiel arrived. God sent Ezekiel to speak to the House of Israel. We see a distinction between the two houses maintained throughout the scriptures, and especially in Book of Ezekiel.

In Ezekiel we see this idea of God Himself gathering His sheep.

> "For thus says the Lord GOD: 'Indeed I Myself will search for My sheep and seek them out. As a shepherd seeks out his flock on the day he is among his scattered sheep, so will I seek out My sheep and deliver them from all the places where they were scattered on a cloudy and dark day'" (Ezek. 34:11, 12).

In the days of Ezekiel, some Jews had been taken to Babylon. The majority of the Jews were back in the land of Judea. They were not yet scattered. So now, to whom was God speaking? He says specifically in Ezekiel 20:39 that He was speaking to the House of Israel:

"And I will bring them out from the peoples and gather them from the countries, and will bring them to their own land…" (Ezek. 34:13). "I will seek what was lost and bring back what was driven away, bind up the broken and strengthen what was sick; but I will destroy the fat and the strong, and feed them in judgment" (Ezek. 34:16).

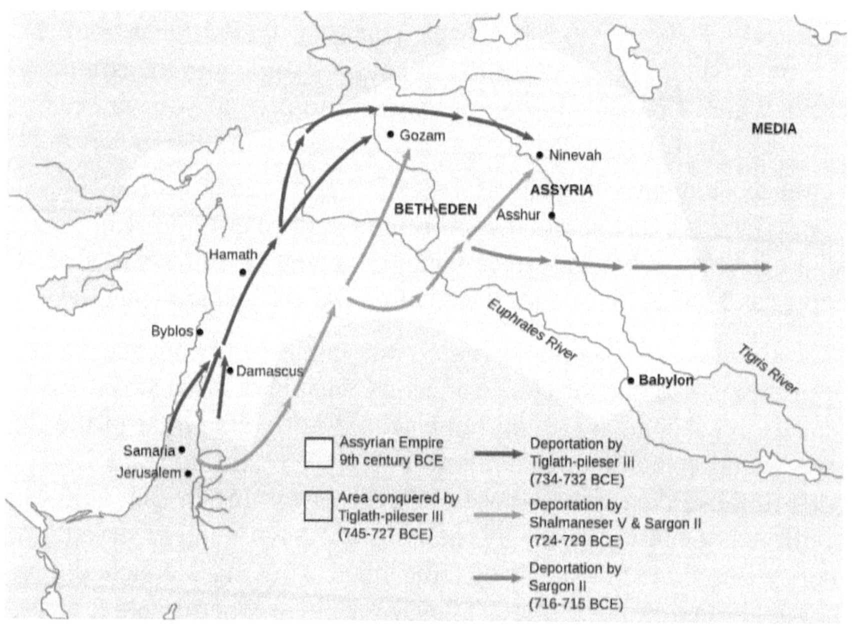

Figure 10 Deportation of the Northern Kingdom of Israel by the Assyrian Empire.[15]

"And *as for* you, O My flock," thus says the Lord GOD: "Behold, I shall judge between sheep and sheep, between rams and goats (Ezek. 34:17). Jesus used this same imagery in Matthew 25:

"When the Son of Man comes in His glory, and all the holy angels with Him, then He will sit on the throne of His glory. All the **nations** will be gathered before Him, and He will separate them one from another, as a **shepherd divides *his* sheep from the goats** (Matt. 25:31, 32).

---

[15] commons.wikimedia.org/wiki/File:Deportation_of_Jews_by_Assyrians.svg

Now in Ezekiel 37 we read: "…say to them, 'Thus says the Lord GOD: "Surely I will take the stick of Joseph…" (Ezek. 37:19). [Remember, Joseph is the father of Ephraim and Manasseh]. "… which *is* in the hand of **Ephraim**, and the **tribes of Israel,** his companions; and I will **join them with it, with the stick of Judah**, and make them one stick, and they will be one in My hand" (Ezek. 37:19).

If we do not have distinction between the two houses, then there is no way we can have a reunification of the two houses. That is why it is so important to follow the narrative of the two houses that God has laid out in His Word. Scripture is replete with the distinction between these two houses. How are they then brought back together in the last days? The "last days," began with the death, burial, and resurrection of Jesus.

> "Then say to them, 'Thus says the Lord GOD: "Surely I will take the children of Israel from **among the nations**, wherever they have gone, and will gather them from every side and bring them into their own land; and I will make them one nation in the land, on the mountains of Israel; and one king shall be king over them all; they shall no longer be two nations, nor shall they ever be divided into two kingdoms again (Ezek. 37:21, 22).

Here again is the mention of two nations becoming one nation. If we don't have two nations, as so commonly has been taught, then there is no way they can be brought back to become one nation. If we miss this point, then much of our theology will be off, some of our soteriology will to be off and a lot of our eschatology will be off; and the list of theological errors goes on and on. These errors could lead to conclusions such as anti-Semitism, Calvinism versus Arminianism, etc.

Continuing now in Ezekiel:

> "Moreover I will make a covenant of peace with them, and it shall be an everlasting covenant with them; I will establish them and multiply them, and I will set My sanctuary in their midst forevermore. My tabernacle also shall be with them; indeed I will be their God, and they shall be My people" (Ezek. 37:26, 27).

Again, this language is used to indicate that they were not His people. "The nations also will know that I, the LORD, sanctify Israel, when My sanctuary is in their midst forevermore" (Ezek. 37:28). God never divorced the southern kingdom of Judah, but He did divorce the northern kingdom of Israel. Here He speaks of bringing them back:

"The Gentiles shall know that the **house of Israel** went into captivity for their iniquity; because they were unfaithful to Me, therefore I hid My face from them. I gave them into the hand of their enemies, and they all fell by the sword (Ezek. 39:23). "Therefore thus says the Lord GOD: 'Now I will bring back the captives of Jacob, and have mercy on the **whole house of Israel'**" (Ezek. 39:25).

The nations will understand what happened to the house of Israel (not the house of Judah). Though God will bring back both houses and have mercy on the whole house of Israel (all twelve tribes).

"When I have brought them back from the peoples and gathered them out of their enemies' lands then they shall know that I *am* the LORD their God, who sent them into captivity among the nations, but also brought them back to their land, and left none of them captive any longer and I will not hide My face from them anymore; for I shall have poured out My Spirit on the house of Israel,' says the Lord GOD" (Ezek. 39:27-29).

The significance of God's separate dealings with the two houses cannot be over emphasized. God divorced and send away the northern kingdom of Israel. However God never divorced the southern kingdom of Judah though He did judge them for 70 years and then He brought them back but He never divorced them. He never scattered them throughout the nations. Many Jews did not return to Israel when they had the chance to return under Cyrus. Hence, they chose to remain outside the land.

"For a mere moment I have forsaken you, but with great mercies I will gather you" (Isa. 54:7). "But I will gather the remnant of My flock out of all countries...." (Jer. 23:3). [This is the same language Jesus used: that He would bring His flock together.] ....where I have driven them, and bring them back to their folds; and they shall be fruitful and increase (Jer. 23:3 cont.).

"In His days Judah will be saved, and Israel will dwell safely; now this *is* His name by which He will be called: THE LORD OUR RIGHTEOUSNESS" (Jer. 23:6).

He will be the one who will do this in His day. The Lord Himself will do this. That is why we understand that Jesus is the second person of the Godhead. He is God the Son. He is the incarnation. He is Emmanuel. He came and He died for His wife, Israel, which He had divorced to bring her back. Notice what he says in Jeremiah:

"I will be the God of **all the families of Israel**, and they shall be My people" (Jer. 31:1). "The people who survived the sword found grace in the wilderness—Israel, when I went to give him rest" (Jer. 31:2). "Yes, I have loved you with an everlasting love; therefore with lovingkindness I have drawn you (Jer. 31:3).

This is one of those verses that people love to use as sort of a personal verse; and that is okay. But it is really talking about the northern kingdom of Israel. God goes on to see her as a virgin! "Again I will build you, and you shall be rebuilt, O virgin of Israel!" (Jer. 31:4). How could God say such a thing to a nation that had cheated on Him so many times? The way in which that could happen would be for the original contract—that original marriage covenant that we call the Old Covenant—for that to be destroyed and for a new covenant to be issued. That New Covenant, the new marriage contract, was issued at the cross. Now there can be a completely new marriage between God and His people. The New Kingdom, the New Covenant, is that accord between the House of Israel, the House of Judah, and of course, God Himself.

"You shall yet plant vines on the mountains of Samaria..." (Jer. 31:5). "Arise, and let us go up *to* Zion, to the LORD our God" (Jer. 31:6). "Behold, I will bring them from the north country, and gather them from the ends of the earth" (Jer. 31:8).

This is clearly talking about the northern kingdom due to the reference to Samaria, the capitol of the northern kingdom. Jesus said He would send out His angels to gather His elect from the ends of the earth. So He will do exactly that.

"Behold, I will gather them **out of all countries** where I have driven them in My anger, in My fury, and in great wrath; they shall be My people, and I will be their God; then I will give them one heart and one way, that they may fear Me forever, and I will make an everlasting covenant with them, that I will not turn away from doing them good; but I will put My fear in their hearts so that they will not depart from Me" (Jer. 32:37-40).

The promise to gather both houses is reiterated throughout the prophets.

"I will strengthen the **house of Judah**, and I will save the **house of Joseph**. I will bring them back, because I have mercy on them. They shall be as though I had not cast them aside; *those of* Ephraim shall be like a mighty man, I will whistle for them and **gather** them, for I will redeem them; and they shall increase as they once increased. They shall live, together with their children, and they shall return. I will also bring them back from the land of Egypt, and gather them from Assyria. I will bring them into the land of Gilead and Lebanon, until no *more room* is found for them" (Zech. 10:6-10).

These are the promises that God has given. Such promises are also in Jeremiah 50: "But I will bring back Israel to his home, and he shall feed on Carmel and Bashan; his soul shall be satisfied on Mount Ephraim and Gilead" (Jer. 50:19).

Again, this is the northern kingdom of Israel. This is not talking about the southern kingdom in those days.

PEACE BETWEEN THE TWO HOUSES

"In those days and in that time," says the LORD, "The iniquity of **Israel** shall be sought, but *there shall be* none; and the sins of **Judah**, but they shall not be found; for I will pardon those whom I preserve" (Jer. 50:20).

Why is Judah mentioned here? Because Judah also sinned. But God never divorced Judah. He did divorce the northern kingdom, the ten tribes. He divorced them and sent them away. Maintaining the distinction between the two houses is imperative for us to see how God is going to bring them back together and make them one nation. Additionally, Jeremiah is also showing joint status as adulterers is wiped away. Israel's utter hopeless situation as a divorcee was annulled and Judah's status as adulterous wife was cancelled. Furthermore, the House of Judah and House of Israel had become one again and the wall of separation between them has been removed.

They are no longer "aliens from the Commonwealth of Israel, and strangers from the covenants of promise, having no hope, and without

God in the world" (Eph. 2:12). Through Yeshua is Israel's and Judah's peace, "who has made both one and has broken down the middle wall of separation" (Eph. 2:14).

God's first marriage was with His special treasure— United Israel. His new marriage is with his special treasure, Israel and Judah— reunited. Yeshua did all that was necessary to restore His bride Israel, just as He promised in Hosea to Israel, whom He divorced.

> "I will **betroth** you to Me forever; Yes, I will betroth you to Me in righteousness and justice, in lovingkindness and mercy; I will betroth you to Me in faithfulness, and you shall know the LORD" (Hos. 2:19, 20).

There is much of this talk about how the Church is the bride of Christ. According to Hosea, the northern kingdom is the one that He will betroth to himself, because He divorced her, sent her away, and said, you are no longer My wife. And yet in the same book, in the same chapter, in Chapter 1 and continuing in Chapter 2, He says, "I will bring you back." It is over for now but I will bring you back one day, and will betroth you. You, My wife, you will become My bride. So how many brides does God have? Just one.

From what we have seen in Scripture, the ten northern tribes were dispersed and swallowed up; they were mingled with every nation on the face of the earth.

Not to make too much or too little of the genetic part, it is reasonable to suspect that everyone who is not part of Judah probably has just a little bit of Ephraimite blood in them. Can that be proven? No. But it is a legitimate assumption.

Does that automatically make us part of the kingdom? No, it does not. But it does make us eligible. It is still a matter of faith and of personal repentance. We must believe in Jesus as our personal Lord and Savior. That does not change. But now we understand how we fit into the bigger picture. The New Covenant was not a new concept that suddenly appeared in the New Testament. It was a long-awaited fulfillment of Old Testament prophecy concerning Israel. Yet from the early centuries of the Church, this idea arose that God had a new Elect called the Church, and that Israel was out of the picture. Nevertheless, we have seen from Scripture that the New Covenant is all about the restoration of these two houses. And we who are not Judah have to come in as part of Ephraim. This was God's plan and why Ephraim was mingled throughout the entire world.

Now you may ask, "Why did God not divorce Judah also if she also played the harlot?" She certainly deserved to be divorced, but God made a promise to David. He made a promise that even if his descendants sinned, He would discipline them, but He would not put them away. This promise was the only reason that Judah was not also divorced. Point in case, God even said in Jeremiah 3, "Wayward Israel was actually better than you [Judah] because they did not do what you've done."

Israel had proven themselves to be more righteous than Judah. Nevertheless, in 1 Kings it says:

"… when Jeroboam went out of Jerusalem, that the prophet Ahijah the Shilonite met him on the way; and he had clothed himself with a new garment, and the two *were* alone in the field. Then Ahijah took hold of the new garment that was on him, and tore it into **twelve** pieces and he said to Jeroboam: 'Take for yourself **ten** pieces, for thus says the LORD, the God of Israel: "Behold, I will **tear the kingdom** out of the hand of Solomon and will give **ten tribes to you** (but he shall have one tribe for the sake of My servant David, and for the sake of Jerusalem, the city which I have chosen out of all the tribes of Israel), because they have forsaken Me, and worshiped Ashtoreth the goddess of the Sidonians, Chemosh the god of the Moabites, and Milcom the god of the people of Ammon, and have not walked in My ways to do *what is* right in My eyes and *keep* My statutes and My judgments, as *did* his father David. However **I will not take the whole kingdom** out of his hand, because I have made him ruler all the days of his life **for the sake of My servant David**, whom I chose because he kept My commandments and My statutes. But I will take the kingdom out of his son's hand and give it to you—ten tribes. And to his son I will give one tribe, that My servant David may always have a lamp before Me in Jerusalem, the city which I have chosen for Myself, to put My name there. So I will take you, and you shall reign over all your heart desires, and you shall be king over Israel"'" (1 Kgs. 11:29-37).

This scripture speaks of the twelve tribes, ten of which would be given to Jeroboam. He was given ten out of twelve tribes, the lion's share of Greater Israel. Rehoboam in the south received Judah plus Benjamin, plus a smattering of Levites. That was simply because God had made a promise to David. That was it. There was no other reason except for God's promise to David, which we will discuss further in the next chapter.

Chapter 2: Judah and the Davidic Covenant

To understand fully the covenantal status of Judah up until the time of Christ, this chapter will endeavor to take a closer look at God's promise to David. This promise to "establish the throne of David forever" was an unconditional agreement; and in this regard, the Davidic Covenant stands as a precursor to the New Covenant. In fact, the eternality and indelibility implied by the Davidic promise is the very aspect preached by Paul to Pisidian Antioch:

> "And that He raised Him from the dead, no more to return to corruption, He has spoken thus: 'I will give you the sure mercies of David'" (Acts 13:34).

The "sure mercies of David," according to the first mention of the phrase in Isaiah, had everything to do with the extension of life: "Incline your ear, and come to Me. Hear, and your soul shall live; and I will make an everlasting covenant with you—the **sure mercies of David**" (Isa. 55:3). It is necessary to stress the eternal nature of this covenant because some would assert that the Davidic Covenant was actually withdrawn by God because of Judah's sin.

God's Oath to David

The Davidic promise was born out of Kind David's desire to build a house for the Lord. It is recorded that once David's kingdom was fully established, and having made peace with the surrounding nations, David was moved to fulfill the prophecy that God would place His name, to dwell, within a chosen location rather than continuing to dwell from place to place in the portable Tabernacle. At first, Nathan the prophet told David to proceed with all that was on his heart. But afterward, the Lord spoke to Nathan and instructed him to return to David with these words:

> "Also the Lord tells you that He will make you a house..."
> "When your days are fulfilled and you rest with your fathers, I will set up your seed after you, who will come from your body, and I will establish his kingdom. He shall build a house for My name, and I will establish the throne of his kingdom forever. I will be his Father, and he shall be My son.

If he commits iniquity, I will chasten him with the rod of men and with the blows of the sons of men. But **My mercy shall not depart from him**, as I took it from Saul, whom I removed from before you. And your house and your kingdom shall be established forever before you. Your throne shall be established forever" (Excerpts 2 Samuel 7:11-16).

We have reviewed the biblical witness to the Davidic Covenant in 1st Kings and 2nd Samuel. There are, however, more than "two or three" witnesses to this promise. Psalms 89 is quite extensive but is quoted below nearly in its entirety for three purposes:

1. To acknowledge that God's promise to David was treated as a covenant (v. 3, 28, 34, & 39).
2. The promise was made with the solemnity of a sworn oath (v. 3, 35, & 49).
3. Verses 38-51 are not God's acknowledgement of a broken covenant, but are rather the accusations of the psalmist, followed by an appeal to the irrevocable promise of God.

Psalms 89:

3 "I have made a **covenant** with My chosen,
I have **sworn** to My servant David:
4 'Your seed I will establish forever,
And build up your throne to all generations.' " Selah

19 Then You spoke in a vision to Your holy one,
And said: "I have given help to one who is mighty;
I have exalted one chosen from the people.
20 I have found My servant David;
With My holy oil I have anointed him,
21 With whom My hand shall be established;
Also My arm shall strengthen him.
22 The enemy shall not outwit him,
Nor the son of wickedness afflict him.
23 I will beat down his foes before his face,
And plague those who hate him.

24 "But My faithfulness and My mercy shall be with him,
And in My name his horn shall be exalted.
25 Also I will set his hand over the sea,

And his right hand over the rivers.
26 He shall cry to Me, 'You are my Father,
My God, and the rock of my salvation.'
27 Also I will make him My firstborn,
The highest of the kings of the earth.
28 My mercy I will keep for him forever,
And My **covenant** shall stand firm with him.
29 His seed also I will make to endure forever,
And his throne as the days of heaven.

30 "If his sons forsake My law
And do not walk in My judgments,
31 If they break My statutes
And do not keep My commandments,
32 Then I will punish their transgression with the rod,
And their iniquity with stripes.
33 Nevertheless My lovingkindness I will not utterly take from him,
Nor allow My faithfulness to fail.
34 My **covenant** I will not break,
Nor alter the word that has gone out of My lips.
35 Once I have **sworn** by My holiness;
I will not lie to David:
36 His seed shall endure forever,
And his throne as the sun before Me;
37 It shall be established forever like the moon,
Even like the faithful witness in the sky." Selah

38 But You have cast off and abhorred,
You have been furious with Your anointed.
39 You have renounced the covenant of Your servant;
You have profaned his crown by casting it to the ground.
40 You have broken down all his hedges;
You have brought his strongholds to ruin.
41 All who pass by the way plunder him;
He is a reproach to his neighbors.
42 You have exalted the right hand of his adversaries;
You have made all his enemies rejoice.
43 You have also turned back the edge of his sword,

And have not sustained him in the battle.
44 You have made his glory cease,
And cast his throne down to the ground.
45 The days of his youth You have shortened;
You have covered him with shame. Selah

46 How long, Lord?
Will You hide Yourself forever?
Will Your wrath burn like fire?
47 Remember how short my time is;
For what futility have You created all the children of men?
48 What man can live and not see death?
Can he deliver his life from the power of the grave? Selah

49 Lord, where are Your former lovingkindnesses,
Which You **swore** to David in Your truth?
50 Remember, Lord, the reproach of Your servants—
How I bear in my bosom the reproach of all the many peoples,
51 With which Your enemies have reproached, O Lord,
With which they have reproached the footsteps of Your anointed.

Yes, according to v.49b, these sure mercies—"Your former lovingkindnesses,"—were sworn to David in truth. In fact, God's oath to David, that through his seed He would "establish forever and build up your throne to all generations" is one of the few oaths by God recorded in the Bible:

- "By myself I have **sworn**, declares the LORD. Because you have done this, and have not withheld your son, your only son, I will surely bless you. I will surely multiply your offspring as the stars of Heaven and as the sand on the seashore. And these your seed shall possess the gate of their enemies. And in your seed shall all the nations of the earth be blessed, because you have obeyed my voice" (Gen. 22:16-18).

- "For forty years I was grieved by that generation. I said, 'These people go astray in their hearts and do not acknowledge my ways.' So I **swore** in my anger, 'They shall not enter my rest'" (Ps. 95:10-11).

- "The LORD says to my Lord, 'Sit at my right hand until I make your enemies your footstool'... The LORD has **sworn** and will not change his mind, 'You are a priest forever after the order of Melchizedek'" (Ps. 110:1, 4)

We find yet another witness to the Davidic Covenant embedded within Isaiah 9:6-7, emphasis added:

For unto us a Child is born,
Unto us a Son is given;
And the **government will be upon His shoulder**.
And His name will be called
Wonderful, Counselor, Mighty God,
Everlasting Father, Prince of Peace.
Of the increase of His government and peace
There will be no end,
Upon the throne of David and over His kingdom,
To order it and establish it with judgment and justice
From that time forward, even forever.
The zeal of the Lord of hosts will perform this.

But now, let us touch back to the previous chapter and Hosea's account of God's dealings with the unfaithfulness of the two houses. Recall that the Northern Kingdom was held fully accountable for its sin. Judah, on the other hand, was not held fully accountable for its sin. This distinction is made in the opening chapter:

"… Then God said to him: 'Call her name Lo-Ruhamah, for I will no longer have mercy on the house of Israel, but I will utterly take them away. **Yet I will have mercy on the house of Judah**, will save them [Judah] by the Lord their God, and will not save them by bow, nor by sword or battle, by horses or horsemen'" (Hosea 1:6-7 Emphasis added).

The implication of God's mercy toward Judah would appear to be the "sure mercies of David" extrapolated to include the entire House of Judah. This conclusion is affirmed most certainly in Hosea 11:12, where it is stated:

"Ephraim has encircled Me with lies, and the house of Israel with deceit; but **Judah still walks with God**, even with the Holy One who is faithful" (Hosea 11:12, Emphasis added).

"Judah still walks with God." Because of Judah's covenant relationship—imputed through the Davidic Covenant as it may be—Judah is said to walk with God. Isn't this mercy afforded by right relationship the very same fellowship-based mercy that John spoke of in 1st John Ch. 1? "But if we walk in the light as He is in the light, we have fellowship with one another, and the blood of Jesus Christ His Son cleanses us from all sin." Obviously, the fellowship in the "person" of Christ and the perfect cleansing of Christ's blood were beyond the scope of the Jews' knowledge during the Second Temple period. But the principle of walking—being in good standing—with God, and thereby receiving supernatural assistance, is very much in view in Hosea 1:6-7 wherein: the Lord their God will save them, "not by bow, nor by sword or battle, by horses or horsemen." Furthermore, this salvation was extended even though Judah could not say they had not sinned, nor could they say they had no sin (1st John 1:8, 10).

"But Judah still walks with God, even with the Holy One who is faithful." The concept expressed here is that a covenant may be prolonged by God's sovereignty even though the human party to the contract has failed to perform. Perhaps Paul, a member of the House of Judah through the line of Benjamin, observing God's dealings with Judah—perhaps even looking expressly to Hosea 11:12—captured the essence of this maxim:

"If we are faithless, He remains faithful; He cannot deny Himself" (2 Tim. 2:13).

Despite the severity of God's chastening that would cause the psalmist to declare: "You have renounced the covenant of Your servant" (Ps. 89:39), this human observation was simply not true, as will be demonstrated in the next section.

More verses confirming the Davidic covenant (emphasis added):

"And behold, you will conceive in your womb and bring forth a Son, and shall call His name Jesus. He will be great, and will be called the Son of the Highest; and the Lord God will give Him the <u>throne of His father David</u>. And He will reign over the <u>house of Jacob forever</u>..." (Luke 1:32-33). [The "house of Jacob" would be indicative of all twelve tribes of Israel].

"But you, Bethlehem, in the land of Judah, are not the least among the rulers of Judah; for out of you shall come a Ruler who will shepherd <u>My people Israel</u>."

GOD'S FORGIVENESS OF JUDAH

In keeping with Solomon's Temple dedication petitions, which God endorsed by fire and which remained in effect during the time of Judah's captivity in Babylon, Daniel prayed toward Jerusalem with the full expectation that Judah would indeed receive God's forgiveness:

"O my God, incline Your ear and hear; open Your eyes and see our desolations, and the city which is called by Your name; for we do not present our supplications before You because of our righteous deeds, but because of Your great mercies. O Lord, hear! **O Lord, forgive!** O Lord, listen and act! Do not delay for Your own sake, my God, for Your city and Your people are called by Your name" (Daniel 9:18-19).

God, in fact, did receive and answer Daniel's prayer, according to the prophecies in the remainder of Daniel Ch. 9. Ezra and Nehemiah returned to the Land with God's approval and blessing. Remembering that Judah was estranged but never divorced, Judah was completely forgiven after her 70 years of chastening. This forgiveness is affirmed by the following verses (emphasis added):

Isa. 40:2 "Speak comfort to Jerusalem, and cry out to her, That her warfare is ended, That **her iniquity is pardoned**; For she has received from the LORD's hand Double for all her sins."

Isa. 44:21-22 "Remember these, O Jacob, And Israel, for you are My servant; I have formed you, you are My servant; O Israel, you will not be forgotten by Me! **I have blotted out, like a thick cloud, your transgressions,** and like a cloud, your sins. Return to Me, for I have redeemed you."

Ps. 85:1-2 "Lord, You have been favorable to Your land; You have brought back the captivity of Jacob. **You have forgiven the iniquity of Your people;** You have **covered all their sin. Selah.**"

In order for the psalmist of Psalms 103 to admonish the hearers to "forget not all His benefits," the benefits listed must have been experience and memorable to the people. In other words, God did not withhold His grace and forgiveness—to be "dispensed" in a later age.

Psalms 103:
Bless the Lord, O my soul;
And all that is within me, bless His holy name!
2 Bless the Lord, O my soul,
And forget not all His benefits:
3 Who **forgives all your iniquities** . . .
7 He made known His ways to Moses*[see verse 8, Exod. 34:6],
His acts to the children of Israel.
8 ***The Lord is merciful and gracious,**
Slow to anger, and abounding in mercy.
9 He will not always strive with us,
Nor will He keep His anger forever.
10 He has not dealt with us according to our sins,
Nor punished us according to our iniquities.
11 For as the heavens are high above the earth,
So great is His mercy toward those who fear Him;
12 **As far as the east is from the west,**
So far has He removed our transgressions from us.
13 As a father pities his children,
So the Lord pities those who fear Him.
14 For He knows our frame;
He remembers that we are dust . . .
17 But **the mercy of the Lord is from everlasting to everlasting**
On those who fear Him,
And His righteousness to children's children,
18 To such as keep His covenant,
And **to those who remember His commandments to do them.**

Imputed righteousness is not something new under the New Covenant. Just like the Abrahamic Covenant through which "all Israel" is blessed (Heb. 6:14), God's Elect have always enjoyed the benefits of Psalms 103. Jesus, the Lord, "is the same yesterday, today, and forever" (Heb. 13:8). It is God's nature to forgive and indeed that is one of the lesser-known names of God. In Psalms 99:8, it is revealed that God is "God Who Forgives." This passage will be further examined in the next section.

THE REALITY OF OLD TESTAMENT FORGIVENESS

There is this notion within dispensational teaching that God dealt with sin differently in the Old Testament times—before Christ's sacrifice. The idea is advanced that the sins of the Old Testament saints were only covered; but through the cross, sins are actually "taken away." Whereas in reality, the words "covered" and "forgiven" are used interchangeably throughout the Old Testament. Paul gives us an example of this equivalence in his quotation of Psalms 32 in the fourth chapter of Romans (emphasis added):

5 But to him who does not work but believes on Him who justifies the ungodly, his faith is accounted for righteousness, 6 just as David also describes the blessedness of the man to whom God imputes righteousness apart from works:

7 "Blessed are those whose lawless deeds are **forgiven**,
And whose sins are **covered**;
8 Blessed is the man to whom the Lord shall not impute sin."

Verse 7 plainly equates "forgiven" and "covered." The verses below demonstrate that the forgiveness of sins was just as complete in the Old Testament as it is under the New Covenant:

Ps. 51:1 Have mercy upon me, O God, According to Your lovingkindness; According to the multitude of Your tender mercies, **Blot out my transgressions. 2 Wash me thoroughly from my iniquity**, And **cleanse me from my sin**.

Isa. 1:18-19a "Come now, and let us reason together," Says the Lord, "**Though your sins are like scarlet, They shall be as white as snow**; Though they are red like crimson, They shall be as wool. 19 If you are willing and obedient . . ."

Isa. 34:25 "I, even I, am He who **blots out your transgressions** for My own sake; And I will **not remember your sins**."

Isa. 38:17 Indeed it was for my own peace that I had great bitterness; But You have lovingly delivered my soul from the pit of corruption, For You have **cast all my sins behind Your back**.

Micah 7:18-19 could not be clearer that God's mercy—the subduing of our iniquities—is synonymous with the "casting away" our sins:

Who is a God like You,

Pardoning iniquity

And passing over the transgression of the remnant of His heritage?

He does not retain His anger forever,

Because **He delights in mercy**.

He will again have compassion on us,

And will subdue our iniquities.

You will **cast all our sins**

Into the depths of the sea.

In all of these instances of forgiveness listed above, there is absolutely no distinction from the forgiveness prophesied under the New Covenant: "For I will forgive their iniquity, and their sin I will remember no more" (Jer. 31:34). In Psalms 99:6-8 below, we find that **God bears, forgives, and carries away sins, because that is who He is:**

Moses and Aaron were among His priests,

And Samuel was among those who called upon His name;

They called upon the Lord, and He answered them.

He spoke to them in the cloudy pillar;

They kept His testimonies and the statutes He gave them.[16]

You answered them, O Lord our God;

You were to them God-Who-Forgives (אֵל נֹשֵׂא , El Nasah),

Though You took vengeance on their deeds.

---

[16] Note: Moses, Aaron, and Samuel were said to have kept the Law of God.

El Nasah [*Nasa*] definition:[17]

נָשָׂא (v) heb

to lift, bear up, carry, take

(Qal)

to lift, lift up

to bear, carry, support, sustain, endure

to take, <u>take away</u>, <u>carry off</u>, <u>forgive</u>

Thus it is the very nature—Name—of God to "forbear" (Rom. 3:25), to carry off ("remove" [Ps. 103:12]), and "forgive," as in the verses quoted above).

PROPITIATION, GRACE, MERCY, AND FORGIVENESS

Below we will look at the Greek words that have been translated into English as, "forgive," "pardon," and "mercy." Note how these words—like "covered" and "cast away" (above)—are often used interchangeably.

Hebrews 9:22 "And according to the law almost all things are purified with blood, and without shedding of blood there is no **remission** (ἄφεσις [*aphesis*])."

[STRONGS NT 859: ἄφεσις [*aphesis*]

ἄφεσις, ἀφέσεως, ἡ (ἀφίημι);

1. release, as from bondage, imprisonment, etc.: Luke 4:18 (19) (Isaiah 61:1f; Polybius 1, 79, 12, etc.).

2. ἄφεσις ἁμαρτιῶν forgiveness, pardon, of sins (properly, the letting them go, as if they had not been committed (see at length Trench, § xxxiii.)), remission of their penalty: Matthew 26:28; Mark 1:4; Luke 1:77; Luke 3:3; Luke 24:47; Acts 2:38; Acts 5:31; Acts 10:43; Acts 13:38; Acts 26:18; Colossians 1:14][18]

Numbers 14:19-21 "**Pardon** (ἄφες, *aphes*) the iniquity of this people, I pray, according to the greatness of Your **mercy** (ἔλεός), just as You have **forgiven** (ἵλεως) this people, from Egypt even until now.

---

[17] https://www.sefaria.org/Psalms.99.8. Source: Open Scriptures on GitHub; Creator: Based on the work of Larry Pierce at the Online Bible

[18] https://biblehub.com/thayers/859.htm

Then the Lord said: "I have **pardoned (Ιλεως)**, according to your word . . ." (Greek from LXX). Notice that forgiveness and pardon [near the end of the passage] are based on the same Greek stem; *hileōs* "merciful." Yet, "pardon" at the beginning of the passage is translated from the Greek *aphesis*, to forgive (see Strong's above).

1 John 1:9 "If we confess our sins, He is faithful and just to **forgive (ἀφῇ,** *aphe*) us our sins and to cleanse us from all unrighteousness."

2 Chron. 6:25 "then hear from heaven and **forgive (ἵλεως,** *hileōs*) the sin of Your people Israel, and bring them back to the land which You gave to them and their fathers.

Exodus 32: 32 "Yet now, if You will **forgive (ἀφεῖς,** *aphaes*) their sin . . ."

More examples: See 1 Kings 8:30-50; Ps. 25:18; Ps. 32; Ps. 86:5.

Despite the wealth of verses quoted above, Hebrews 9:26 and 10:4 are often used to imply that sins were not really taken away until the cross.

Hebrews 9:26 "… once at the end of the ages, He has appeared to **put away (ἀθέτησιν,** *athetēsin*) sin by the sacrifice of Himself." [Dodson's Concise Lexicon; **ἀθέτησιν,** "nullification, abrogation."]

Hebrews 10:4 "For it is not possible that the blood of bulls and goats could **take away (ἀφαιρεῖν,** *aphairei*) sins."

Then how were sins cast away and cast behind in the Isaiah and Micah passages quoted above? Sins have always been forgiven and forgotten by God's sovereign determination to do so—by the dispensation of God's mercy. (This is the true doctrine of dispensation). Righteousness, blamelessness, and faultlessness are imputed by God. The sacrifice of animals, without repentance and without God's acceptance could never accomplish anything except to fulfill an empty requirement, a legalistic duty.

From the time of Able—until God discouraged animal sacrifices because of man's desecration of these sacrificial services—animal sacrifices *were* **prescribed and accepted by God.**

To cover all the bases on the subject of sacrifices, we cannot overlook what is said about Christ's sacrifice in Hebrews 10:5-7:

5 Therefore, when He came into the world, He said: "**Sacrifice** and **offering** You did **not desire**, But a body You have prepared for Me. 6 In burnt offerings and sacrifices for sin You had no pleasure. 7 Then I said, 'Behold, I have come—In the volume of the book it is written of Me—To do Your will, O God.'"

The quote selected by the author of Hebrews presents an interesting wrinkle in time. By quoting Psalms 40 and then stating that these words were spoken when Christ entered the world, the writer of Hebrews is either claiming the psalmist was privy to a Christophany (a manifestation of Jesus before the incarnation); or, the psalmist experienced a vision of words spoken by Jesus in the future, but never recorded in any of the Gospels.

Psalms 40:
6 Sacrifice and offering You did not desire;
My ears You have opened.
Burnt offering and sin offering **You did not require**.
7 Then I said, "Behold, I come;
In the scroll of the book it is written of me.
8 I delight to do Your will, O my God,
And Your law is within my heart."

As a side note, but pertinent to an important discussion within this book, verse 8 of Psalms 40 affiliates delighting to do the will of God with having God's law within the heart. The verse—clearly speaking of Christ—stands to contradict any doctrine that would claim Jesus came to take away the Law. No, He came to take away sin!

Now, let us examine this passage from Hebrews. God certainly **did** for a time **require** the sacrificial offerings, which were prescribed in His law. What **was required**—and only available through the incarnate Son of God—was the sacrifice by which Satan's reign of death and his rule over this world could be defeated. The sacrificial death of the Son of the Godhead was also **required** to satisfy the death of the husband toward the remarriage of unfaithful Israel. (See the next chapter, "Why Did Jesus Have to Die?").

Chapters 9 and 10 of the book of Hebrews make the following points about the superiority of Christ's sacrifice:

- Accomplished by the precious blood of the Only Begotten Son.
- Permanence—Once for All.
- Able to cleanse the conscience by changing the heart—"a new creation."
- Blood of bulls and goats **inferior, but not ineffective.**

Bulls and goats slaughtered irreverently and without repentance would not invoke God's determination to forgive. (Similar to the casual drinking of wine and eating of bread apart from recognition of the body and blood of Christ—1 Cor. Ch. 11.) The Old Testament sacrifice of bulls and goats, when offered according to the prescribed preparation and expectation of forgiveness, was effective to achieve God's determination of forgiveness.

God's prescription of sacrifices

The references in the book of Hebrews to God's displeasure with animal sacrifices **must** relate to the time subsequent to God's declarations that such sacrifices would **no longer** be received, as in the following passages[19]:

Jeremiah 6:20 "What do I care about incense from Sheba or sweet calamus from a distant land? Your burnt offerings are not acceptable; your sacrifices do not please me."

Psalm 50:9-13 "I have no need of a bull from your stall or of goats from your pens, for every animal of the forest is mine, and the cattle on a thousand hills. I know every bird in the mountains, and the creatures of the field are mine. If I were hungry I would not tell you, for the world is mine, and all that is in it. Do I eat the flesh of bulls or drink the blood of goats?"

Isaiah 1:11-13 "The multitude of your sacrifices - what are they to me?" says the LORD. "I have more than enough of burnt offerings, of rams and the fat of fattened animals; I have no pleasure in the blood of bulls and lambs and goats. When you come to appear before me, who has asked this of you, this trampling of my courts? Stop bringing meaningless offerings! Your incense is detestable to me. New Moons, Sabbaths and convocations - I cannot bear your evil assemblies."

---

[19] Source: Tekton Apologetics Ministry; *www.tektonics.org*

God was pleased with Abel's sacrifice; Leviticus 1:9 (also Leviticus 23:27) "He is to wash the inner parts and the legs with water, and the priest is to burn all of it on the altar. It is a burnt offering, an offering made by fire, an aroma **pleasing to the LORD."**

In Article IV of the *Apology*, Melanchthon explains that similar passages in Psalm 50 and Jeremiah 7 condemn, not the divinely ordained sacrifices themselves, but rather "the wicked belief of those who did away with faith in the notion that through these works they placated the wrath of God," those who offered "sacrifices with the notion that on account of them they had a gracious God, so to say, *ex opere operato* [meaning "from the work performed."]

God *did* approve of the Israelites' offerings, when they were offered properly and sincerely, not hypocritically. God looks upon the heart; and, as stated in 1 Samuel 15:22, obedience is more important to God than sacrifice. Jesus quoted from Hosea, that mercy is better than sacrifice (Hosea 6:6, Mt 12:7).

The context of Jeremiah 6 and Isaiah 1 (above) reveals that God did not accept the Israelites' offerings because they were sinning and were not repentant. Jeremiah 6:16-20 shows that the Israelites were disobedient and were rejecting God's teaching. Likewise, Isaiah 1:2-4 describes the Israelites' current sins and 1:15-19 makes it even clearer as God tells the Israelites what they need to do to be right with him again. Psalm 50 (above) does not present a contradiction since it merely states that God does not depend on offerings for sustenance, and the Bible does not say anywhere that God is dependent on offerings. Forgiveness is ultimately based on God's determination to forgive, with His full knowledge of His sacraments, the attitude of man's heart during their observance; and, whether God Himself had declared His rejection of certain forms of sacrifice due to man's duplicity.

So far, this book has demonstrated that the Bible speaks prolifically regarding the two houses of Israel and makes a distinction between God's dealings with each. We have also shown the durability of God's covenant with the line of David, and made a connection between the Davidic Covenant and God's grace toward Judah. The next chapter reveals that the cross of Christ not only applies to personal redemption, but that it also has far reaching consequences in the rectification of a spectrum of issues; from the fall of creation, to the fall of both houses of Israel.

CHAPTER 3: WHY DID JESUS HAVE TO DIE?

Many of us heard the gospel message that Jesus died for our sins. Of course, this raises the question of why exactly did Jesus need to die? Sometimes, we can very simplistically say, "Jesus died for my sins. He went to the cross to pay for the sins of the people." These are both true. It is great to give a very condensed version. When we are on the street or sharing with somebody, that is fine.

Sometimes we need to look deeper to really understand in more detail what His death accomplished and why it was imperative. Some of the corrections have already been realized in our lives, and some we will need to wait until the second coming of Jesus. The chiasm entitled "The History of Redemption" helps us visualize what was accomplished at the cross.

We start off with God in perfect harmony with His creation. We see this in Genesis 2:3. Then Adam disobeys. As a result of that sin, all creation falls into bondage. Adam dies physically—or genetically. The heavenly Jerusalem and earth separate. This is a dimensional separation between the two realms. Adam loses the spirit that God breathed into him. And then, a few millennia later, God chooses and marries a United Israel. God then divorces the northern kingdom, and chastises Judah for adultery. These are the seven consequences for which Jesus had to die.

The fulcrum of human history is when Jesus went to the cross, because His blood would harmonize all these things. These are the seven issues that required reconciliation that really stand out in Scripture. We see a very clear picture of these issues going bad, and then a clear picture of things becoming right again. So His blood would correct all these things: the relationship will be restored with His bride, His wife—that is Israel. And then the united Israel will be restored. Then the spirit that God breathed into Adam will be restored to mankind. The heavenly Jerusalem and the earth will not remain separate but will come back together. Adam will then be restored— mankind restored, physically/genetically. Creation itself will be liberated from the bondage of corruption. At that time, Adam-Mankind will be in harmony with God once again. At this point we come full circle, back to where we started. God is in perfect harmony with His creation. All things in heaven and earth will be back together.

Let us now begin in Genesis 2:3. God is in perfect harmony with His creation. "Then God saw everything that He had made, and indeed *it was* very good. So the evening and the morning were the sixth day" (Gen. 1:31). "Then God blessed the seventh day and sanctified it, because in it He rested from all His work which God had created and made" (Gen. 2:3). Everything is good, very good. There is no dissonance, no disharmony. Everything is just the way it ought to be. God and creation are happy together. But we know very shortly thereafter, Adam disobeys. And this is the risk that God had to take. God created Adam and Eve in His image, in His likeness. Not only in a physical sense, not only in a characteristic sense, but having freewill. And as is necessary for freewill to happen, there must be real opportunity to choose. Of course, we know the story; we know that Adam chose poorly. So Adam disobeyed in Genesis Chapter Three.

"So when the woman saw that the tree *was* good for food, that it *was* pleasant to the eyes, and a tree desirable to make *one* wise, she took of its fruit and ate. She also gave to her husband with her, and he ate" (Gen. 3:6).

Three words, "and he ate," changed the course of history.

"Then the eyes of both of them were opened, and they knew that they *were* naked; and they sewed fig leaves together and made themselves coverings" (Gen. 3:7).

CREATION FALLS INTO BONDAGE

As a result of Adam's disobedience, creation itself fell into bondage. Adam was taken from the *adamáh*, from the earth, from the dirt. And whatever Adam did, happened to everything else. He was the federal head. What he chose to do had a direct impact on the very soil—the material that he was drawn from. The Earth is subjugated to him. He is the lord over it; and whatever he does, will happen to it. So when Adam fell, when he disobeyed and fell into death, so too did the entire planet, the entire cosmos, fall into disarray and bondage.

"Then to Adam He said, 'Because you have heeded the voice of your wife, and have eaten from the tree of which I commanded you, saying, "You shall not eat of it": 'Cursed *is* the ground for your sake; in toil you shall eat *of* it all the days of your life'" (Gen. 3:17).

It was not as though God took His wand, so to speak, and cursed the ground. But God was declaring, "Adam, now the ground is cursed because of what you did." Because God had made man to have dominion over the planet, when he sinned and went into death, so too did the earth.

We see also in Isaiah 24:

"The earth is also defiled under its inhabitants, because they have transgressed the laws, changed the ordinance, broken the everlasting covenant. Therefore the curse has devoured the earth, and those who dwell in it are desolate. Therefore the inhabitants of the earth are burned, and few men *are* left" (Isa. 24:5, 6).

Romans 8:20 says:

"For the creation was subjected to futility, not willingly, but because of Him who subjected *it* in hope" (Rom. 8:20).

ADAM DIES PHYSICALLY/GENETICALLY

We see, then, that Adam died physically or genetically.

"'In the sweat of your face you shall eat bread till you return to the ground, for **out of it you were taken**; for **dust** you *are,* and **to dust you shall return**.' And Adam called his wife's name Eve, because she was the mother of all living. Also for Adam and his wife the LORD God made tunics of skin, and clothed them. Then the LORD God said, 'Behold, the man has become like one of Us, to know good and evil'" (Gen. 3:19-22).

It was imperative that Adam and Eve actually know good and evil. One may say, "Wait a second." Does that mean God wanted them to eat from the tree of the knowledge of good and evil?" No. He had said not to eat from it. But there were always two options involved with the tree of the knowledge of good and evil. And either choice would give you the knowledge of good and evil. We know they chose to eat from the tree and by doing so, they gained the knowledge of good and evil. But they also could have chosen Option A, which was a much better option, not to eat from the tree of the knowledge of good and evil. If they had done so, they would have also exercised their own freewill.

They could have said, "You know what Satan? I know we could eat from it, but we are not going to." And by doing that, God might have said, "Hey, look, man has become like one of us, knowing good and evil." It is a good thing to be like God. That is why He made us in His image, and in His likeness, because He wants us to be like Him. Though He wants us to make good choices, He will not force us in our decisions. He cannot force us any more than people can make their own children choose correctly. They can't be forced to make good decisions. Forcing someone to make certain choices does not help them learn to make the correct choices on their own.

As a parent, we want a child to make good choices. We will encourage a child to make good choices. We might discipline a child to help him make good choices, but only the child can make the good choice. No matter how much we might threaten and discipline, and maybe spank or take away the keys to the car; we still can't make the child do the right thing. And God cannot make us do the right thing. That is what's so crazy about this. If He were to make us do the right thing, then it would no longer be freewill.

So He can only give us the opportunity to do this or that. And of course, Adam and Eve chose poorly. But had they done the right thing, God would have said, "Look, man has become like one of us, knowing good and evil. Now let him stretch out his hand and take from the tree of life and live forever." But that is not what happened. He said:

> "'And now, lest he put out his hand and take also of the tree of life, and eat, and live forever'— therefore the LORD God sent him out of the garden of Eden to till the ground from which he was taken. So He drove out the man; and He placed cherubim at the east of the Garden of Eden, and a flaming sword, which turned every way, to guard the way to the tree of life" (Gen. 3:22-24).

Adam died physically; he started the process of death, though his body would not give up the ghost for another 930 years. Nevertheless, his body entered a genetic transformation where it became full of death. It was corrupted, started decaying from that moment on. It was a slow decay for sure. But the process began right then. We are told in Romans:

> "Therefore, just as **sin** came into the world **through one man**, and **death** through sin, and **so death spread** to all men because all sinned—for sin indeed was in the world before the law was given, but sin is not counted where there is no law. Yet death reigned from Adam to Moses, even over those whose sinning was not like the transgression of Adam, who was a type of the one who was to come. But the free gift is not like the trespass. For if many died through one man's trespass…" (Rom. 5:12-15 ESV).

Adam also lost the spirit that God breathed in him.

> And the LORD God formed man *of* the dust of the ground, and breathed into his nostrils the breath of life; and man became a living being (Gen. 2:7).

In this passage, the word "breathed into" is *vayipakh* in the Hebrew. The Greek equivalent used in the Greek Septuagint is the word *enephusesen*. We find that same word used in John 20:22 when Jesus shows up and He breathes upon (literally, "breathes into") the disciples, and says, "Receive the Holy Spirit." It is the same breath that God breathes into people when they are born again of the Spirit (See John 3:5-6). It is the very Spirit of God. He is breathing the Holy Spirit into them. So there in the beginning, Adam was filled with the Holy Spirit; but he lost that Spirit. That was the first thing he lost, the Holy Spirit. And mankind would not enjoy the indwelling of the Holy Spirit until some 4,000 years later when Jesus would come and breathe it into His followers. So Adam lost the Spirit of God. He died genetically and physically. And then heavenly Jerusalem and the Earth are separated, accounting for the dimensional shift between the two realms.

HEAVENLY JERUSALEM AND EARTH SEPARATED

Before the fall, the terrestrial realm and the spiritual realm were one. This seems very odd to us because all we have ever known is this terrestrial realm. We do not know about the other dimension, though the rabbis have long known about the existence of ten or eleven dimensions. Quantum Physics is catching up and discovering that there must be eleven dimensions. We will not go into that now. However, the two dimensions, (realms), which we can comprehend, previously existed as one realm. They were both occupying the same plane, if you will.

And we see evidence of this in scripture, where God says: "You cannot see My face; for no man shall see Me, and live" (Exo. 33:20).

Yet Adam walked with God in the cool of the day. God was right there. He created Adam with the capability to be in His presence. It was sin that brought about the wall of separation, now represented as the "smoke" that surrounds God. A thick darkness surrounds Him, and it is there to protect us from God. It is not that God thinks, "Oh, you guys can't be allowed to see Me because I'm just too good for you." It is because, if He were to expose all His glory to us, we would simply melt. If the mountains are going to melt before the glory of the Lord, before the presence of the Almighty, what would happen to us?

When Jesus comes and His enemies are standing before Him, Scripture says those enemies will melt. Their eyes will melt in their sockets. They will literally melt from the very presence of the Lord. So then, we should say, "Hallelujah!" because there is, currently, smoke surrounding God's throne to protect us from God's incredible glory. We know that there is also electricity and fire from His waist up, and from His waist down. There is a fiery stream coming out from God's throne. This is what it means to be in God's presence.

Currently, we are not able to sustain His presence. It is impossible. But before the fall, it was possible. Do you think the earth was burning up when God made it? Of course not. The earth was able to sustain God's presence because there was perfect harmony between the two realms. There was no sin, no division, no decay, and no death had come in. But now death is in the very members of the earth itself. We cannot be in God's presence in our current condition. We now understand why there is a veil that separates heaven and earth.

- Stephen gazed into heaven, and saw the glory of God, and he said, "Look, I see the heavens **opened**" (Acts 7:55).
- "Now the heavens were **opened** and behold a white horse," (Rev. 19:11).
- the heavens were **opened** and I saw visions of God" (Ezek. 1:1).
- And as Jesus comes up out of the water at His baptism: "the heavens were **opened**" (Matt. 3:16).

There is a veil, a dimensional shield, if you will, that is between heaven and earth; and it is protecting us from God. One day that veil will go away. It will roll up like a scroll.

GOD CHOOSES/MARRIES UNITED ISRAEL

Now over the course of time, God chose, and married, United Israel. He had a plan to be present in this world, to manifest His glory, to show His goodness, and to work through humanity. He chose His "elect" through the United Kingdom of Israel. He entered into a special relationship with them and they got married. We see that they got married in the book of Ezekiel.

He says in Ezekiel 16:

"'When I passed by you again and looked upon you, indeed your time *was* the time of love; so I spread My **wing** [hem of garment] over you and covered your nakedness. Yes, I swore an **oath** to you and entered into a **covenant** with you, and you became Mine,' says the Lord GOD" (Ezek. 16:8).

Here God is speaking to the two houses of Israel that used to be one. He says, "We got married. We entered into a covenant relationship, and you became mine." To spread a wing over somebody, that is what Ruth requested of Boaz, to spread his wing over her. That is what God did to Israel. He married her. He married Israel. And notice the language in the following verses that speak of an adulterous wife:

> "Surely, *as* a **wife** treacherously departs from her husband, so have you dealt treacherously with Me, O **house of Israel**," says the LORD (Jer. 3:20).

> "Then those of you who escape will remember Me among the nations where they are carried captive, because **I was crushed by their adulterous heart** which has departed from Me, and by their eyes which play the harlot after their idols; …" (Ezek. 6:9).

At their wedding on Mount Sinai, the groom and bride exchanged vows. God, the husband, expressed His love for His bride Israel when He vowed, "If you will indeed obey My voice and keep My covenant, then you shall be a special treasure to Me above all people, for all the earth is mine." A special treasure. Can you imagine God saying to Israel, "My little special treasure?" He uses that kind of lovey-dovey language—sweetheart, honey, and all that. Give Me My special treasure. God is saying how much He loves Israel. They exchanged vows. He says,

> "… LORD [Yehovah] your God; the LORD your God has **chosen** you to be a people for Himself, a special treasure above all the peoples on the face of the earth. The LORD did not set His love on you nor choose you because you were more in number than any other people, for you were the least of all peoples; but because the **LORD loves** you, and because He would keep the oath which He swore to your fathers, the LORD has brought you out with a mighty hand, and redeemed you from the house of bondage, from the hand of Pharaoh king of Egypt" (Deut. 7:6-8).

They recorded their vows in what we would call a *ketubah*, a marriage contract. And it is just a mere four chapters in Exodus, Chapters 20 through 23. And then it says, "Then Moses took the book of the covenant, and read in the hearing of the people" (Exo. 24:7). This marriage contract came with some prenuptial agreements in case of infidelity. But everything that God gave was good. He gave ten words, or ten commandments, and they were for her good. "And now Israel, what does the LORD, your God require of you, but to fear the LORD your God, to walk in all His ways and to love Him." That is what He desires from us - to fear Him, walk in His ways, and to love Him. He was saying, "You express your love for Me through the doing of these things." Now you are not doing these things just as a checklist, as if to say, "Well, I did that, I did that." But because you love Me. These are the ways that you can express your love to Me."

Every relationship has these things. There are some things that your wife or your husband likes when you do them, and there are things that they don't like for you to do. So what do you do? Do you just have a list? Do you think, "Well, if I just do these things, then we are going to have a perfect marriage?" It probably won't work that way. But if you do not or if you just disregard the list, it is not going to help your marriage at all. Let's just be honest. If you do the things the other does not like, it will hurt your relationship. On the other hand, if you refuse to do the things the other likes, that will not help your marriage either. So do those things, but make sure the actions are all founded in love. Love God, serve him with all your heart, soul, and keep his commandments statutes that He commanded for our good. This is what God is asking of us.

And so Israel said, "I do." "All Yehovah said we will do and be obedient" (Exod. 24:7). All she needed to do was to love Him by remaining faithful to Him. He also promised that if they would be faithful, Israel would be a special treasure above all the people of the earth. Their marriage contract was cut and the vows were ratified with blood.

> "And Moses took the blood, sprinkled *it* on the people, and said, 'This is the blood of the **covenant** which the LORD has made with you according to all these words'" (Exod. 24:8).

They were married. Unfortunately, Israel did not remain faithful. In a marriage, a lot of things can go wrong. You should have grace for leaving socks around and burnt toast. But the one thing that will wreck a marriage is infidelity. This is what God experienced with Israel. The kingdom of Israel was divided; and God divorced the northern kingdom and chastised Judah for her adultery.

> "Bring **charges** against your mother, bring charges; for she is **not My wife**, nor am I her Husband! Let her put away her

harlotries from her sight, and her adulteries from between her breasts" (Hos. 2:2).

"Then I saw that for all the causes for which backsliding Israel had committed adultery, I had **put her away** and given her a **certificate of divorce**; yet her treacherous sister Judah did not fear, but went and played the harlot also" (Jer. 3:8).

Israel was unfaithful to her husband from the beginning. His wife, United Israel, was then divided into two kingdoms, the kingdom of Judah in the South, which included the tribes of Benjamin, Levi, and of course, Judah; and the kingdom of Israel in the north, which included the other 10 tribes. And it was the kingdom in the north that became known as "Israel" because they were the vast majority—ten tribes were there. God gave the northern kingdom to Jeroboam. He left a remnant in Judah for the sake of David, but the larger kingdom was in the north.

So God took the kingdom away from the house of David, except for a tiny portion, because He had made promises to David. This division took place around 932 BC. But, of course, things went from bad to worse. The kingdom of Israel in the north continued to go after false gods with great vigor. And so God said, "Tell northern Israel that she is not my wife, nor I her husband." Yehovah could only have divorced Israel, if he had been wed to Israel. There is no way to divorce somebody if you've never been married. And yet, God divorced.

THE CERTIFICATE OF DIVORCE

"Then I saw that for all the causes for which backsliding Israel had committed adultery, I had put her away and given her a certificate of divorce; yet her treacherous sister Judah did not fear, but went and played the harlot also" (Jer. 3:8).

> "…that I made with their fathers in the day *that* I took them by the hand to lead them out of the land of Egypt, My covenant which they broke, though I was a husband to them, says the LORD" (Jer. 31:32).

A broken relationship. And so after 700 years, God gave them a certificate of divorce. It says, "Therefore Yehovah was very angry with Israel and removed them from His sight. **There was none left but the tribe of Judah alone**" (2 Kgs. 17:18 Emphasis added).

This is the backdrop for why Jesus had to die. These are the seven things in Scripture that had to be reconciled at the cross. It wasn't just one. The two houses are an important part of what we have just read, but it is not the only thing. God had to deal with the very degeneration, the decay in our human body, the decay that is in the planet itself, the separation of heaven and earth. How do you bring these components back together? Even if God were to just restore Israel, how do you overcome death? How do you get God back into this plane of existence without torching it?

These are the real, big problems and there is only one way to do it. That is what is so incredible about the blood of Jesus. It changed everything. It harmonizes all things in heaven and earth. Colossians 1:20 explains: "… and by Him to **reconcile all thing**s to Himself, by Him, whether things on earth or things in heaven, having made peace **through the blood of His cross**" (Col. 1:20).

> " …that in the dispensation of the fullness of the times He
> might gather together in one all things in Christ, both which are
> in heaven and which are on earth—in Him" (Eph. 1:10).

Acts 3:21 further expounds: "… whom heaven must receive [speaking of the Lord Jesus] **until the times of restoration of all things**, which God has spoken by the mouth of all His holy prophets since the world began" (Acts 3:21).

Jesus had to be taken up until the restoration of all things. At the second coming of Jesus, we will see the restoration of all things. We will see the restoration of heaven and earth. The first thing that the blood of Yeshua restored was that relationship with His bride.

God says in Hosea 2:19, "She is not my wife, nor I her God." He says:

> "I will **betroth** you [speaking to the kingdom of Israel] to Me
> forever; yes, I will betroth you to Me in righteousness and justice,
> in lovingkindness and mercy; I will betroth you to Me in
> faithfulness, and you shall know the LORD" (Hosea 2:19, 20).

I can only imagine that the angels were scratching their heads when God said this. They might have said, "Wait a second, how can You divorce her, and then remarry her and yet, keep Your own law? Because You said

"When a man takes a wife and marries her, and it happens that she finds no favor in his eyes because he has found some uncleanness in her, and he writes her a certificate of divorce, puts it in her hand, and sends her out of his house, (Deut 24:1) "when she has departed from his house, and goes and becomes another man's wife, (Deut 24:2) "if the **latter** husband detests her and writes her a **certificate of divorce,** puts it in her hand, and sends her out of his house, or if the latter husband dies who took her as his wife, (Deut 24:3) "then her **former husband** who divorced her **must not** take her back to be his wife after she has been defiled; for that is an abomination before the LORD, and you shall not bring sin on the land which the LORD your God is giving you as an inheritance. (Deut 24:4)

The angels must have been confused. In addition, the prophets might have said, "We don't get it. How is He going to do this?"

Angels were looking into these things. Peter tells us: "… the things which have now been reported to you through those who have preached the gospel to you by the Holy Spirit sent from heaven—things which angels desire to look into" (1 Peter 1:12).

They desired to know but they could not see it. How do you put this puzzle together? There is a piece we are missing. And indeed, the piece that they could not see was that Messiah would come to die. Even though it was in the pages of Scripture, they still did not understand. It was all there, but nobody could see it. Hallelujah! "The stone that the builders rejected has become the chief cornerstone. This is the Lord's doing and it is marvelous in our eyes" (Ps. 118:22). Nobody could see it. They saw it happening but they did not know why.

What do all these things mean? God says in Jeremiah—in the same chapter where He gives a certificate of divorce:

"'Only **acknowledge** your **iniquity**, that you have transgressed against the LORD your God, and have scattered your charms to alien deities under every green tree, and you have not obeyed My voice,' says the LORD" (Jer. 3:13) "'Return, O backsliding children,' says the LORD; 'for I am **married** to you. I will take you, one from a city and two from a family, and I will bring you to Zion'" (Jer. 3:14).

All that is required to come back into relationship with God is right here in Scripture. God says to acknowledge your iniquity, that you've transgressed against Me. That is it. You do not need a degree in theology. You do not need to be versed in Hebrew, or Greek or any of that stuff. Just acknowledge your iniquity.

Remember the conversation of the thieves on the crosses beside Jesus: "Hey, brother, we are up here because we deserve it. But this man, He has done nothing wrong." Then looking to Jesus one of them said, "Lord, remember me when You come into Your kingdom." How much theology do you think that thief really had? He was probably your average Jew with an average knowledge of theology. But he wasn't a scribe or a Pharisee or Sadducee, or an expert in the law. He had no advanced degree. He probably had no clue what the "hypostatic union" meant, or how to describe the triunity of God. He did not know any of these complex doctrines. All he knew was, "I've committed iniquity; that is why I'm up here. And I also believe that this Nazarene has a solution; I have no more to go on than that. I've got nothing to lose, but everything to gain." That is the essence of the good news— that Jesus died for our sins. And that is very good news indeed. Hallelujah, for that!

Once again, how could God accomplish this? The former husband who divorced Israel must not take Israel back to be his wife after she has been defiled—for that is an abomination before Yehovah. The only way that the wife (northern Israel) could be released from her fate of having been put away (Hebrew, *"shlichah"*) and divorced (*"kritut"*), was for her husband, God, to die. That was the only way. There was no other solution. The great mystery was that the Husband died, and yet He lives.

That is why the angels may have thought, "Wait a second, God marries, divorces, and somebody has to die. I don't get it. God is eternal. He does not die. How can this be?" The only solution to this dilemma was to annul/dissolve the original marriage contract. Paul understood this when he used the law to explain. He reminded the Jews who knew the law that the law only has jurisdiction over a person until their death.

"Or do you not know, brethren (for I speak to those who know the law), that the law has dominion over a man as long as he lives? For the woman who has a husband is bound by the law to *her* husband as long as he lives. But if the husband dies, she is released from the **law of *her* husband**" (Rom. 7:1, 2).

She was not released from the Torah itself, but from the "law of her husband," from that contract which is called a marriage contract by which she entered into that law. She would be released from that law if he died. That is how she was released. Paul goes on to explain how the wife is freed from the law of the husband—the marriage contract.

"So then if, while *her* husband lives, she marries another man, she will be called an adulteress; but **if her husband dies**, she is **free from <u>that</u> law**, so that she is no adulteress, though she has married another man" (Rom. 7: 3).

That is what God called Israel, an adulterous wife. But if the husband died, she is free from that law, from the marriage contract, so that she is not adulterous though she has married another man. Who was the other man that she has now married? The one that rose from the dead. Thus, Paul was not suggesting the Torah, the Law, has been done away with, not at all.

"Therefore, my brethren, you also have become dead to the law through the body of Christ, that you may be married to another—to Him who was raised from the dead, that we should bear fruit to God" (Rom. 7: 4).

Remember, if the husband dies, she is released from the law of her husband. We are not under the old marriage contract, the old covenant. There was nothing wrong with that marriage contract, by the way. It was a good contract. It was not the marriage contract that had issues. It was one of the two parties that had issues, namely Israel, not God. God was good. But Israel did not keep the stipulations of the contract. She went whoring again and again… after other false gods. God could have ended it the first time but He graciously said, "I know you've got issues, how can I work with you?" But finally, He said, "Okay, that is it. We are divorcing. Sorry, can't take it any longer." God's patience shows His grace.

Then Paul tells us in Colossians 2:14, "having wiped out the handwriting of requirements…"

God's righteous requirement was death, because of adultery—that is what she deserved. Death because of adultery. That was the handwriting against her. And that was penalty that was against us, which was contrary to us; and which He has taken that out of the way, having nailed it to the cross. It is unfortunate that many of our Christian brothers think that it was the Torah, "The Law," that God nailed to the cross. It was not. The Torah is good. It is perfect. It is eternal, spoken by God, by His own mouth. Of course it is good. You cannot nail that to the cross. That is inconceivable. And yet, some people think that.

Progressing in our chiasm, God has restored His relationship with His bride; and calls her His bride once again. The next step in restoration was to take these two, and make them one— the northern kingdom and the southern kingdom that were split needed to be made one again. It would be the United Israel restored. We see in Ezekiel 37:

> As for you, son of man, take a stick for yourself and write on it: "For Judah and for the children of Israel, his companions." Then take another stick and write on it, "For Joseph, the stick of Ephraim, and *for* all the house of Israel, his companions." Then join them one to another for yourself into one stick, and they will become one in your hand. And when the children of your people speak to you, saying, "Will you not show us what you *mean* by these?"— say to them, "Thus says the Lord GOD: 'Surely I will take the stick of Joseph, which *is* in the hand of Ephraim, and the tribes of Israel, his companions; and I will join them with it, with the stick of Judah, and make them one stick, and they will be one in My hand'" (Ezek. 37:16-19).

How could God take these two kingdoms that have separated and make them one again? They have centuries of enmity between them. This seems impossible. And yet this is what God promised to do.

We then have the spirit restored to Adam. John 20:22: "When He had said this, He breathed on them and said to them 'receive the Holy Spirit.'" That was one of the things that Jesus has accomplished. He has given the Holy Spirit to those who believe in Him by faith. We have seen that it is the exact same language used in Genesis 2:7.

The heavenly (New) Jerusalem and Earth were separated but now they are brought back together. They are no longer separated. The heavens shall be rolled up like a scroll when the sky recedes, like a scroll when it is rolled up. "And He will destroy on this mountain the surface of the covering cast over all people, and the veil that is spread over all nations" (Isa. 25:7).

Isaiah says: "Oh, that You would rend the heavens! That You would come down!" (Isa. 64:1). That veil is similar to curtains when they open. Jesus will make His appearance. This is the exciting news, that that veil between heaven and earth is going to come down. And the two dimensions (realms) will become one dimension (realm) again. The transition from the realm we see now will be fiery indeed. At that time Adam, or mankind, will be restored physically, genetically. We will no longer die. That is one of the last things that God had to resolve.

"For as in Adam all die, even so in Christ all shall be made alive. But each one in his own order: Christ the firstfruits, afterward those *who are* Christ's at His coming" (1 Cor. 15:22, 23).

"It is sown a natural body, it is raised a spiritual body. There is a natural body, and there is a spiritual body" (1 Cor. 15:44).

"For as by one man's disobedience many were made sinners, so also by one Man's obedience many will be made righteous" (Rom. 5:19).

We all died because we are carbon copies of Adam. We all have his DNA inside of us. We all have his decaying, degenerate, corrupt DNA. Every time we make babies, we are making a copy of a copy of a copy… So we are worse off than Adam was; we are mutants. But we will not be mutants forever. That is the good news. God is going to resolve this. He is going to make us new. It is very interesting that two evolutionists did a study called *Why Y?* They looked at the Y chromosome and they suggested that the Y chromosome contains a record of an event in the life of the man who had passed on the current Y chromosome.

Could not the man who had the record of the event have been Adam himself—that Adam had his DNA, his Y chromosome, mixed up and that has been passed from generation to generation? We all die because of Adam. The good news is that we will be reborn with the seed of Messiah.

"Yet it pleased the LORD to bruise Him; He has put *Him* to grief. When You make His soul an offering for sin, He shall see *His* **seed** [sperma]…" (Isa. 53:10).

Now Jesus did not have physical children with a woman as the gnostic gospels propose. They are wrong. However, we are told that He has seed. We are also told in 1 John 3:9:

"Whoever has been born of God does not sin, for **His seed** remains in him; and he cannot sin, because he has been born of God."

Therefore, according to 1 John 3:9, when we believe in God we are actually given His seed, His seed is in us. First Peter tells us: "…having been born again, not of corruptible seed... (1 Pet. 1:23).

Corruptible seed is the garden variety—man plus woman makes baby. That is the corruptible seed; corruptible in the sense that people physically die, degenerate, and decay. It happens. When you are in your 20's you don't believe it, but as time goes on you begin to see that it is true.

"…, not of corruptible seed but incorruptible, through the word of God which lives and abides forever,…" (1 Pet. 1:23).

We are promised a new seed. That is good news. Because our seed, our DNA, is corrupted. It is definite that we will be given new seed. We will be reborn with a new image.

"Truly, truly I tell you, Jesus says, **unless a person is born from above**, he cannot see the kingdom of God" (John 3:3). "That which is born from flesh is flesh, and that which is born from The Spirit is spirit" (John 3:6). "Do not be astonished that I said to you that all of you must be born again" (John 3:7).

"Therefore, if anyone *is* in Christ, *he is* a new creation; old things have passed away; behold, all things have become new" (2 Cor. 5:17). "For in Christ Jesus neither circumcision nor uncircumcision avails anything, but a new creation" (Gal. 6:15).

At this point one may say, "Wait a second. Where's my new body?" It is on hold, on layaway. It is reserved in heaven for you. It is a present reality, but it is on hold. We don't get it just yet. There is a reason for that, but it is beyond the scope of this discussion.

But God makes the promise: "Your dead shall live;…Awake and sing, you who dwell in dust; …" (Isa. 26:19). He says:

Therefore prophesy and say to them, "Thus says the Lord GOD: 'Behold, O My people, I will open your graves and cause you to come up from your graves, and bring you into the land of Israel. Then you shall know that I *am* the LORD, when I have opened your graves, O My people, and brought you up from your graves. I will put My Spirit in you, and you shall live, and I will place you in your own land. Then you shall know that I, the LORD, have spoken *it* and performed *it*,' says the LORD" (Ezek. 37:12-14).

We see here the glorious day when the bones come together and sinews begin to grow on them, flesh comes back upon these bones. This will not be the same man that died. He will be a new and improved man from that day forward. Creation itself will be liberated from the bondage of corruption. Again, the very earth, the dirt, the soil has corruption, has degeneration in it. Paul says:

> For the **earnest expectation** of the **creation** eagerly waits for the revealing of the sons of God…because the **creation** itself also will be **delivered** from the **bondage of corruption** into the glorious liberty of the children of God. For we know that the whole creation groans and labors with birth pangs together until now. Not only *that*, but we also who have the firstfruits of the Spirit, even we ourselves groan within ourselves, eagerly waiting for the adoption, the redemption of our body (Rom. 8:19-23).

When the alpha particle escapes from a piece of granite, the granite decays and becomes faintly radioactive. What that tells us is that piece of rock is ever so slowly falling apart. God will take all the alpha particles and stick them back where they need to go so that the very dirt itself will not die anymore. Can you imagine how glorious the earth will be? It is a beautiful place now, but imagine when there is no more death in the dirt itself! How wonderful, vibrant, lush, and glorious it will be. The ground was cursed because of what Adam did and brought forth thorns and thistles.

In Isaiah 55, it says:

- "Instead of the thorn shall come up the cypress tree, and instead of the brier shall come up the myrtle tree" (Isa. 55:13).
- "Sing, O heavens, for the LORD has done *it!* Shout, you lower parts of the earth; break forth into singing, you mountains, O

forest, and every tree in it!" "For the LORD has redeemed Jacob, and glorified Himself in Israel" (Isa. 44:23).

- "The wilderness and the wasteland shall be glad for them, and the desert shall rejoice and blossom as the rose; it shall blossom abundantly and rejoice..." (Isa. 35:1, 2).
- "Break forth into joy, sing together, you waste places of Jerusalem" (Isa. 52:9)!
- The earth itself will be radically transformed. "And the weaned child shall put his hand in the viper's den" (Isa. 11:8). "They shall not hurt nor destroy in all My holy mountain, for the earth shall be full of the knowledge of the LORD as the waters cover the sea" (Isa. 11:9).

That day is coming when the relationship with the animals will be restored. When Adam sinned, the earth fell into decay. When the earth fell into decay, the things that came up out of the earth fell into decay, because it says: "Let the earth bring forth the living creature..." (Gen. 1:24). It means that the earth and the animals were connected to Adam's sin. When he sinned, death entered the world, death entered into animals which is when they started to eat each other, etc. When humans are restored, and the earth is restored, then the animals will of necessity be restored to their original state. Then Adam will be in harmony with God. What a glorious day that will be!

> "And I heard a loud voice from heaven saying, 'Behold, the tabernacle of God *is* with men, and He will dwell with them, and they shall be His people. God Himself will be with them *and be* their God'" (Rev. 21:3).

No more veil of separation between heaven and earth. No more distance between the New Jerusalem and us. No more problems between animals and humans. No more thorns and thistles on the planet. No more divorce between Israel and God. No more separation between Judah and Israel. All of these things will be brought together; and they were all made possible by the blood of Yeshua. That is powerful blood. That is very, very powerful blood.

Moreover I will make a covenant of peace with them, and it shall be an everlasting covenant with them; I will establish them and multiply them, and I will set My sanctuary in their midst forevermore. My tabernacle also shall be with them; indeed I will be their God, and they shall be My people. The nations also will know that I, the LORD, sanctify Israel, when My sanctuary is in their midst forevermore (Ezek. 37:26-28).

Now we come back to where we started; God in perfect harmony with His creation. All things in heaven and earth have been restored because of the blood of Jesus. "For behold, I create new heavens and a new earth; and the former shall not be remembered or come to mind" (Isa. 65:17).

These seven things are why Yeshua had to die. Although the simplistic explanation "Jesus died for my sins," is true, there is so much more than that. The problem was bigger than just one person. It entailed the massive divorce between God and everything He had created. God had to bring it together and the only way to do it was for the incarnate Son to die, shedding His own blood. No substitute would ever be sufficient. We have a good God, do we not?

As has been stated from the onset of this book, the authors desire to dispel any notion that being chosen, elect, or in good covenantal standing is the equivalent of being saved from the wrath to come, which is accomplished only in Jesus the Messiah. Therefore, the following chapter is included at this point, before proceeding to develop the premise of Judah's good standing during the Second Temple period. Understanding "election" is just as important as knowing the history of the two houses in our discussion of Judah's national status as being chosen, and continuing on the national basis to "be My people" up until the time of Judah's national rejection of Christ.

A consequence of not maintaining the distinction between the house of Israel and the house of Judah led to predestinationism, commonly known as Calvinism. The progression is very simple. If God's plan switched from the Jews to the church and the church became the new Israel, then the concept of election is not one of national election but personal, individual election. In this chapter we will see that biblical election refers to God having chosen all Israel (both houses) and has absolutely nothing to do with individual (private) salvation, contrary to the teaching of Calvinism.

Calvin summarizes this foundational doctrine in his book *Institutes of the Christian Religion* (Book 3 Chapter 21): "Of the eternal election, by which God has predestinated some to salvation, and others to destruction." He qualifies his summary by stating:

> The **predestination** by which God adopts some to the hope of life, and adjudges others to **eternal death**, no man who would be thought pious ventures simply to deny…By predestination we mean the eternal decree of God, by **which he determined with himself** whatever he wished to happen with regard to every man. All are not created on equal terms, but **some are preordained to eternal life**, others to **eternal damnation**; and, accordingly, as **each has been created for one or other of these ends**, we say that he has been predestinated to life or to death. (Calvin Institutes 3:21:5: 06)

Calvinist James White reiterates Calvin's words demonstrating that Calvin meant what he said. White states: "God elects a specific people unto Himself without reference to anything they do. This means the basis of God's choice of the elect is solely within Himself. His grace, His mercy, His will. It is not man's actions, works, or even foreseen faith, that "draws" God's choice. God's election is unconditional and final." (James R. White, *The Potter's Freedom*, Amityville, NY: Calvary Press, 2000, p. 39) This is also echoed by Loraine Boettner, in *The Reformed Doctrine of Predestination*:

> The Doctrine of absolute Predestination of course logically **holds that some are foreordained to death** as truly as others are foreordained to life. The very terms 'elect' and 'election' imply the terms 'non-elect' and 'reprobation'.

When some are chosen out, others are left not chosen. The high privileges and glorious destiny of the former are not shared with the latter…Those who hold the doctrine of Election but deny that of Reprobation can lay but little claim to consistency. To affirm the former while denying the latter makes the decree of predestination an illogical and lop-sided decree. The creed which states the former but denies the latter will resemble a wounded eagle attempting to fly with but one wing. (Loraine Boettner, *The Reformed Doctrine of Predestination*, 1932, from 2000 Bible Study Centre™ DIGITAL LIBRARY pp. 104-5).

The good news, however, is that "election, elect, chosen" (and the derivatives) are terms that **have nothing to do with one's eternal destiny**. Scripture does speak at length of "the elect" and "the chosen" but these terms are devoid of the Calvinistic sense of someone who has been chosen to receive eternal life. The term elect and its derivatives therefore are not salvific in meaning but simply refer to persons or things that are chosen for a particular purpose and the purpose has nothing to do with eternal life. Once the definition of the word is established biblically, the foundation of Calvinism will be undermined and will collapse and arguing the tenants of TULIP will become inapplicable.

The word "elect" (Greek verb: eklegomai ἐκλέγομαι; Hebrew verb: bakhar בָּחַר) means to choose, select. The elect or chosen (as nouns or adjectives) are those people or things that have been elected, selected, or chosen for a particular purpose by someone. Scripture bears witness that elect and its derivatives have nothing to do with someone being chosen specifically to eternal life.

THE ELECTION OF PRIESTS, KINGS, AND DISCIPLES

In the Old Testament we see times when God **chose**, and people chose. God chose Levi to minister forever "… the LORD your God has **chosen** [*bakhar* בָּחַר Greek LXX *eklexetai* εκλεξηται] him…" (Deut. 18:5, see also 1 Chr. 15:2). God chose Saul to be the first king of Israel. What is fascinating about King Saul is that he was chosen both by God and by the people: "…Samuel said to all the people, 'Do you see him whom the LORD has **chosen**'" (1 Sam. 10:24). The Hebrew and Greek are the same roots as above.

Two chapters later he was chosen by the people: "…here is the king whom you have chosen and whom you have desired. And take note, the LORD has set a king over you" (1 Sam. 12:13). Saul's election by God had nothing to do with eternal life. Saul was chosen, elected by God for the purpose to be king over Israel and with that he had all of the potential to be a good king and for his lineage to be the lineage of the Messiah. "Why then did you not obey the voice of the LORD? … Behold, to obey is better than sacrifice, and to heed than the fat of rams. For rebellion is as the sin of witchcraft, and stubbornness is as iniquity and idolatry. Because you have rejected the word of the LORD, He also has rejected you from being king" (1 Sam. 15:19, 22-23).

It is only after repeated disobedience that Saul is rejected, and David is chosen to take his place. Saul's election by God to be king had nothing to do with eternal life and his removal from being king, likewise, had nothing to do with eternal life—he was simply removed from his post. Saul is analogous to Judas in many ways, because both he and Judas were chosen, yet they both forfeited their election. "Jesus answered them, 'Did I not choose [eklegomai ἐκλέγομαι] you, the twelve, and one of you is a devil?'" (John 6:70). God elected David to be king and passed over the other seven sons of Jesse. "The LORD said to Samuel, 'Do not look at his appearance or at his physical stature, because I have refused him' … Neither has the LORD **chosen** this one…the LORD has **not chosen** these" (1 Sam. 16:7-10). The choosing or election had nothing to do with eternal life according to the Calvinist definition: God chose David because of what He saw in the heart; and, He chose him to be king—not for the purpose of eternal life. See Luke 6:13; John 13:18, 15:16, 19; Acts 1:2, 24, 15:7 concerning Jesus choosing the disciples, one of whom was a devil (John 6:70).

THE ELECTION OF MESSIAH AND ANGELS

God's election of Messiah further demonstrates that the term "election" is devoid of the Calvinistic concept of eternal life. Jesus, the Messiah-God-Incarnate, certainly has no need of salvation or eternal life; He is the source of life! "Behold! My Servant whom I uphold, My Elect One [LXX: *eklektos* εκλεκτος] in whom My soul delights! I have put My Spirit upon Him… (Isa. 42:1, see also Isa. 49:7).

This very title was used of Jesus on the cross "…the rulers with them sneered, saying, 'He saved others; let Him save Himself if He is the Christ, the chosen of God'" (Luke 23:35). Peter further confirms God's election of the Messiah: "Coming to Him as to a living stone, rejected indeed by men, but chosen by God and precious" (1 Pet. 2:4, see also 1 Pet. 2:6). Jesus was unquestionably chosen, elected, predestined by God to be the Messiah, but His election was not for His salvation. He was chosen by the Father to give us eternal life! In a similar fashion we find that angels can be elected – demonstrating that "elect" does not mean chosen to eternal life (see also Heb. 2:16 regarding the fact that God only offers salvation to mankind): "I charge you before God and the Lord Jesus Christ and the elect angels…" (1 Tim. 5:21).

The Election of Jerusalem

God also elected (chose) Jerusalem to be His city, proving that election has nothing to do with eternal life. "Yet I have chosen Jerusalem, that My name may be there, and I have chosen David to be over My people Israel" (2 Chr. 6:6), "…the city which You have chosen…" (1 Kgs. 8:44), "…and for the sake of Jerusalem, the city which I have chosen…" (1 Kgs. 11:32), "…the city which I have chosen for Myself, to put My name there" (1 Kgs. 11:36), "For the LORD has chosen Zion; He has desired it for His dwelling place" (Ps. 132:13). In all these verses we see that God has chosen or elected Jerusalem for a purpose and the word election does not entail eternal life.

The Election of False Gods and Foolish Things

In Corinthians we learn that God has chosen foolish, weak, base and despised things: "But God has chosen the foolish things of the world to put to shame the wise, and God has chosen the weak things of the world to put to shame the things which are mighty; and the base things of the world and the things which are despised God has chosen, and the things which are not, to bring to nothing the things that are," (1 Cor. 1:27-28, see also James 2:5).

Not only is election used to describe God's choosing of people, places, and things for His special purposes, it is used for men's choosing of the true God and of false gods. "So Joshua said to the people, 'You are witnesses against yourselves that you have chosen the LORD for yourselves, to serve Him…'" (Josh. 24:22).

"Go and cry out to the gods which you have chosen; let them deliver you in your time of distress" (Judg. 10:14). Jesus points out others who chose poorly in the Gospel of Luke: "Jesus noticed how the guests chose the places of honor, He told them a parable. He said to them…'when you are invited…do not take the place of honor'" (Luke 14:8).

Our conclusion from the above verses is that election has nothing to do with predestination to eternal life. God chose priests, kings and Jerusalem for His purposes and man chose both God and idols. We would be wrong to try to insert the concept of predestination into the term election.

THE ELECTION OF ISRAEL

While election is made by God and men of people and places, there is a usage that stands out uniquely in Scripture: God's chosen people, the elect, are the Israelites. The title "chosen/elect" concerning Israel is found in no less than eight verses. The use of the title "elect" to describe Israel becomes very important when we venture into the New Testament because it clears up many theological, soteriological, and eschatological issues.

"Seed of Israel His servant, you children of Jacob, His chosen ones" (1 Chr. 16:13)!

"Blessed is the nation whose God is the LORD, the people He has chosen as His own inheritance" (Ps. 33:12).

- "Seed of Abraham His servant, you children of Jacob, His **chosen** ones" (Ps. 105:6)!
- "He brought out His people with joy, His **chosen** ones with gladness" (Ps. 105:43).
- "For the LORD has **chosen** Jacob for Himself, Israel for His special treasure" (Ps. 135:4).
- "For Jacob My servant's sake, and Israel My **elect**…" (Isa. 45:4).
- "I will bring forth descendants from Jacob, and from Judah an heir of My mountains; My **elect** shall inherit it, and My servants shall dwell there" (Isa. 65:9).
- "For as the days of a tree, so shall be the days of My people, and My **elect** shall long enjoy the work of their hands" (Isa. 65:22).

The verses above demonstrate how God has specifically called Israel, Jacob, the Seed of Abraham, His chosen. Thus the term "the chosen" or "My chosen" and "the elect" is a reference to ethnic Israel. This point is proven by Paul who, in a synagogue on the Sabbath day in Antioch, read from the Law and Prophets and then spoke to his fellow Jews: "Men of Israel, and you who fear God, listen: 'The God of this people Israel chose our fathers...'" (Acts 13:16, 17). Thus, the election of Israel was true in the Old Testament and the New Testament as well.

THE "FEW CHOSEN" ARE ISRAELITES

With the definition of "the elect/chosen" established, we are now ready to proceed to the teachings of Jesus, Whom, we must remember, was Himself Jewish. In Matthew 22 Jesus, speaking with the Pharisees, compares the Kingdom of Heaven to a king who prepared a wedding feast for his son. Those that were invited to the wedding feast were not interested in coming, so the king sent his servants out calling everyone who would come. That the invited guests to the wedding were the Israelites is certain. Jesus Himself confirms this in His rebuke to the Pharisees: "And I say to you that many will come from east and west, and sit down with Abraham, Isaac, and Jacob in the kingdom of heaven" (Matt. 8:11).

There are also many passages in the Old Testament that speak of the Messianic age in which the descendants of Abraham, Isaac, and Jacob would be God's special people (see for example: Isa. 2, 4, 11, 60-66). Therefore, Jesus' statement "For many are called, but few are chosen," (Matt. 22:14, see also Matt. 20:16) must be interpreted in light of who are the chosen—that is Israel! The chosen, elect (Israel) were the ones to whom the promise of the Messianic Age was first given. However, when the bridegroom came, they were not willing to come and therefore God the Father gave instruction for all (the many) to be called to the feast. Understanding who the elect are unlocks the passage for us. Knowing that the elect is Israel completely rules out any Calvinistic interpretation of the passage. Note that both the called and chosen still needed salvation as indicated by the wedding garment; and he who was found in the feast without a garment was cast out.

THE ELECT IN PETER'S EPISTLES ARE ISRAELITES

Peter used the term elect to describe Israel. We know so because Peter says as much: "Peter, an apostle of Jesus Christ, to the pilgrims of the Dispersion in Pontus, Galatia, Cappadocia, Asia, and Bithynia, **elect** according to the foreknowledge of God the Father, in sanctification of the Spirit, for obedience and sprinkling of the blood of Jesus Christ…" (1 Pet. 1:1-2). The word "dispersion" (Greek *diaspora* διασπορά) was used to describe the scattering among the nations that God had promised to Israel if they would not follow Him (Lev. 26:33; Deut. 4:27; Neh. 1:8, etc., the LXX uses the same Greek word as the NT). James, in his epistle, could not be any clearer that the diaspora is Israel when he says: "To **the twelve tribes** which are scattered abroad [*en te diaspora* εν τη διασπορα]: Greetings" (James 1:1). The twelve tribes are of course Israel, and they are in the diaspora – the same group to which Peter was addressing his letter.

At the end of his first epistle, Peter further establishes that part of the elect were none other than Jewish believers, who were also in the diaspora. He writes (in the NKJV) "She who is in Babylon, **elect** together with [you,] greets you" (1 Pet. 5:13). Now at first glance it appears that Peter might be referring to some woman by the use of the word "she" (aute αὐτή) – which by the way, is absent from the Greek text. The word in the text is the feminine article (he ἡ) which is referencing back to something that was already addressed in the letter. We know that the something in question is also elect and is an adjective modifier to the something because "elect" is feminine singular (*suneklekte* συνεκλεκτὴ).

The question is, however, what is the something that the article and adjective refer to? The answer is found by considering to whom the feminine something is sending greetings. That takes us back to the first chapter, where Peter established already that he was writing to the pilgrims who were in the diaspora. Diaspora is a singular feminine word and hence it fits the bill perfectly. Certain translations, like the NET Bible for example, have translated the feminine article in 1 Peter 5:13 not as "she" but as "the church". Their selection at first appears justified since Peter is obviously writing to believers in Jesus and, of course, the word (*ekklesia* ἐκκλησία) is singular feminine. The weakness of the translation, however, is proven by the fact that the word "ekklesia" does not appear even once in either of Peter's epistles. The word diaspora does appear and fits in both number and gender.

Lastly, we must acknowledge two important points: 1) Peter was the apostle to the Jews. In Galatians 2:7-9 Paul states that he "was entrusted with the gospel to the uncircumcised just as Peter was to the circumcised" (Gal. 2:7); 2) Babylon was the third largest Jewish center in the ancient world. When the Jews were given leave under Cyrus to return to Israel in 536 BC, only a small remnant returned, while many thousands stayed in Babylon. The writing of the Babylonian Talmud gives concrete proof of the fact that Babylon was a major center of Jewish life and culture. Since Peter was the apostle specifically appointed to take the Gospel to the Jews, finding him in Babylon (not Rome!) in the company of Jews is simple enough to grasp. Whether or not Peter ever ventured to Rome, as church history would have us believe, is therefore in question—though it remains outside of the scope of this brief study. Nevertheless, we see that Peter is writing from Babylon, in the company of other Jews (the elect) to fellow elect who were also in the diaspora (that is, not living in Israel). Realizing that Peter is the apostle to the (elect) Jews and is writing from Babylon to other (elect) Jews facilitates the interpretation of the two epistles.

In 1st Peter chapter two, Peter writes concerning these elect in the diaspora: "you also, as living stones, are being built up a spiritual house, a holy priesthood, to offer up spiritual sacrifices acceptable to God through Jesus Christ. But you are a chosen generation [note: the Greek word is genos (race) not genea (generation) see: NASB], a **royal priesthood**, a **holy nation**, His own **special people**, that you may proclaim the praises of Him Who called you out of darkness into His marvelous light" (1 Pet. 2:5, 9). These same words were used repeatedly in the Old Testament to describe Israel:

- "Now therefore, if you will indeed obey My voice and keep My covenant, then you shall be a **special treasure** to Me above all people; for all the earth is Mine" (Ex. 19:5). See Ps. 135:4.

- "'And you shall be to Me a **kingdom** of **priests** and **a holy nation**.' These are the words which you shall speak to the children of Israel" (Ex. 19:6).

- "For you are a **holy people** to the LORD your God; the LORD your God has chosen you to be a people for Himself, a **special treasure** above all the peoples on the face of the earth" (Deut. 7:6). See also Deut. 14:2.

Now Peter addresses the House of Israel: "You **once were not a people**, but now you are God's people. You were shown no mercy, but now you have received mercy" (1 Pet. 2:10). The passage is taken from Hosea 1:9 where God, speaking to the house of Israel: "Then the LORD said: "Name him 'Not My People' (Lo-Ammi), because **you are not my people** and I am not your God" (Hos. 1:9). Peter is demonstrating that their previous divorce has been undone in Jesus Christ. This truth is given by God through Hosea, "However, in the future the number of the people of Israel will be like the sand of the sea which can be neither measured nor numbered. Although it was said to them, '**You are not my people**,' it will be said to them, 'You are children of the living God!'" (Hos. 1:10, see also Hos. 2:23)

ELECT BUT NOT SAVED

Thus, when we read in 2nd Peter: "Therefore, brethren, be even more diligent to make your call and election sure, for if you do these things you will never stumble" (2 Pet. 1:10) – we know that Peter is talking to Israelites and that they were elected apart from their salvation. Therefore, this is not a Calvinistic call for us to, somehow, make sure that we have been chosen to eternal life! It is rather a fulfillment of the plethora of times God told the house of Israel that he would bring them back and make them his people once again.

However, their election is by no means an absolute guarantee that they will inherit eternal life. Paul corroborates this fact so clearly in 2nd Timothy: "Therefore I endure all things for the sake of the **elect**, that they also **may obtain the salvation** which is in Christ Jesus with eternal glory" (2 Tim. 2:10). Note well that Paul must endure for the elect, the Israelites, so that they too might be saved. As we have seen, election has nothing to do with salvation. Furthermore, election is generally a term used of Israel, which is of course, God's chosen people. This is confirmed yet again in Romans 11 where Paul states: "Concerning the gospel they are enemies for your sake, but concerning the election they are beloved for the sake of the fathers" (Rom. 11:28).

Part of the challenge of understanding the book of Romans is recognizing that Paul is speaking to the believers in Rome who are both Jewish and Gentile (non-Jewish). We learn that from the way that he addresses his readers: "…the gospel of Christ … is the power of God to salvation for everyone who believes, for the Jew first and also for the Greek" (Rom. 1:16). "Jew and Greek" is a combination that he uses throughout the book; see for example Romans 2:9, 10; 10:12. In Romans 2:17 Paul speaks specifically to the Jews, "Indeed you are called a Jew, and rest on the law, and make your boast in God" (Rom. 2:17). Paul then asks what advantage the Jew has (Rom. 3:1) and he answers his question with, "Much in every way! Chiefly because to them were committed the oracles of God" (Rom. 3:2). In Chapter Four Paul speaks of Abraham who was their father according to the flesh: "…Abraham our father, as pertaining to the flesh…" (Rom. 4:1 KJV). Thus, Paul was essentially describing Abraham as "our genetic (birth) father." The NET Bible confirms that translation: "Abraham, our ancestor according to the flesh" (Rom. 4:1 NET). Finally, Paul bridges the apparent polemic between the Jews and Greeks of the Roman church with the following conclusion: "For there is no distinction between Jew and Greek, for the same Lord over all is rich to all who call upon Him" (Rom. 10:12).

Having seen that the book of Romans was written in large part to the Jews, (see also Acts 18:2 and Romans 16:3 concerning Roman Jews) as well as Gentiles, we can now see that the many uses of the word "elect" are not references to salvation, predestination, etc. Rather, they are references to the Israelites (elected by God) "to whom pertain the adoption, the glory, the covenants, the giving of the law, the service of God, and the promises; of whom are the fathers and from whom, according to the flesh, Christ came…" (Rom. 9:4-5). Therefore, Paul's question, "Who shall bring a charge against God's elect?" (Rom. 8:33) is not Calvinistic (predestined to eternal life) but is a reference to Israel whom God elected (see above: 1 Chr. 16:13, Ps. 33:12, Ps. 105:6, Ps. 105:43, Ps. 135:4, Isa. 45:4, Isa. 65:9, Isa. 65:22). This concept is consistent throughout the book. Romans 9-11 is the great defense of Scripture, par excellence, that God has not cast away His people.

Paul begins the section by showing how God began with Abraham and then chose Isaac over Ishmael, and then Jacob over Esau. Speaking of the two nations in Rebecca's womb, Paul says, "for the children not yet being born, nor having done any good or evil, that the purpose of God according to election [*ekloge* εκλογη] might stand, not of works but of Him who calls" (Rom. 9:11). The election has nothing to do with Calvinistic predestination, but with God choosing Jacob rather than Esau to be the one who would receive the oracles of God, etc.

ELECTION OF GRACE

Paul continues in Romans 11, "Even so then, at this present time there is a remnant according to the election [*ekloge* εκλογη] of grace" (Rom. 11:5). This was spoken concerning the encounter of Elijah and the 400 Israelite prophets of Baal. Just when Elijah thought all was lost, God informed him that He had reserved 7,000 that had not followed the evil ways of Baal. Thus, in like manner, Israel—who had been chosen, elected by God to be the conduit of blessing to the world— in large part, had rejected that special calling. This concords with what Jesus stated in Matthew 22:14 that, "few [the Israelites] are chosen" and that small group had, for the most part, rejected the special RSVP.

Paul continues, "What then? Israel has not obtained what it seeks; but the elect [*ekloge* εκλογη] have obtained it, and the rest were blinded" (Rom. 11:7). It must be noted that the word "elect" here is in fact feminine singular– demonstrating that it is not speaking of "the elect ones" (masculine plural eklektoi εκλεκτοι) but the abstract noun "election". This means that in both Romans 11:5 and 11:7 the term is "election"—thus God's action of selecting Abraham, Isaac, Jacob to the be the recipients of the promises (Rom. 9:4-5). (The Wesley translation properly maintains the nuance of the noun "the election [*ekloge* εκλογη] hath obtained..." Rom. 11:7 Wesley.) The entire context of the elect and election has to do with Israel as evidenced by Paul's following statement of how the house of Israel "have not stumbled so as to fall... on the contrary, because of their stumbling, salvation has come to the Gentiles to make the Jews jealous" (Rom. 11:11).

The biblical "election of grace" is not Calvin's idea of God choosing some to eternal life and others to eternal damnation; it is rather God choosing Israel, which was based purely on God's grace and not on Israel's righteousness. Moses plainly stated this early in their national history: "It is not because of your righteousness or the uprightness of your heart that you go in to possess their land, but because of the wickedness of these nations that the LORD your God drives them out from before you, and that He may fulfill the word which the LORD swore to your fathers, to Abraham, Isaac, and Jacob" (Deut. 9:5).

That the election of grace is referring to God's choosing of the fathers is further established in Chapter 11:

"Now if their stumbling means riches for the world, and if their fall means riches for the Gentiles, how much more will their full inclusion mean! For if their rejection means the reconciliation of the world, what will their acceptance mean but life from the dead?" (Rom. 11:12, 15)

Israel had been scattered and assimilated in the nations which thereby translated into riches for the Gentiles (nations). However, the election of grace, that is God's making promises to Abraham, Isaac, and Jacob and their seed, was an irrevocable call, which is why Paul says about the unbelieving Jews: "Concerning the gospel they are enemies for your sake, but concerning the election they are beloved for the sake of the fathers. For the gifts and the calling of God are irrevocable" (Rom. 11:28-29). Paul probably had Jeremiah 31:35-37, among other passages, in mind when speaking of the irrevocability of God's promise. God had called Israel to Himself; and would never let them go completely. "God has not cast away His people whom He foreknew" (Rom. 11:2). Peter also confirms that God foreknew the Israelites: "to the pilgrims of the Dispersion elect according to the foreknowledge of God the Father" (1 Pet. 1:2). God chose Abraham, Isaac, Jacob, and their descendants for a special purpose. His choosing them (election) had nothing to do with the Calvinistic idea of predestination to eternal life and eternal damnation. Though Israel was elected, the Israelites were not automatically saved.

FOREKNOWLEDGE

Foreknowledge is a companion of election – but just like election, foreknowledge is a general reference to God having known the Israelites beforehand. Consider Paul's definitive statement: "So I ask, God has not rejected His people, has He? Absolutely not! For I too am an Israelite, a descendant of Abraham, from the tribe of Benjamin. God has not cast away His people whom He foreknew [*proginosko* προγινώσκω]" (Rom. 11:1-2). The word "foreknow," like election, has nothing to do with having predestined someone to eternal life or eternal damnation as Calvin suggested. "Foreknow" and "foreknowledge" are simply: a verb and a noun of the same basic stem.

Look at the following verses that demonstrate that knowing something ahead of time is not only possible for God, but for man as well; and it does not entail the Calvinistic concept whatsoever: "They knew me from the first [*proginosko* προγινώσκω], if they were willing to testify…" (Acts 26:5), "You therefore, beloved, since you know [this] beforehand [*proginosko* προγινώσκω], beware lest you also fall from your own steadfastness…" (2 Pet. 3:17). Certainly neither of those two examples carries any sense of Calvinistic predestination.

Peter speaks of Jesus being foreknown before the beginning of the world; and is just now made known: "He was foreknown [*proginosko* προγινώσκω] before the foundation of the world but was manifested in these last times for your sake" (1 Pet. 1:20 NET). We witnessed before how Peter was addressing the Israelites in his epistle, whom he states to be elect according to God's knowing beforehand: "…to the pilgrims of the Dispersion…elect according to the foreknowledge [*prognosis* πρόγνωσις] of God the Father…" Therefore, when we come to Romans 8, we ought not to jump to the Calvinistic definition but to the God-foreknew-Israel definition.

"And we know that all things work together for good to those who love God, to those who are the called according to His purpose. For whom He foreknew [*proginosko* προγινώσκω], He also predestined to be conformed to the image of His Son, that He might be the firstborn among many brethren. Moreover whom He predestined these He also called; whom He called…" (Rom. 8:28-30). Even the act of calling we find spoken of concerning Israel in the book of Isaiah:

"But now, thus says the LORD, who created you, O Jacob, and He who formed you, O Israel: fear not, for I have redeemed you; I have called you by your name; you are Mine." (Isa. 43:1, see also: 54:6; 1 Pet. 1:15, 2:9, 5:10).

Insofar as we Gentiles are grafted into the olive tree, then we share in the common purpose that God has for His elect—Israel. "You, being a wild olive tree, were grafted in among them, and with them became a partaker of the root and fatness of the olive tree," (Rom. 11:17). Paul's usage of the olive tree is not happenstance. He was drawing it from Jeremiah who clearly identifies the olive tree as Judah:

"The LORD called your name, **Green Olive Tree**, Lovely and of Good Fruit. With the noise of a great tumult He has kindled fire on it, And its **branches** are **broken** (Jer. 11:16)." "For the LORD of hosts, who planted you, has pronounced doom against you for the evil of the **house of Israel** and of the **house of Judah**, which they have done against themselves to provoke Me to anger in offering incense to Baal" (Jer. 11:17).

Once we have the identities of the house of Israel and the house of Judah, we see that Paul's writings are continually speaking of their restoration on a national level. Failing to identify the two houses, leads to replacement theology and then the error of Calvinism.

OTHER VERSES ON ELECTION

There remain a number of verses that speak of the elect in the New Testament. In light of all that we have studied, we can confidently know that they have nothing to do with the Calvinistic idea of predestined to salvation or damnation. Furthermore, in almost all of the cases, understanding them to be a reference to the Israelites, God's chosen people, is warranted. Let's briefly consider those remaining verses. When Jesus spoke of God avenging "His own elect who cry out day and night to Him" (Luke 18:7), He was talking about the Israelites.

"Rufus, chosen in the Lord," (Rom. 16:13) may be speaking of him being Jewish. This would make the most sense given that of the many other (obviously) believing brothers and sisters in the chapter, only Rufus is called elect. Why would Paul refer to only him as being elect if the Calvinistic definition of election were true? Were the others not also heirs of eternal life? Understanding that elect/election is not salvation but is a reference to Israel, the passage makes complete sense.

Ephesians 1:4 ought to be viewed in light of the chosen people, Israel: "just as He chose us in Him before the foundation of the world, that we should be holy and without blame before Him in love," (Eph. 1:4). We know that Paul traveled to Ephesus and there spent three months reasoning with the Jews in the synagogues (Acts 19:1-8). Thus, Ephesians seems to be according to the paradigm, "for the Jew first and then the Gentile."

The elect in Colossians is also a reference to Israelites: "...as the elect of God, holy and beloved..." (Col. 3:12). Paul is viewing the believers in that place as part of the commonwealth of Israel (Eph 2:12) and hence part of God's chosen.

The letter to the Thessalonians is also a letter to the Jews first and then the Gentiles. In Acts 17 we read, "they came to Thessalonica, where there was a synagogue of the Jews. Then Paul, as his custom was, went into them, and for three Sabbaths reasoned with them from the Scriptures... and some of them were persuaded and ... joined Paul and Silas" (Acts 17:1, 2, 4). With that in mind, we can see why Paul would say, "we give thanks to God always for you all, making mention of you in our prayers... knowing, beloved brethren, your election by God" (1 Thess. 1:2, 4). Once again, election is not Calvinistic in its definition, but referring to the Israelites. Likewise in Titus 1:1, Paul speaks of the faith of God's elect, which very possibly was a reference to the faith of the Jewish house.

The Apostle John wrote to "the elect lady and her children..." (2 John 1:1). Though there is debate whether this is addressed to an individual woman and her immediate family, or to the larger community, is not material for this study. However, the term elect points a community who are part of the commonwealth of Israel.

CONCLUSION

We thus come to the end of our study having seen that elect and election have nothing to do with salvation, predestined to eternal life or death, nor any Calvinistic definition whatsoever. God elected priests, kings, disciples, Messiah, angels, and Jerusalem – all of which had nothing to do with being predestined to salvation. We also saw that elected/chosen was used of foolish things and of false gods (on man's part) – again, the term had nothing to do with being predestined to salvation.

We then came to the election of Israel and saw that no less than eight verses in the Old Testament God declared Israel to be His elect! When we turned to the New Testament, we could see that elect/election/chosen was never there as a reference to being predestined to salvation; in fact, nearly every reference of the elect was to Israel. We looked at the epistles of Peter and found the mention there of elect was to the children of Israel.

Finally, we considered the term foreknowledge/foreknow and found that it is not a salvific term but simply God, or even man, knowing something in advance. With all that we have seen, we must therefore conclude that election is not salvation. The definition that Calvin gave "Of the eternal election, by which God has predestinated some to salvation and others to destruction," is completely lacking in Scripture. Election has nothing to do with salvation or damnation. It is simply God or man making a choice. However, biblical election is a reference to the house of Israel and the house of Judah which God has put back together through the cross of Jesus.

Now, with the meaning of the term "election" resolved, we are ready to dive into the heart of our thesis: Judah's covenantal standing in the Second Temple period. The next chapter establishes the assertion of the book's subtitle by citing many scriptural witnesses. Many readers will have previously been taught that Judah was cut off and rejected together with the Israel. Other readers may not have given much thought about or seen the importance of understanding the Jew's relationship to God from the time of Ezra to Christ. However, the impact of reading the Prophets and the Psalms will be forever enhanced by understanding this historical reality.

So far, we have seen that God's narrative about the two houses of Israel and His specific dealings with each house are not at all obscure within the Scripture. Moreover, we have demonstrated that neither "election" nor national covenants equate to individual salvation unto eternal life. Furthermore, we trust that we have made it perfectly clear that there is only one New Covenant entered into through the blood of Jesus Christ by which the constituents of each of the two houses must be saved (Acts 4:12). These caveats, unfortunately, must precede our deeper discussion of Judah's national standing because distinguishing between national standing and Messianic salvation is a fine line—a distinction defined by Scripture nonetheless.

THE WORDS OF JESUS

The first passage we will examine contains a remark made by Jesus to His disciples, following His Triumphal Entry into Jerusalem:

> If I had not come and spoken to them, they **would have no sin**, **but now** they have no excuse for their sin. He who hates Me hates My Father also. If I had not done among them the works which no one else did, they would have no sin; **but now** they have seen and also hated both Me and My Father" (John 15:22-24).

Twice within these three verses, Jesus makes the conditional statement: "they would have no sin." Because of this statement, the passage immediately stands out as a contradiction to one of the primary assumptions within Christian Soteriology; namely, that "all have sinned and fall short of the glory of God" (Rom. 3:23). The Apostle John doubles down on this postulate: "If we say that we have no sin, we deceive ourselves, and the truth is not in us" (1 Jn. 1:8) "If we say that we have not sinned, we make Him a liar, and His word is not in us" (1 Jn. 1:10).

Clearly, Jesus' words, quoted in the John 15 passage above, cannot be applied in the context of individual, personal, sin. But the passage makes perfect sense when applied to Judah's covenantal standing. The antecedent to the "they," who would have no sin, refers to the national Jewish leadership to whom Jesus came repeatedly during the feasts and to whom He had just come, prior to His Last Supper. The passage also expresses that if Jesus had not spoken to "them," and if Jesus had not performed convincing miracles, "they would have no sin."

The key to interpreting this passage both logically, and in keeping with Christian doctrine on sin, is to consider the stipulation spoken to Moses about the one like Moses who would come.

"I will raise up for them a Prophet like you from among their brethren, and will **put My words in His mouth**, and He shall speak to them **all that I command Him**. And it shall be that **whoever will not hear My words**, which He speaks in My name, I will require it of him" (Deut. 18:18-19, emphasis added).

Now consider that Jesus had also spoken these words to them:

"He who rejects Me, and **does not receive My words**, has that which judges him—**the word that I have spoken** will judge him in the last day. For I have not spoken on My own authority; but the Father who sent Me gave Me a command, what I should say and what I should speak" (Jn. 12:48-49).

When Jesus said they would be judged by "the word that I have spoken," He may have simply been referring to the words spoken to Moses in Deuteronomy Ch. 18, because Jesus is Lord—the Lord of the Old Testament.

What Jesus appears to have communicated to the Jews was that the House of Judah was still in good standing at the coming of Messiah. However, they would not continue to walk with a good conscience toward God if they were to reject the reality that a Prophet like Moses *had* come, bearing the words of the Father and performing substantiating signs. The inconsistency of claiming to be without guilt while rejecting Messiah would also appear to be what Jesus was conveying when he told the Pharisees—again, the national Jewish leadership —, "If you were blind, you would have no sin; but now you say, 'We see.' Therefore your sin remains" (Jn. 9:41).

Before turning to the Old Testament for evidence of Judah's covenantal standing, we will examine two other comments by Jesus that support the assumption that a righteous remnant was present at the time of Christ. Reading from Matthew's gospel:

Now it happened, as Jesus sat at the table in the house that, behold, many tax collectors and sinners came and sat down with Him and His disciples. And when the Pharisees saw it, they said to His disciples, "Why does your Teacher eat with tax collectors and sinners?"

When Jesus heard that, He said to them, "Those who are well have no need of a physician, but those who are sick. But go and learn what this means: 'I desire mercy and not sacrifice.' For **I did not come to call the righteous**, but sinners, to repentance" (Matt. 9:10-13).

Granted, verse 13 could be interpreted from the standpoint that there were, in reality, none righteous; and that Jesus desired to draw the attention of the Pharisees to that fact. But if there were truly no righteous people existing at the time of Christ, then there would have been no reason at all for Jesus to address specifically, "the righteous." Moreover, an awareness of precisely whom Jesus did come to call seems to persistent in the mind of Matthew, because his gospel alone mentions Jesus' retort to His disciples regarding a Canaanite woman:

"But He answered and said, 'I was not sent except to the lost sheep of the house of Israel'" (Matt. 15:24).

We shall once again rely on the thirty-fourth chapter of Ezekiel to establish the precedent for the Shepherd of Israel:

For thus says the Lord God: "Indeed **I Myself** will search for **My sheep** and seek them out. **As a shepherd** seeks out his flock on the day he is among his scattered sheep, **so will I seek out My sheep and deliver them from all the places where they were scattered**... And I will bring them out from the peoples and gather them from the countries, and will bring them to their own land... **I will seek what was lost**..." (Excerpts, Ezek. 34:11-16).

From Ezekiel we can conclude that the house of Israel that Jesus referenced was not "all Israel"—all twelve tribes—, but was the House of Israel that had been scattered and which had not yet been brought back into the Land. In short, these "lost sheep of the house of Israel" excluded the sheep of the House of Judah, which were already back in the Land; and, as logic further implies, the Jews were not considered to be lost at that time.

The significance of these passages from Matthew is that the House of Judah was still under covenant, and were therefore, as a nation, not considered to be sinners. This classification also agrees with Paul's assessment conveyed in Galatians 2:15: "We who are Jews by nature, and **not sinners of the Gentiles [Nations]**."

Once again, as in Jesus' statement, "they would have no sin," Paul was not contradicting the doctrine of man's fallen nature; but stating the fact that the Jews were born under covenant and that devout Jews desired (in their hearts) to remain under covenant through obedience to the Law. (More will be said about obedience to the Law as this chapter progresses.)

THE NEW COVENANT

Now we will revisit the Old Testament passage that speaks of the new covenant; only this time, we will give special attention to what is said, and not said, about the two houses of Israel.

Jeremiah 31:

31 "Behold, the days are coming, says the Lord, when I will make **a new covenant** with the house of **Israel** and with the house of **Judah**—

32 not according to the covenant that I made with their fathers in the day that I took them by the hand to lead them out of the land of Egypt, My covenant which they broke, though I was a husband to them, says the Lord.

33 But this is the covenant that I will make with the **house of Israel** after those days, says the Lord: I will put My law in their minds, and write it on their hearts; and I will be their God, and they shall be My people.

34 No more shall every man teach his neighbor, and every man his brother, saying, 'Know the Lord,' for they all shall know Me, from the least of them to the greatest of them, says the Lord. For I will forgive their iniquity, and their sin I will remember no more."

Verses 31 and 32 expressly address both houses of Israel. Both houses broke the covenant made in the wilderness and both houses, therefore, needed a new covenant—the benefits of that new covenant in the blood of Messiah have already been covered in previous chapters of this book. Verse 33, however, by omission, supports the position that the House of Judah—as a nation—was not predisposed to break God's commandments. Verse 33 indicates that only the House of Israel needed to have the law put into their minds and written on their hearts.

This interpretation—that these endowments concerning the law were directed to the House of Israel, alone—is overwhelmingly validated by the last phrase of verse 33: "and I will be their God, and they shall be My people." The House of Judah was never divorced by God and, therefore, never ceased from being God's people.

A second witness to the fact that the House of Israel had spiritual needs above and beyond those of Judah is found in chapters 11 and 36 of the book of Ezekiel. In both cases, God is obviously addressing the House of Israel. This distinction between Judah and Israel is made ever so clear in Ezekiel 11:15: "Son of man, your brethren, your relatives, your countrymen, and all the house of Israel in its entirety, are those about whom the inhabitants of Jerusalem have said, 'Get far away from the Lord; this land has been given to us [the Jews] as a possession.'" Thus the Jews were well aware of the difference between the two houses and spoke in agreement with prophecy that the House of Israel would be sent "far away"—far off.

What we find in Ezekiel 36:22-28 is similar to what was prophesied about the House of Israel in Jeremiah 31:33:

> "Therefore say to the house of Israel, 'Thus says the Lord God: "I do not do this for your sake, O **house of Israel,** but for My holy name's sake, which you have profaned among the nations wherever you went. And I will sanctify My great name, which has been profaned among the nations, which you have profaned in their midst; and the nations shall know that I am the Lord," says the Lord God, "when I am hallowed in you before their eyes. For I will take you from among the nations, gather you out of all countries, and bring you into your own land. Then I will sprinkle clean water on you, and you shall be clean; I will cleanse you from all your filthiness and from all your idols. I will give you a new heart and put a new spirit within you; I will take the heart of stone out of your flesh and give you a heart of flesh. I will put My Spirit within you and cause you to walk in My statutes, and you will keep My judgments and do them. Then you shall dwell in the land that I gave to your fathers; **you shall be My people**, and I will be your God."

Note: as in other citations addressing the House of Israel, the passage ends with: "you shall be My people, and I will be your God."

Do the passages above, directed toward the House of Israel, indicate by omission that the House of Judah did not need to have the law written on their hearts, because it was already written there? Do we find evidence in Scripture that this might indeed be the case? Consider Zachariah and his wife Elizabeth and also Simeon (not to mention Nicodemus, Joseph of Arimathea, and the Jewess Mary, mother of Jesus):

> "There was in the days of Herod, the king of Judea, a certain priest named Zacharias, of the division of Abijah. His wife was of the daughters of Aaron, and her name was Elizabeth. And they were both **righteous** before God, walking in all the commandments and ordinances of the Lord **blameless**" (Luke 1:5-6).

> "And behold, there was a man in Jerusalem whose name was Simeon, and this man was **just** and **devout**, waiting for the Consolation of Israel, and **the Holy Spirit was upon him**" (Luke 2:25).

Paul commented on just such Spirit-endowed Jews in his opening chapters of Romans: "but he is a Jew who is one inwardly; and circumcision is that of the heart, in the Spirit, not in the letter; whose praise is not from men but from God" (Rom. 2:29). Yes, "he is a Jew." If, as mainstream theologies suggest, no Jews met these criteria, Paul would have never used such a Jew as a model to the Church of a genuine spirit-led walk that is pleasing to God!

So then, were all Jews living during the Second Temple Period deemed to be righteous? And after Christ's finished work, were all the members of both houses of Israel saved? These would seem to be the very questions Paul sought to address in Chapter 11 of his letter to the Romans (below). In effect, Paul was attempting to explain how certain of God's promises and prophecies could be fulfilled, and yet at the same time, appear to be unfulfilled or only partially fulfilled.

Romans Chapter 11 with commentary:

> 1 I say then, has God cast away His people? Certainly not! For I also am an Israelite, of the seed of Abraham, of the tribe of Benjamin. 2 God has not cast away His people whom He foreknew…

Paul gives himself—a member of Judah through his Benjamite ancestry—as his first proof that the Jewish House had not been completely "cast away." He later concedes (v. 15), for the sake of a conditional argument, that some within Judah might indeed be cast away.

> …Or do you not know what the Scripture says of Elijah, how he pleads with God against Israel, saying, 3 "Lord, they have killed Your prophets and torn down Your altars, and I alone am left, and they seek my life"? 4 But what does the divine response say to him? "I have reserved for Myself seven thousand men who have not bowed the knee to Baal." 5 Even so then, at this present time there is a remnant according to the election of grace. 6 And if by grace, then it is no longer of works; otherwise grace is no longer grace. But if it is of works, it is no longer grace; otherwise work is no longer work.

In the absence of theological instruction regarding the covenantal standing of Judah, it is easy to equate this "election of grace" with faith in Messiah. Indeed, such a deduction fits nicely with other New Testament discussions contrasting faith with works. Consider, instead, that the election of grace refers to Judah's right standing—albeit, for the sake of David—despite the fact that Judah had been as unfaithful as Israel, or more so. But God continued to choose (elect) the House of Judah although their works did not merit, did not earn, this special grace.

> 7 What then? Israel has not obtained what it seeks; but the elect have obtained it, and the rest were blinded. 8 Just as it is written: "God has given them a spirit of stupor, eyes that they should not see and ears that they should not hear, to this very day."
>
> 9 And David says: "Let their table become a snare and a trap, a stumbling block and a recompense to them. 10 Let their eyes be darkened, so that they do not see, and bow down their back always."

In verses 7-10 Paul selects verses pertinent to those who willfully oppose God and specifically to those who approved the crucifixion without remorse (Ps. 69). What Israel sought was restoration in all its fullness according to the Messianic prophecies: the gathering; God with us; the Lord our Righteousness; the Lord is there; etc. Here is where the stumbling block of Deuteronomy 18:18 became a factor in individual salvation. And thus, many individuals from the House of Judah stumbled. But those chosen among the chosen—the elect—with eyes to see "have obtained it."

11 I say then, have they stumbled that they should fall? Certainly not! But through their fall, to provoke them to jealousy, salvation has come to the Gentiles.

Because so many Jews refused to hear the good news of God's kingdom and manifest king, their Messiah and Lord standing before them, the focus of evangelism turned to the lost among the Nations (the Gentiles).

12 Now if their fall is riches for the world, and their failure riches for the Gentiles, how much more their fullness! 13 For I speak to you Gentiles; inasmuch as I am an apostle to the Gentiles, I magnify my ministry, 14 if by any means I may provoke to jealousy those who are my flesh and save some of them.

Contrary to Supersessionism (Replacement Theology), not all of Judah had fallen. There remained a remnant that Paul will later refer to as the "natural branches." These Jews represented the majority of the nascent church for a good deal of the first century. Furthermore, rather than writing the House of Judah off, Paul was looking forward to the time when the house of Judah nationally would overcome the "stumbling block" and come to faith in Jesus.

15 For if their being cast away is the reconciling of the world, what will their acceptance be but life from the dead?

Verse 15 is particularly problematic as traditionally translated. The first phrase, which is the hypothesis of this conditional statement, is translated correctly. It is merely restating a truth from Verse 11: *"...to provoke them to jealousy, salvation has come to the Gentiles."*

They—many of the Jews—were cast away because of transgressions. These transgressions included disobedience to the Law and the disobedience of rejecting Jesus. Unfortunately, this translation indicates that the Jews will be accepted in the future, but had not been accepted at the time that Romans was written.

The Greek text is presented below. This verse contains no textual variants among the major Byzantine and Alexandrian source texts.

15 εἰ γὰρ ἡ ἀποβολὴ αὐτῶν καταλλαγὴ κόσμου, τίς ἡ πρόσλημψις εἰ μὴ ζωὴ ἐκ νεκρῶν;

The verse contains no forms of the word, "to be." In fact, the verse contains no words in verb form. The "is," "will," and "be" have been placed in the English text according to the theological bent of the translators. Young's Literal Translation reads as follows:

15 for if the casting away of them [is] a reconciliation of the world, what the reception—if not life out of the dead? (YLT).

Young's Literal Translation does contain an implied "is," most likely to support the participle "gloss" of ἀποβολὴ (casting away). But it is not really there in the original text.

As written by Paul, the verse has nothing whatsoever to do with time. Literally, in poor English, the verse reads, *"For if their casting away, reconciliation of the world, what the reception if not life from the dead."* The verse simply consists of an action and a result, a second action and a second result, with the condition that if the first pair were true, the second pair is certainly true. In the absence of any *real* verbs, whatever verbal tense might be imagined applying to the hypothetical, should for consistency, be applied to the conclusion.

Young's translation would be more accurate by either removing the bracketed [is] from the one statement, or adding the same [is] to the other side of the conditional. The logical take away for the reader of the original Greek text—who was actually witnessing both the Jews' stumbling and the reconciliation of the world in real time—would have been:

"For if their casting away IS the reconciliation of the world, what IS their reception but life from the dead."

Those of the House of Judah and the House of Israel who believed in Jesus—the entire early Church for approximately two decades until

Gentiles slowly began to join the Church—obviously believed both statements to be true! The Jews were cast away—but by the grace of God were never divorced; but, the "obedient" Jews were already being received/accepted.

THE HOLINESS OF JUDAH

16 For if the **firstfruit** is **holy**, the **lump** is also **holy**; and if the **root** is **holy**, so are **the branches**. 17 And if some of the branches were broken off, and **you, being a wild olive tree**, were grafted in among them, and with them became a partaker of the root and fatness of the olive tree, 18 do not boast against the branches. But if you do boast, remember that **you do not support the root**, but the **root supports you**.

Here Paul employs the analogy of the olive tree found in Jeremiah Ch. 11. Because of Paul's precedent set in 1 Cor. 15:20, the holy "firstfruit" seems intuitively to be a reference to Christ. Consider, however, that verse 16 may simply present two conditional statements by which Paul might support the logic of his example of the branches in the verses which follow in the passage. This proposition is supported by the fact that what is, "first," is being compared to the "lump" (Gr. *Phurama*). In all but one instance in the New Testament, *phurama* refers to meal or dough, (in the exception, it refers to "clay"). The root, on the other hand, is further defined in verse 18 by the fact that this "root" supports the wild olive branch.

Before attempting to identify the various parts of the olive tree, it is imperative to establish how the olive was defined by Jeremiah in the first place. This citation from Jeremiah Chapter 11 is so important in defining the tree and its parts that it must be included in our text.

Jeremiah Chapter 11 with emphasis added:

1 The word that came to Jeremiah from the Lord, saying, 2 "Hear the words of this covenant, and **speak to the men of Judah and to the inhabitants of Jerusalem**; 3 and say to them, 'Thus says the Lord God of Israel: "Cursed is the man who does not obey the words of this covenant 4 which I commanded your fathers in the day I brought them out of the land of Egypt, from the iron furnace, saying, 'Obey My voice, and do according to all that I command you; so shall you be My people, and I will be your God,' 5 that I may establish the oath which I have sworn

to your fathers, to give them 'a land flowing with milk and honey,' as it is this day.""'"

And I answered and said, "So be it, Lord."

6 Then the Lord said to me, "Proclaim all these words **in the cities of Judah and in the streets of Jerusalem**, saying: 'Hear the words of this covenant and do them. 7 For I earnestly exhorted your fathers in the day I brought them up out of the land of Egypt, until this day, rising early and exhorting, saying, "Obey My voice." 8 Yet they did not obey or incline their ear, but everyone followed the dictates of his evil heart; therefore I will bring upon them all the words of this covenant, which I commanded them to do, but which they have not done.'"

9 And the Lord said to me, "A conspiracy has been found among the **men of Judah and among the inhabitants of Jerusalem**. 10 They have turned back to the iniquities of their forefathers who refused to hear My words, and they have gone after other gods to serve them; the **house of Israel and the house of Judah** have broken My covenant which I made with their fathers."

11 Therefore thus says the Lord: "Behold, I will surely bring calamity on them which they will not be able to escape; and though they cry out to Me, I will not listen to them. 12 Then the **cities of Judah** and the **inhabitants of Jerusalem** will go and cry out to the gods to whom they offer incense, but they will not save them at all in the time of their trouble. 13 For according to the number of your cities were your gods, **O Judah**; and according to the number of the streets of **Jerusalem** you have set up altars to that shameful thing, altars to burn incense to Baal.

14 "So do not pray for this people, or lift up a cry or prayer for them; for I will not hear them in the time that they cry out to Me because of their trouble.

15 "What has My beloved to do in My house,
Having done lewd deeds with many?
And the holy flesh has passed from you.
When you do evil, then you rejoice.
16 The Lord called **your** name,
Green Olive Tree, Lovely and of Good Fruit.

With the noise of a great tumult
He has kindled fire on it,
And **its branches are broken**.

17 "For the Lord of hosts, who planted you, has pronounced doom against you for the evil of the house of Israel and of the house of Judah, which they have done against themselves to provoke Me to anger in offering incense to Baal."

Here we find that: "The Lord called **your** name, **Green** Olive Tree." It is critical to identify exactly who the Lord designated a "Green Olive Tree." The prophet was instructed to speak the words of Jeremiah Chapter 11 specifically to Judah in the streets of Jerusalem. There are two incidental references to the House of Israel within that text. To be sure, the covenant made by God and broken by both houses obviously involves all twelve tribes of Israel. However, at the time of Jeremiah, the House of Israel was divorced, "not My people," and—temporarily—out of covenant. The House of Judah was, so to speak, the last man standing.

Figure 11 Olive tree near the Garden of Gethsemane

Those who have seen old olive trees are aware that much of the tree is typically dead and that the dead branches have broken away altogether. Yet, there remains a living green portion which is viable. The Lord did indeed plant but one olive tree, consisting of all twelve tribes of Israel, but in Jeremiah's declaration Judah is represented as the green portion that was left; thus, the emphasis on the adjective, "Green." Perhaps Jesus made a reference to Judah, still under covenant by God's grace, when on His way to be crucified He spoke to the **daughters of Jerusalem**, "For if people do these things when the **tree is green**, what will happen when it is dry?" (Luke 23:31 NIV). "Green" represented national Judah while still in good standing under the grace extended because of the Davidic Covenant. The verse also predicts that Judah will become "dry" on the national level at some point after the cross.

The branches of the House of Israel were already dry when Jeremiah wrote. That is why, while mentioning the sins of both houses, the passage specifies that God was speaking to Judah—still under covenant and therefore **still green**. The entity addressed in the second person by God, and called "Green Olive Tree," was the House of Judah, including the cities of Judah, and specifically, Jerusalem—The Lord called **your** name, Green Olive Tree. The significance of this observation is that the entire "green" olive tree is Judah. The entire living part of the tree: roots, branches, and "fatness." Whatever roots, and branches of the Ten Tribes that were still attached to the tree were dead; having no sap, and no fatness; they were dried up. The conclusion that the Green Olive is Judah by no means conflicts with those who see Christ as the Firstfruit, as He is indeed the Lion of the tribe of Judah. Thus, by Paul's olive tree analogy and the words of Christ, Judah is declared to be green—viable, elect, and under covenant—near the end of the Second Temple period.

What is implied, then, as the basis for the discussion about the branches? That the firstfruit of Judah *is* holy; and, the root of Judah *is* holy. Regardless of the doctrinal conclusions that have been applied within various Messianic movements, the passage effectively communicates the holiness of Judah—even at the time of Paul's ministry. Thus, we find this passage to be one of the most powerful proof texts affirming the continued good standing of Judah, a remnant nevertheless.

"Some," but not all, of the natural branches of Judah had been broken off according to Jer. 11:16. And who are the wild branches? "And you, being a wild olive tree." Paul has already ascribed the identity of "you" in verse 13: "For I speak to you Gentiles [you of the Nations]."

Then what does Paul mean by the statement: "you do not support the root, but the root supports you?" He simply means what he had written concerning all twelve tribes of Israel in Romans 9:4: "To them belong the adoption as sons, the glory, the covenants, the giving of the law, the temple worship, and the promises." There can be no clearer statement that believers in Yeshua are indeed the heirs of the Abrahamic promises than Hebrews 6:13-18 (emphasis added):

> "For when God made a **promise to Abraham**, because He could swear by no one greater, He swore by Himself, saying, 'Surely blessing I will bless you, and multiplying I will multiply you.' And so, after he had patiently endured, he obtained **the promise**. For men indeed swear by the greater, and an oath for confirmation is for them an end of all dispute. Thus God, determining to show more abundantly to the **heirs of promise** the immutability of His counsel, confirmed it by an oath, that by two immutable things, in which it is impossible for God to lie, **we might have strong consolation**, who have fled for refuge to lay hold of **the hope set before us**."

Paul's statement: "you do not support the root, but the root supports you," further supports the assumption that the Green Olive is the House of Judah. It has already been established that the "you" in this statement are Gentiles, represented by the wild branches. If the Gentiles (Nations) represent the House of Israel on a spiritual level, as suggested by Commonwealth Theology, then Paul seems to be saying that the Nations/House of Israel do not support Judah, but Judah (the green part of the tree that has continued to live throughout the Northern Kingdom's estrangement) supports you. On the other hand, if the Green Olive Tree represents all twelve tribes of Israel—God's original "planting," then Paul's statement becomes nonsense, basically saying: You, now part of the twelve tribes, don't support the twelve tribes, but the twelve tribes support the ten tribes—who would then be part of the twelve.

Continuing in Romans Ch. 11:

19 You will say then, "Branches were broken off that I might be grafted in." 20 Well said. Because of unbelief they were broken off, and you stand by faith. Do not be haughty, but fear. 21 For if God did not spare the natural branches, He may not spare you either. 22 Therefore consider the goodness and severity of God: on those who fell, severity; but toward you, goodness, if you continue in His goodness. Otherwise, you also will be cut off. 23 And they also, if they do not continue in unbelief, will be grafted in, for God is able to graft them in again. 24 For if you were cut out of the olive tree, which is wild, by nature, and were grafted contrary to nature into a cultivated olive tree, how much more will these, who are natural branches, be grafted into their own olive tree?

Going back to verse 16b: "and if the root is holy, so are the branches," if the root (Judah) is *not* holy, then neither are the branches. And neither would the branches of a wild olive tree become holy by being grafted into an unholy tree. Unless Judah was indeed holy at the beginning of the first century, this entire discussion of the olive tree would be rendered meaningless! The remainder of verses 19-24 above is self-explanatory.

25 For I do not desire, brethren, that you should be ignorant of this mystery, lest you should be wise in your own opinion, that blindness in part has happened to Israel until the fullness of the Gentiles has come in. 26 And so all Israel will be saved, as it is written:

"The Deliverer will come out of Zion,
And He will turn away ungodliness from Jacob;
27 For this is My covenant with them,
When I take away their sins."

Paul's focus broadens from verse 25 through the end of the chapter to include "all Israel"—both houses. The meaning of the "fulness of the Gentiles" has been well covered in previous chapters. In verse 26, Paul alludes to the manner or the process through which all Israel will be saved. Paul begins by quoting Isaiah 59:20 from the Greek Septuagint version of the Old Testament: Καὶ ἥξει ἕνεκεν Σιων ὁ ῥυόμενος καὶ ἀποστρέψει ἀσεβείας ἀπὸ Ιακωβ; literally, "And the Deliverer will come for the sake of Sion [Zion] and will turn away ungodliness from

Jacob." (Note: the Masoretic text reads "he will come to those who turn away from transgression.") Yes, this is what was believed by the Early Church among the nations—that the Deliverer had come for Zion's sake! For Jerusalem, Judea, and all Israel. The Nations were delivered out of the overflow of Messiah's ministry, as confirmed by Isaiah 49:6:

> "Indeed He says,
> 'It is too small a thing that You should be My Servant
> To raise up the tribes of Jacob,
> And to restore the preserved ones of Israel;
> I will also give You as a light to the Gentiles,
> That You should be My salvation to the ends of the earth.'"

Also of note is the fact that, "When I take away their sins," does not appear in the Isaiah 59:20 passage. This phrase has been added by Paul in order to establish the timing of *when* the Deliverer would come and *when* the sins of "all Israel" would be taken away. If the assumption is made that the narrative of Isaiah Ch. 59 flows over into Isaiah Ch. 60—and it seems appropriate that the arrival of the Deliverer would coincide with the rising of the Light by which "the Gentiles will come to your light" (Isa. 60:3)— then Paul would appear to be announcing the fulfillment of the prophecy of the coming of Messiah. This line of interpretation is overwhelmingly confirmed by Paul's inclusion of the first phrase of Isaiah 59:21: "For this is My covenant with them." How can we be certain that this is the New Covenant in the blood of Jesus? By examining Isaiah 59:21 in its entirety:

> "As for Me," says the Lord, "this is My **covenant** with them: My Spirit who is upon you, and My words which I have put in your mouth, shall **not depart from your mouth**, nor from the mouth of your descendants, nor from the mouth of your descendants' descendants," says the Lord, "from this time and forevermore."

What comes immediately to mind are the words of Jesus: "Heaven and earth will pass away but My words will never pass away." Observe, however, that it was not only "My words" but also "My Spirit" that would be "upon" and remain forever. This prophecy by Isaiah pre-dated the prophecies by Jeremiah and Ezekiel and formed the basis— in the Writings—for their prophecies regarding the indwelling Spirit at the time of the New Covenant.

"when I will make a new **covenant** with the house of Israel and with the house of Judah… I will **put My law in their minds**, and **write it on their hearts;** and I will be their God, and they shall be My people. (Jer. 31:31, 33, see also Ezek. 36:26)

Thus, we are not still waiting for the fulfillment of Isaiah's Deliverer; Paul was merely quoting the future tense—"will be saved"—contained in this Septuagint prophecy. Christ's words have already been spoken. The Spirit has already been given. And, the Gentiles have already come to His light! So then, has all Israel been saved? No more than all Gentiles have come to His light. Although several prophecies point to a mass conversion at the time of Christ's second coming, until then—although the Deliverer has come—salvation is an ongoing process. As Paul prefaced this entire conversation: "But they have not all obeyed the gospel. For Isaiah says, 'Lord, who has believed our report?' So then faith comes by hearing, and hearing by the word of God" (Rom. 10:16-17).

28 Concerning the gospel they are enemies for your sake, but concerning the election they are beloved for the sake of the fathers. 29 For the gifts and the calling of God are irrevocable. 30 For as you were once disobedient to God, yet have now obtained mercy through their disobedience, 31 even so these also have now been disobedient, that through the mercy shown you they also may obtain mercy. 32 For God has committed them all to disobedience, that He might have mercy on all.

The Deuteronomy 18:18 mandate has added a new, but permanent, dimension to disobedience. The House of Israel, now among the Nations (Gentiles) was cast away—divorced—for their disobedience to the covenant in the wilderness. The leadership of the house of Judah, in unbelief to the Gospel that Jesus is Lord and Christ, find themselves in disobedience to Deuteronomy 18, so that Jews and Gentiles alike are all in need of the mercy—and all of the other benefits described in the previous chapters—afforded by the cross. But the notion that the mercies and grace of the New Covenant would be withheld on the national level from holy Judah, while at the same time being freely dispensed to the wild olive tree—the House of Israel among the Nations, or the Church—is absolutely ludicrous.

Zechariah 10:6, emphasis added: "I will strengthen Judah and save the tribes of Joseph. I will restore them because I have compassion on them. <u>They will be as though I had not rejected them</u>, (JUST as IF I [they] had not sinnED: "JUSTIFIED")

To sum up Paul's olive tree analogy using English slang: If Judah ain't holy, ain't nobody holy! Nevertheless, we must reiterate that being chosen (elect) and remaining under both the Sinaitic and Davidic covenants—by God's grace—does not equate to personal, Messianic salvation unto eternal life. Furthermore, as stated in previous chapters, both houses of Israel were in need of the New Covenant as declared by Jeremiah, "… I will make a new covenant with the house of Israel and with the house of Judah…"

CHAPTER 6: THE STIGMA OF A HOLY PEOPLE

Indeed, the Lord has proclaimed to the end of the world: "Say to the daughter of Zion, 'Surely your salvation is coming; behold, His reward is with Him, and His work before Him.'" And they shall call them The Holy People, The Redeemed of the Lord; and you shall be called Sought Out, A City Not Forsaken. (Isa. 62:11-12)

The Jews—indeed all belonging to the "Commonwealth of Israel"—comprise God's holy people. By definition, "holy" means that the Elect are "set apart" from all other peoples on earth. From the beginning, "All Israel" had been intended to set an example, to be a testimony, a light to the Gentiles. There are, in reality, only two spiritual kingdoms, the kingdom of light and the kingdom of darkness. Those of the kingdom of darkness inadvertently, naturally, bear the fruit of the flesh: "Now the works of the flesh are evident, which are: adultery, fornication, uncleanness, lewdness, idolatry, sorcery, hatred, contentions, jealousies, outbursts of wrath, selfish ambitions, dissensions, heresies, envy, murders, drunkenness, revelries, and the like; of which I tell you beforehand, just as I also told you in time past, that those who practice such things will not inherit the kingdom of God" (Gal. 5:19-21).

It is human nature to be envious, jealous, and contentious. It is only natural that the unredeemed (heathen) nations should be resentful, even hostile, toward God's people. Thus, Paul's adage: "Yes, and all who desire to live godly in Christ Jesus will suffer persecution" (2 Tim. 3:12). And again, Paul's rhetorical questions: "For what fellowship has righteousness with lawlessness? And what communion has light with darkness?" Whereupon he paraphrases Isaiah 52:11: "Therefore, come out from among them and be separate, says the Lord." In truth, God's people are separate. They have, from their calling, been marked, sealed—given a "stigma" in the eyes of the world.

Furthermore, the Living God—the one true God—stands above and in contrast to all other authorities on earth. Thus, it is said to the Lord of all the earth, the King of kings:

> The Lord said to my Lord,
> "Sit at My right hand,
> Till I make Your enemies Your footstool."
> The Lord shall send the rod of Your strength out of Zion.

Rule in the midst of Your enemies!...
The Lord is at Your right hand;
He shall execute kings in the day of His wrath.
He shall judge among the nations,
He shall fill the places with dead bodies,
He shall execute the heads of many countries.
(Psalms 110:1-2;5-6)

Although this Psalm was penned by King David prior to the building of the First Temple, the nations surrounding the Promised Land were acquainted with such prophecies even before Joshua's campaign to drive out the inhabitants of Canaan. Balaam the son of Beor prophesied: "His king shall be higher than Agag, and his kingdom shall be exalted. God brings him out of Egypt; He has strength like a wild ox; He shall consume the nations, his enemies; He shall break their bones and pierce them with his arrows" (Num. 22:7b-8).

It is interesting to note that "The Nations" are said to be God's enemies; yet God established the nations and promised, through Abraham, that the nations would be blessed. "Praise the Lord, all you Gentiles! Laud Him, all you peoples! For His merciful kindness is great toward us, and the truth of the Lord endures forever" (Ps. 117). This seeming conundrum is resolved by Messiah (Isa. 49) and will be addressed in the latter chapters of this book. For now, let it suffice to say that the nations and their rulers who remain un-submitted to the Holy One of Israel will also remain as His enemies until they are reconciled, which is clearly prophesied in Scripture to be completed at the end of the Age.

During the Second Temple Period, because the land of Israel was the locus of important trade routes, and also a strategic battleground for the rising and falling empires surrounding her, Judah could not avoid interaction with the Nations. She endured under the Persians, Alexander's expansion, Seleucia, Ptolemy, and finally Rome. And all these international superpowers interacted with Judah while the Jews carried on their own internal conflicts. The primary civil divisions being between: the Hellenists and the Orthodox (Traditionalists); the Sadducees and the Pharisees; and, the Zealots and the so-called "Peace Party"—those who were willing to live at peace with a Roman governing presence among God's people.

According to historian Edward Flannery, anti-Semitic attitudes by the Nations toward the Jews became obvious during the struggle between the Hellenizers and the Traditionalists.

> It was the Jews' refusal to accept Greek religious and social standards that marked them out...The first clear examples of anti-Jewish sentiment can be traced back to Alexandria in the 3rd century BCE. Alexandria was home to the largest Jewish community in the world... Manetho, an Egyptian priest and historian of that time, wrote scathingly of the Jews and his themes are repeated in the works of Chaeremon, Lysimachus, Poseidonius, Apollonius Molon, and in Apion and Tacitus.[20]

> Manetho wrote that the Jews were expelled [as] Egyptian lepers who had been taught by Moses "not to adore the gods." Agatharchides of Cnidus wrote about the "ridiculous practices" of the Jews and of the "absurdity of their Law," and how Ptolemy Lagus was able to invade Jerusalem in 320 BC because its inhabitants were observing the Sabbath.[21]

The first century Roman historian Tacitus wrote: "Moses prescribed for them a novel religion quite different from those of the rest of mankind. Among the Jews all things are profane that we hold sacred; on the other hand, they regard as permissible what seems to us immoral...The other practices of the Jews are sinister and revolting..."[22]

So, just as would be expected, the peculiar people of God, along with their proprietary laws and customs, were repulsive to the on-looking world. But to make matters worse, the Jewish House was never able to fulfill the vision of Psalms 133: "Behold, how good and how pleasant it is for brethren to dwell together in unity." During the Hellenization of the Holy Land a sharp division formed between the "orthodox"/traditional" Jews and those Jews who welcomed the modernization and lifestyle implemented within the Grecian Empire of Alexander the Great.

THE MACCABEAN REVOLT

---

[20] Flannery, Edward H. *The Anguish of the Jews: Twenty-Three Centuries of Antisemitism.* Paulist Press, first published in 1985; this edition 2004, pp. 11–12.

[21] ibid, p. 25.

[22] Tacitus, *Histories*, Book 5:4.1; 5.1

What turned into the Maccabean Revolt had many "moving parts." Some of the points of contention were:

- The secular appointment of the High Priest;
- The participation of outside forces in internal affairs (such as Rome by invitation); and,
- The formation and identity of the Sadducee and Pharisee parties.

Understanding the dynamics of this war coincides with the study of the intrusion of ungodly powers into the affairs of God's people, which is the focus of the next chapters of this book. Therefore, we will take the time to review some historical sources to gain a general understanding of this chain of events. "What began as a civil war took on the character of an invasion when the Hellenistic kingdom of Syria sided with the Hellenizing Jews against the Traditionalists."[23]

Readers of the New Testament without the historical knowledge imparted by the apocryphal writings might assume that Rome had gained control of the Holy Land by invasion. When in fact, the Roman Empire was invited to join in league with Judea. Judas Maccabeus was completely enamored by Rome's seeming virtue and the humility of Rome's leaders, as follows:

> "Judas had heard about the Romans and their reputation as a military power. He knew that they welcomed all those who joined them as allies and that those who came to them could be sure of the friendship of Rome... ... no Roman ever tried to advance his own position by wearing a crown or putting on royal robes. 15 They created a senate, and each day 320 senators came together to deliberate about the affairs of the people and their well-being. 16 Each year they entrusted to one man the responsibility of governing them and controlling their whole territory. Everyone obeyed this one man, and there was no envy or jealousy among them" (1 Maccabees 8:1;14-16).

The Roman–Jewish Treaty was an agreement made between Judas Maccabeus and the Roman Republic. In 161 BC. Judas Maccabeus sent

---

[23] Wood, Leon James (1986). *A Survey of Israel's History*. Zondervan. p. 357.

two emissaries: Eupolemus, son of John, son of Accos; and Jason, son of Eleazar, to establish a treaty of friendship with the Roman Senate; as follows:

"May all go well with the Romans and with the nation of the Jews at sea and on land forever, and may sword and enemy be far from them. If war comes first to Rome or to any of their allies in all their dominion, the nation of the Jews shall act as their allies wholeheartedly, as the occasion may indicate to them. To the enemy that makes war they shall not give or supply grain, arms, money, or ships, just as Rome has decided; and they shall keep their obligations without receiving any return. In the same way, if war comes first to the nation of the Jews, the Romans shall willingly act as their allies, as the occasion may indicate to them. And to their enemies there shall not be given grain, arms, money, or ships, just as Rome has decided; and they shall keep these obligations and do so without deceit. Thus, on these terms the Romans make a treaty with the Jewish people. If after these terms are in effect both parties shall determine to add or delete anything, they shall do so at their discretion, and any addition or deletion that they may make shall be valid" (I Maccabees chapter 8:17–20).

Emil Schürer, in his work, *A History of The Jewish People in The Time of Jesus Christ*, describes how the Jewish religious purists began to isolate themselves. They at first affiliated themselves with the Maccabees, but then Schürer summarizes how the Purists eventually came to be at odds with the governors of Judah:

It appears that during the Greek period, when the chief priests and rulers of the people took up an increasingly lax attitude towards the law, they united themselves more closely into an association of such as made a duty of its most punctilious observance. When then the Maccabees raised the standard to fight for the faith of their fathers, these "pious" took part in the conflict, but only as long as the faith and the law were actually contended for. When this was no longer the case, and the object of the contest became more and more the national independence, they seem to have retired.

Hence, we no longer hear of them under Jonathan and Simon. Not till John Hyrcanus do they again appear, and then under the name of "Pharisees," no longer indeed on the side of the Maccabees, but in hostile opposition to them. The course of affairs had brought it to pass, that the priestly family of the Maccabees should found a political dynasty. The ancient high - priestly family had been supplanted. The Maccabees or Hasmonaeans had entered into its political inheritance. But with this, tasks which were essentially political had devolved upon them.

The chief matter in their eyes was no longer the carrying out of the law, but the maintenance and extension of their political power. The prosecution however of these political objects could not but more and more separate them from their old friends the "Chasidim" or "Perushira." Not that they had apostatized from the law. But a secular policy was in itself scarcely reconcilable with that legal scrupulosity and carefulness which the Pharisees required.

It was inevitable, that sooner or later there should be a breach between them and their two opposite pursuits. This breach occurred under John Hyrcanus. At the beginning of his government, he still adhered to the Pharisees, but afterwards renounced them and turned to the Sadducees. The occasion of the breach is related by Josephus in a legendary style. But the fact itself, that this change took place under Hyrcanus, is thoroughly authentic.

And in consequence, we henceforth find the Pharisees the opponents of the Hasmonaean priest - princes. They were such, not only under John Hyrcanus, but also under Aristobulus I., and especially Alexander Jannaeus. Under the latter, who as a fierce warrior entirely disregarded the interest of religion, it came even to open revolution. For six years Alexander Jannaeus with his mercenary troops was in conflict against the people led by the Pharisees.[24]

---

[24] *A History of The Jewish People in The Time of Jesus Christ* (1891) Second Division Vol 2 Schürer, Emil, 1844-1910, pp. 26-26.

This division of Judah was not too dissimilar in nature to the division between the Northern and Southern Kingdoms shortly after the dedication of the First Temple. In both schisms, the sovereignty of the Davidic government was challenged. During this Second Temple Period, this threat to the Davidic order took the form of governmental affiliation with international powers. Eventually, the Zealots, who upheld the vision of Judah's scepter in the hands of a Son of David fought against their fellow countrymen who advocated peace with the Romans.

As in the "Breach of Jeroboam," the sanctity of the Jerusalem Temple as the center for worship was also brought into question. During the earlier schism, Bethel and Dan. were established as alternatives to the Jerusalem Temple. A more subtle degradation of the Second Temple resulted when the high priests began to be appointed by governors. And, at last, the roles of king and priest were combined; and that without regard to lineage—neither regarding the priestly lineage of Aaron nor the kingly lineage of David.

Although most readers of this book are probably familiar with the basic differences between the Pharisees and Sadducees, another quote from Josephus is given below. Of special interest is the fact that the Sadducees were not inclined to regard "the traditions of men," for which the Pharisees, on the other hand, were repeatedly reprimanded by Jesus.

> "The Pharisees had passed on to the people certain regulations handed down by former generations and not recorded in the Laws of Moses, for which reason they are rejected by the Sadducean group, who hold that only those regulations should be considered valid which were written down (in Scripture), and that those which had been handed down by former generations need not be observed. And concerning these matters the two parties came to have controversies and serious differences…"[25]

Although merely a sketch of these historical events is presented at this point in our study, the outcome of these external and internal conflicts is most profound:

---

[25] ibid.

- The offices of king and priest were combined as if to prematurely establish an "order of Melchizedek."
- The king of Judea had placed himself under subjection to a national (Gentile) empire.
- The party of the Sadducees had taken control of the government.

This last point is especially troublesome according to the following assessment by Josephus: "The Sadducees… suppose that God is not concerned in our doing or not doing what is evil; and they say, that to act what is good, or what is evil, is at men's own choice, and that the one or the other belongs so to everyone, that they may act as they please."[26] This, "doing what was right in their own eyes" bears a striking resemblance to the legal method of Cicero, the father of Humanism.

Cicero was rediscovered by Western Europe during the Renaissance and was the one who created the "Humanist" classification of philosophical study. His legal writings had their greatest impact on the West during the Enlightenment. The Humanists incorporated the legal philosophies of Cicero in their experimental political alternatives to the Divine Right of Kings. In the second book of his *De Legibus*, Cicero wrote the following, where he refers to Jupiter as the "divine mind."

> Therefore, as that divine mind is the highest law, so too when it is in man, it has been fully developed in the mind of the wise man. Moreover, when things have been written for peoples variously and to suit the occasion, they hold the name of laws by favor more than by substance. [Those who more precisely inquire about these things] teach that all law that can correctly be called law is praiseworthy, by arguments such as these:

---

[26] Josephus, *Wars of the Jews*, Book II, chapter 8:14, 1895, translated by William Whiston, A.M. Auburn and Buffalo.

It is surely settled that laws have been invented for the health of citizens, the safety of cities, and the quiet and happy life of human beings, and that those who first sanctioned resolutions of this sort showed to their peoples that they would write and provide those things by which, when they were received and adopted, they would live honorably and happily, and that they would of course name "laws" those things that were thus composed and sanctioned. From this it is properly understood that those who have written down orders that were ruinous and unjust to their peoples, since they did the opposite of what they promised and claimed, provided something other than laws, so it can be clear that interpreting the name of law involves the significance and sense of choosing what is just and true."[27]

Even though the dialog above mentions the divine mind, Cicero considered that laws are an invention of man; created to keep men healthy, safe, and happy. However, when laws are judged by men to be harmful or unjust, these laws can and should be set aside. In fact, they cannot even continue to be called laws if they fail the test of man's reasonable judgment. Cicero concludes this discourse by asserting that the selection of what may be correctly called law involves "choosing what is just and true." Cicero's semi-divine / semi-human view of law espoused that God was involved in the promulgation of laws, but that those laws were not truly of God, unless they passed the pragmatic test of their benefit to humanity.

So now we see that Judah's acceptance of the Greco-Roman legal system would eventually lead to the undermining of God's laws. (Just as is occurring today.) But law is not the only area influenced by the power of empires. Theology, and specifically theology pertaining to the Jews, has been swayed since the second century. And not only theology, but the leaders of nation-states would appear also to be under the influence of global ideologies. Sound like conspiracy theories? The next chapter will expose the truth of a system that's been in place for a very long time.

---

[27] Tullius, Marcus, David Fott, Trans. Cicero: *On the Laws*. Ithaca: Cornell University Press. 2014. Print.

Over the last 50 years, much attention has been focused on identifying the hidden powers that are expected to emerge as the One-World Government of the antichrist. There is, in fact, abundant evidence that the wealthy men of the world do hold sway over the course of world affairs. This is only to be expected, as asserted by James: "Do not the rich oppress you and drag you into the courts? Do they not blaspheme that noble name by which you are called?" (James 2:6-7). Certainly, the Hapsburgs Dynasty did go underground around the time that democracy was proposed in Europe and America. But if these royal families did go broke, as purported, why do we still find them represented at such high-level meetings as the Bilderberger's gatherings?

Despite the reality that social and political policy appears to the everyday observer to be pushed down from above, rather than rising from the populous, responses like the article below seem to be intended to quash any serious investigation into the existence of any such "world-ruling" body.

If you were really a member of the global élite, you'd know this already: the world is ruled by a powerful, secretive few. Many of the rest of us peons have heard that in 2004 both candidates for the White House were members of Yale University's secretive Skull and Bones society, many of whose members have risen to powerful positions. But Skull and Bones is small potatoes compared with the mysterious cabals that occupy virtually every seat of power, from the corridors of government to the boardrooms of Wall Street.

Take the Illuminati, a sect said to have originated in 18th century Germany; and which is allegedly responsible for the pyramid-and-eye symbol adorning the $1 bill: they intend to foment world wars to strengthen the argument for the creation of a worldwide government (which would of course be Satanic in nature). Or consider the Freemasons, who tout their group as the "oldest and largest worldwide fraternity" and boast alumni like George Washington. Some think that despite donating heaps of cash to charity, they are secretly plotting your undoing at Masonic temples across the world.

Or maybe, some theorize, the guys pulling the strings aren't concealed in shadow at all. They might be the intelligentsia on the Council on Foreign Relations, a cadre of policy wonks who allegedly count their aims as publishing an erudite bimonthly journal and establishing a unified world government—not necessarily in that order.[28]

Some conspiracy theorists believe the secret elite will become so powerful, so confident, that in the end they will walk brazenly across the world stage in plain view. But what if these secret powers have never been secret at all—but well known and open to view? There was a time, however, when it was easier to expose the Kingdom of Man, in contrast to the Kingdom of God—represented on earth as His Elect, the people of God. Today, many nations around the world "identify" as the people of God. But 2,000 years ago, this was not the case.

At the close of the Second Temple Period, when it was apparent that yet another empire—this time the Roman Empire—was on the verge of taking Israel captive all over again, the Jewish sages were emboldened to identify the Kingdom of Man, once and for all.

UNDER THE BANNER OF THE BIRD

Pertinent citations from 4 Ezra Chapter 11 and The Assumption of Moses, Section 10 are presented below without comment. The objects within these visions/analogies will become clear as this chapter develops.

The Eagle and the Lion—4th Ezra/2 Esdras

2 Esdras 11, Common English Bible (CEB):

The Vision of the Eagle

1 On the second night I had a dream. I saw an eagle, with twelve feathered wings and three heads, rising up from the sea. 2 As I looked, it spread its wings over the whole earth, and all the winds of heaven blew toward it, and the clouds gathered around it.

---

[28] *Time*, "Separating Fact from Fiction: Secret Societies Control the World"; retrieved 5/22/2021.

http://content.time.com/time/specials/packages/article/0,28804,1860871_18608 76_1861005,00.html

3 Out of its wings grew opposing wings. These became small, tiny wings. 4 Its heads were at rest. The middle head was larger than the other heads, but it was also at rest with them.

5 I kept looking and saw the eagle flying with its wings to rule over the earth and over those who lived on the earth. 6 I saw how everything under heaven was made to submit to it, and no one opposed it, not a single creature that lives on the earth... (Verses 7-32 proceed to depict the interactions of various wings and heads—omitted here because they aren't necessary for understanding the symbology of these "bird" representations).

The Vision of the Eagle and the Lion

33 After all this, I watched as the middle head, just like the wings, suddenly disappeared. 34 There were two heads left, however, which also ruled over the earth and over those who live on it. 35 I looked and watched as the head on the right side devoured the one on the left. 36 I heard a voice saying to me, "Look in front of you and consider what you see." 37 I looked and saw something like a lion being roused, roaring out of the forest. I heard how he spoke in a human voice and said to the eagle, 38 "Listen, you, and I will speak to you. The Most High says to you, 39 'Aren't you the last of the four beasts that I made to rule in my world so that I might bring about the end of my times through them? 40 You, the fourth that has come, conquered all the beasts that came before you, ruling over the world with much terror and over the whole world with harsh oppression. You have lived in the world with deceit for so long! 41 You judged the earth, but not in truth, 42 for you have oppressed the meek and injured those who caused no unrest. You hated those who spoke the truth and loved liars. You destroyed the dwellings of those who bore fruit and tore down the walls of those who had done you no harm. 43 Your insolence has ascended to the Most High and your pride to the mighty one. 44 The Most High has reviewed his times. Look! They are finished, and his ages are complete. 45 Therefore, eagle, you must utterly vanish, you and your terrifying wings, your dreadful little wings and your evil heads, and your dreadful talons and all your worthless body.

46 Then the whole earth will be refreshed and restored, set free from your violence, and will hope for the judgment and mercy of him who made it.'"

The Eagle and Israel—Assumption of Moses

The Assumption of Moses, Section 10.

The Church Fathers Clement of Alexandria, Origen, and Didymus believed that Jude 9 was quoted from The Assumption of Moses. The translation below fills in some undecipherable text, rather than skipping the omitted characters in the manner of other translations.[29]

> 7. For the Most High will arise, the Eternal God alone,
> And He will appear to punish the Gentiles,
> And He will destroy all their idols.
> 8. Then thou, O Israel, wilt be happy,
> And thou wilt mount upon the neck[s and wings] of the eagle,
> And (the days of thy mourning) will be ended.
> 9. And God will exalt thee,
> And He will cause thee to approach to the heaven of the stars,
> And He will establish thy habitation among them.
> 10. And thou wilt look from on high and wilt see thy enemies in Ge(henna),
> And thou wilt recognise them and rejoice,
> And thou wilt give thanks and confess thy Creator.

By taking these two early Jewish writings together, we can easily deduce that the "Lion" in 4 Ezra 11 is analogous to "Israel" in The Assumption of Moses Sec. 10. However, in both passages the enemy of God's people is represented with allusions to birds: the headed pairs of wings in Ezra, and the eagle—with necks and wings—in The Assumption. So, who or what do these birds symbolize? This question is not difficult to answer; all the necessary information is provided by studying World History. From the onset of the Age of Man, birds were the primary focus of worship.

---

[29] *The Assumption of Moses* translated from the Latin sixth century MS. by R.H. Charles, M.A., Trinity College, Dublin, and Exeter College. Oxford, London, Adam and Charles Black, 1897.

Figure 12 The Vulture Stone at Göbekli Tepe.

Göbekli Tepe is a c. 12,000-year-old archaeological site in Anatolia, Turkey. The deepest and oldest Layer III is also the most sophisticated with enclosures characterized by different thematic components and artistic representations. Pillar no. 43, the "Vulture Stone," is shown in Figure 12 above. On the left-hand side, a vulture is holding an orb or egg in an outstretched wing.[30]

The older parts of the ancient tell may be more reliably dated to circa 9,000 B.C. For those readers who hold to a roughly 6,000-year-old "new earth" creation position, just appreciate that Göbekli Tepe is considered to be the oldest known site of worship on earth. To "secular" scientists, and those who favor the theory of a recently inhabited old earth, this site is placed on the timeline just at the close of the last Ice Age. The important thing to observe within the scope of our study is the display of various birds.

---

[30] *World History Encyclopedia,*
https://www.worldhistory.org/image/13200/vulture-stone-gobekli-tepe.

Although the vulture is the predominant figure, the Ibis or Crane is easily visible—up and to the right of the vulture and egg. What we behold before our eyes is a real-life example of symbols of worship made like "birds and four-footed animals and creeping things" (Rom. 1:23). And do take notice that Paul begins his list with birds.

Supporting our thesis that the large birds, or birds of prey, were to become the emblems of the Kingdom of Man during this Age, we submit the "prehistoric" archaeological chamber known as the "Cave of the Birds," located just below the surface of the Giza plateau. This location begs the question: Were the pyramids built at this ceremonial site of worship based on the importance of the Tomb of the Birds?

Figure 13 CollinsA2-Gizas Tomb of the Birds

Figure 14 Tomb of the Birds in relation to the Giza Pyramids (underground TOB cave circled).

The explorer and discoverer of the caves was unable to carry out research on the content of the tunnel, being interrupted indefinitely by Egyptian authorities. Below are his initial findings. His expectation, however, regarding the Ibis turned out to be correct.

Identifying what type of birds were interred might well provide some clue as to how the ancient Egyptians viewed the entrance to Giza's cave world. My money would be on the birds being either ibises, indicative of the cult of Thoth (the Greek Hermes), or falcons, suggestive of the cult of Horus or more intriguingly that of Sokar, the guardian of the Memphite necropolis in its role as the Fifth Hour of the duat-underworld as portrayed in the Am-duat funerary text. Other bird types might include the vulture, indicative of the cult of Mut; the goose, the totem of the earth-god Geb, the eagle, examples of which were found recently in a new tomb discovered at Saqqara, or even the crane, which might hint at a very archaic cult indeed.[31]

---

[31] Which Bird Cult? Andrew Collins,
http://www.andrewcollins.com/page/articles/sealed.htm, retrieved 5/21/2021.

More than 4 million sacred ibis mummies have been found in the catacombs of Tuna el-Gebel and 1.75 million have been discovered in the ancient burial ground of Saqqara. The vast majority were votive offerings to the god Thoth, a practice that had its heyday between 450BC and 250BC.[32]

The significance of the Ibis becomes clear when it is understood that the Ibis was central to an Egyptian creation story—a story that wholly contradicts the biblical account. The Ibis, therefore, became a symbol of the Egyptian religion. But the bird symbol was also one of the oldest carvings found on Hittite and Mesopotamian reliefs. Over the course of the next several millennia, the symbol of the bird took on the meaning that is ascribed to it today—the attributes of "kingdom" and "authority." The winged sun or winged disk was a symbol of worship when it first began to be used; but by the time of Judah's King Hezekiah, the winged disk had become synonymous with kingship.

THE WINGED DISK

Figure 15 Benben stone from the Pyramid of Amenemhat III, Twelfth Dynasty. Egyptian Museum, Cairo. *Copyright free image enhanced to feature the winged disk at the top.*

---

[32] "Experts crack mystery of ancient Egypt's sacred bird mummies: DNA analysis helps work out origin of nearly 6 million mummified ibises. https://www.theguardian.com/science/2019/nov/13/experts-crack-mystery-ancient-egypt-sacred-bird-mummies.

The Benben stone is an object that is found in the mythology of ancient Egypt. Note the winged disk at the top of Figure 15. This mythical stone is thought to have been part of a shrine at the temple dedicated to the deity Atum in Heliopolis. The Benben stone is also an architectural term, and is the name given to the tip of an obelisk or the capstone placed on top of a pyramid. In the mythology of ancient Egypt, there are several accounts of the creation of the world. According to this version of the creation story, the universe was brought into being by Atum. It was believed that in the beginning, there was nothing but darkness and chaos. It was out of the dark waters that the primordial hill, known as the Benben arose, on top of which stood Atum. Because the Benben rose from the primeval waters, it has been suggested that this word is associated with the verb 'weben', which is the Egyptian hieroglyph for 'to rise'.[33]

Next, we observe that the winged disk became a prominent icon throughout the eastern Mediterranean reaching into the Fertile Crescent. In early Egyptian religion, the symbol Behedeti represented Horus of Edfu, later identified with Ra-Harachte. As time passed (according to interpretation) all of the subordinated gods of Egypt were considered to be aspects of the sun god, including Khepri.

From roughly 2000 BC, the symbol also appears in the Levant, Mesopotamia, and Asia Minor. It appears in reliefs with Assyrian rulers and in Hieroglyphic Anatolian as a symbol for royalty, transcribed into Latin as SOL SUUS (literally, "his own self, the Sun", i.e., "His Majesty").[34]

---

[33] Ancient Origins.net, Mythical Benben Stone: The Landing Site of Egyptian God Atum. https://www.ancient-origins.net/artifacts-other-artifacts/mythical-benben-stone-landing-site-egyptian-god-atum-006513, Retrieved 5/21/2021.

[34] https://en.wikipedia.org/wiki/Winged_sun

Figure 16 Winged-disk, Susa, Mesopotamia

Figure 17 The seal of Tudhaliya IV (1237–1228 B.C.) is stamped on this 4-inch-high fragment of a letter sent to the king of Ugarit. Although the letter is written in cuneiform, the seal is in Hittite hieroglyphics. Credit: Erich Lessing.

As early as 1900 B.C.E., an Indo-European people began to settle in what is now Turkey. By the 16th century B.C.E., they were powerful enough to invade Babylon. Their might continued to expand until they were a superpower on the level with Egypt and Assyria. The Hittites play a prominent role at key places in the Hebrew Bible: Ephron the Hittite sells Abraham the family burial ground (Genesis 23); Esau married Hittite women, and Rebecca despised them (Genesis 26:34); frequently they are listed as one of the inhabitants of Canaan (e.g., Exodus 13:5; Numbers 13:29; Joshua 11:3).[35]

L'MELEKH—BELONGING TO THE KING

From ca. the 8th century BC, the winged solar disk appears on Hebrew seals connected to the royal house of the Kingdom of Judah. Many of these are seals and jar handles from Hezekiah's reign, together with the inscription l'melekh [LMLK] ("belonging to the king").[36]

---

[35] *Biblical Archaeology*, "Who Were the Hittites?" Ellen White, May 19, 2021; https://www.biblicalarchaeology.org/daily/ancient-cultures/ancient-near-eastern-world/who-were-the-hittites

[36] Deutsch, Robert (July–August 2002). "Lasting Impressions: New bullae reveal Egyptian-style emblems on Judah's royal seals". *Biblical Archaeology Review*. 28 (4): 42–51. Retrieved 12 October 2014.

Figure 18 HEZEKIAH IN THE BIBLE. The royal seal of Hezekiah, king of Judah, was discovered in the Ophel excavations under the direction of archaeologist Eilat Mazar. Photo: Courtesy of Dr. Eilat Mazar; photo by Ouria Tadmor.

The bulla (Figure 18), which measures just over a centimeter in diameter, bears a seal impression depicting a two-winged sun disk flanked by ankh symbols and containing a Hebrew inscription that reads "Belonging to Hezekiah, (son of) Ahaz, king of Judah."[37]

---

[37] King Hezekiah in the Bible: Royal Seal of Hezekiah Comes to Light, https://www.biblicalarchaeology.org/daily/news/king-hezekiah-in-the-bible-royal-seal-of-hezekiah-comes-to-light.

Figure 19 Hezekiah's Seal

"Hezekiah Seal (Figure 19) Proves that Ancient Jerusalem was a Major Judahite Capital." Similar seal impressions had already been found – by thieves. This one uniquely found in situ proves King Hezekiah's connection to the LMLK symbols and the existence of an advanced Judahite administration.[38]

Regrettably, the Hezekiah Seal does not just prove ancient Jerusalem was a major Judahite capital. It also proves that the government of Judah had already been compromised by using the symbology of the Nations— and especially, the bird icon of Egypt and Canaan.

Leviticus 18:2-5: The Lord said to Moses, "Speak to the Israelites and say to them: 'I am the Lord your God. You must not do as they do in Egypt, where you used to live, and you must not do as they do in the land of Canaan, where I am bringing you.

---

[38]https://www.haaretz.com/archaeology/what-the-hezekiah-seal-proves-jerusalem-status-1.5385544.

Do not follow their practices. You must obey my laws and be careful to follow my decrees. I am the Lord your God. Keep my decrees and laws, for the person who obeys them will live by them. I am the Lord.

Although it is said that Hezekiah did what was right in the sight of God, the God who also said not to "take their name on your lips" could not have been pleased with the incorporation of this pagan symbol. Below is a map showing how possessing variations of the King's bird seal showed allegiance to the king.

LMLK seals (with LMLK meaning 'of the king') are ancient Hebrew seals stamped on the handles of large storage jars first issued in the reign of King Hezekiah (circa 700 BC) and discovered mostly in and around Jerusalem. The iconography of the two and four winged symbols are representative of royal symbols whose meaning "was tailored in each kingdom to the local religion and ideology".[39]

---

[39] Na'aman, Nadav. "The lmlk seal impressions reconsidered." Tel Aviv 43.1 (2016): 115.

Figure 20 Sites where LMLK seals were found

This technique of making modifications to the King's seal of authority was eventually copied internationally. Therefore, the "secret society" controlling world affairs has been no secret for at least the last 2,000 years. The long anticipated one-world government has indeed been in place since the onset of the Age of Man. The Coats of Arms image below represents merely a few of the "bird banners" used by nations all over the world. The bird symbol is an unspoken acknowledgment of submission to the king—the Kingdom of Man. There is simply no other way to explain why many otherwise hostile and alienated countries would choose the same mascot.

COAT OF ARMS
EAGLE

Figure 21 Coat of Arms with Eagle.[40]

---

[40] https://www.netclipart.com/down/iixxbmx_coat-of-arms-with-eagle.

Many Jewish historians look to the reign of Herod (the Edomite) as the point of infiltration by outsiders into Judah's government. In the same way, many Christians look to the reign of Constantine as the time when the State took control of the Church. Yet, by recognizing the bird figure as the symbol of national—and international—authority, it can be seen that the influence of the overbearing state is more ubiquitous than could have been initiated by one king or one emperor. Both the Eastern and Western arms of the Christian Church had no reservations about displaying their true LMLK seals of belonging.

Figure 22 Double Eagle insignia of the Byzantine Empire.

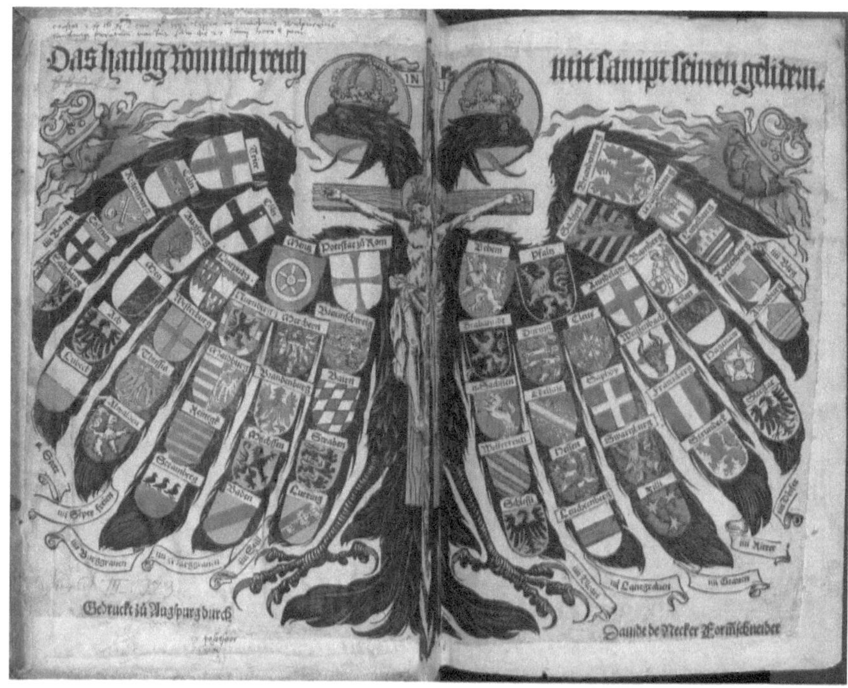

Figure 23 Quaternionenadler, an eagle of the Holy Roman Empire that shows the shields of the member states by rank (1510).

ORIGINS OF THE DOUBLE-HEADED BIRD

Figure 24 Relief representing a two-headed eagle on the sphinx located at the right of the Sphinx Gate, Alaca Höyük, Turkey

The double-headed eagle motif has been used as an emblem by countries, nations, and royal houses in Europe since the early medieval period. Notable examples include the Byzantine House of Palaiologos, the Holy Roman Empire, the House of Habsburg, and the Ruriks and Romanovs of Russia. The Russian use of the double-headed eagle motif (dating from the adoption of it by Ivan III in 1497), though iconographically modeled after the Byzantine, was likely in imitation of the Hapsburgian.[41]

It would appear curious that regional Christian empires would choose for their mascot the Hittite double-headed eagle. The selection of the Hittite eagle is suspect because the "Cradle of Christianity"—Antioch of Syria—lies within the borders of the Ancient Hittite Empire. This possible spiritual connection will be addressed in the next chapter.

Yazılıkaya is an ancient sanctuary that served the Hittite capital of Hattusa, located in modern-day Boğazkale, Turkey. The region (known as the "land of Hatti") was first inhabited by the Hattians, around 2000 BC and was absorbed into a new Hittite state. Hattusa was established as the capital during the 17th century BC by King Hattusilis I. A large sanctuary, Yazılıkaya, was constructed outside the city gates across roofless chambers formed inside a group of rock outcroppings. The chambers depict various rock-cut reliefs portraying the gods of the Hittite pantheon such as the sun-goddess Hebat and the storm-god Teshub, with most of the reliefs dating from restorations by King Tudhaliya IV and king Suppiluliuma II in the late 13th century BC.[42]

---

[41] *The Mesopotamian Origins of the Hittite Double-Headed Eagle.* Jesse D. Chariton, UW-L Journal of Undergraduate Research XIV (2011).

[42] www.heritagedaily.com/2020/09/yazilikaya-the-sanctuary-of-the-hittites/134949, retrieved 7/17/2021.

Figure 25 Yazilikaya double-headed eagle relief[43]

____

[43] Paul Williams Photographer Funky Stock Photos

Among the reliefs is the image of the double-headed eagle, thought to represent the deific daughter and granddaughter of the Tešub, the storm god. Such a record of the progeny and international battles of the "wings" is exactly what is described in the interim verses of the 4 Ezra citation, which were omitted, at the beginning of this chapter. The artwork from the Early Dynastic period of Early Mesopotamia has many double-headed king figures. Figure 25 shows a double-headed winged figure with a humanoid body (possibly representing a deity [or king]).

Figure 26 . Seal impression from Alalakh (Tell Atchana); from Assyrian Colony period (Collon 1987:Illustration 142[44].

Cylinder seals, common in Mesopotamia, are the main design influence on the Hittite stamp seals. The seal impression has imagery with Mesopotamian themes and motifs. The double-headed eagles in each exhibit has elongated necks and wide tails, with long, thin legs.[45]

---

[44] Collon, Dominique. 1987 First Impressions: Cylinder Seals in the Ancient Near East. The University of Chicago. Press, Chicago.

[45] *The Mesopotamian Origins of the Hittite Double-Headed Eagle.* Jesse D. Chariton, UW-L Journal of Undergraduate Research XIV (2011).

Figure 27 Seal impression from Acem Hüyük; Assyrian Colony period (mirrored double headed winged creature—right half of imprint).[46]

"Bicephalous, or double-headed, images constitute a widely distributed class of objects of great variety about whose primordial relationships we know little."[47] This is not the case in the ancient Near East, where the class of objects showing the double-headed eagle is much narrower, namely sculpture and seals, along with Hittite monumental architecture. Recognizing that much of Mesopotamian culture transmitted northwest from the southeast (Sumer) over time, and that the use of the double-headed eagle followed the same route, the relationships of the objects are generally understood, even if the meanings behind the iconography are not.[48]

"And thou wilt mount upon the neck[s and wings] of the eagle" (The Assumption of Moses 10:8). Notice the reference to the "necks" (plural) of the eagle (singular). The 4 Ezra passage quoted at the beginning of this chapter also mentions the two-headed bird; but then, one of its heads is removed. We see this same pattern over time, with the double-headed insignia used in the Old-World symbology of Eastern and Western Christianity. Whereas modern crests typically feature a single-headed bird of prey.

---

[46] Collon, Dominique. 1987 *First Impressions: Cylinder Seals in the Ancient Near East.* The University of Chicago, Press, Chicago.

[47] Mundkur, Balaji, H.-G. Bandi, Stephen C. Jett, George Kubler, William Breen Murray, and Charles R. Wicke 1984 The Bicephalous "Animal Style" in Northern Eurasian Religious Art and Its Western Hemispheric Analogues. *Current Anthropology* 25(4): 451-482.

[48] Jesse D. Chariton.

Amazingly, it would appear that the Jewish sages were spot on in their understanding of Israel's enemies, which more appropriately are the enemies of the Holy One of Israel.

What is revealed by this study of the Kingdom of Man?

- World rulers have affiliated under a common ideology; and this religious system is based upon myths and false deities.
- The camaraderie of the world's nations and empires can be dated to nearly prehistoric times.
- Wings, winged disks, and eagles have been used as a subtle— seemingly harmless—means to show that an entity is under authority (belonging to the king). Unfortunately, the king/deity of the world's nations is Satan, the "ruler of this world."
- Sufficient influence by the heathen nations, on both Jewish and Christian leaders, is revealed by these religions' incorporation of worldly bird symbols.
- The infiltration of worldly/ungodly ideologies has influenced Judaism from ancient times; and this fellowship with the Nations persisted into the Post-Apostolic Early Church; and continues today.

Due to the reign of the "World Rulers" κοσμοκράτορας (*kosmokratoras*—Eph. 6:12) God has allowed for nearly 2,000 years the false doctrines that Judah was forsaken and replaced by a new chosen people, the Church; and more recently with Dispensationalism, that Judah was cut off along with the House of Israel and must wait for the "rapture of the Church." The immediate response, though, of "the prince of the power of the air"—Eph. 2:2—was to "sell" these doctrinal narratives to the public by "scattering" Judah so that they, like the House of Israel, might lose their identity; something that God has never done.

As a point of interest, Göbekli Tepe is not far from Harran—the home of Terah and Laban; and Abraham's stopping point on his way to the land of Canaan. How much influence Göbekli Tepe's literally "Age-old" objects of worship had on Jacob's in-laws is unclear, but we do know that when Rachael set off with Jacob to return to Canaan, she was secretly in possession of Laban's household idols.

Figure 28 Proximity of Antioch, Harran, and Göbekli Tepe[49]

---

[49] Boundary of the Hittite Empire obtained from "Map of the Hittite Empire at its greatest extent," with Hittite rule ca. 1350–1300 BC represented by the green line. https://commons.wikimedia.org/wiki/File:Map_Hittite_rule_en.svg.

We now turn our attention to Antioch, which is also within the boundaries of the ancient Hittite Empire. Who knows what spiritual propensities might have lingered over that metropolis, which may have been responsible for the chain of events that will be covered in this chapter?

Antioch was founded near the end of the fourth century BC by Seleucus I Nicator, one of Alexander the Great's generals. Antioch became the Roman capital of Syria. At the time of Christ Antioch was the third largest city in the Roman Empire, exceeded in population only by Rome and Alexandria. The location of the city was determined using a most unusual method—by means of an eagle no less! An eagle, the bird of Zeus, had carried off a piece of sacrificial meat and the city was founded on the place where the eagle landed with the meat offering, as follows:

> Seleucus came to the city of Antigonia, which had been founded by Antigonus Poliorcetes. The city was surrounded and defended by the river Archeuthas, also called the Iaphthas, which is another river, which flows from the lake. There Seleucus performed a sacrifice to Zeus on the altars erected by Antigonus; he cut the meat and prayed with the priest Amphion for a sign to be given, to show whether he should settle the city of Antigonia, and change its name, or [if] he should abandon the city and found another city somewhere else.

> Suddenly a great eagle came down from the sky and snatched the meat of the offering from the fire on the altar. The eagle flew off by Mount Silpius, where Seleucus followed it and found the consecrated meat, with the eagle poised over it. When Seleucus and the priest and the augurs saw this marvel, they said, "We must settle here, and not in Antigonia; the city must not be there, because the gods do not wish it." And then he consulted with them as to where he might safely build the city, because he was worried by the streams and winter torrents, which came down from Mount Silpius.

He laid the foundations of the city at the bottom of the valley opposite the mountain, by the great river Dracon which was renamed Orontes, where there was a village called Bottia,[50] opposite Iopolis. After Amphion, the high priest, had sacrificed a virgin girl called Aemathe between the city and the river, Seleucus [founded the city] on the 22nd day of the month of Artemisius which is also May, at the first hour of the day as the sun was rising, and he called the city Antioch, after the name of his son Antiochus Soter.[51]

Figure 29 3D reconstruction of ancient Antioch, one of the four great metropolises of the Roman Empire.[52]

---

[50] For further reading on the Bottia/Zeus connection, see *Corrupting the Image 2*, by Dr. Douglas Hamp.

[51] John Malalas, Book 8, pp.199–202.

[52] Source: reddit;
https://www.mapmania.org/map/1995/3d_reconstruction_of_ancient_antioch_one_of_the_four_great_metropolises_of_the_roman_empire.

Recall—from the chapter before last—the observation that "the Hellenistic kingdom of Syria sided with the Hellenizing Jews against the Traditionalists." This alliance not only affected the Holy Land; Syria became a refuge and a gathering place for Hellenistic Jews, who may have sought to distance themselves from the traditionalist (Torah observant) Jews of Judea. As a result, Antioch became the main center of Hellenistic Judaism at the end of the Second Temple period. Antioch was called "the cradle of Christianity" because of the pivotal role it played in the emergence of both Hellenistic Judaism and early Christianity.[53] In fact, Antioch contained the largest settlement of Hellenistic Jews in all of Europe, nearly on par with Alexandria in Egypt.

To gain an understanding of Hellenistic Judaism we consult *jewishencyclopedia.com*[54]:

> Post-exilic Judaism was largely recruited from those returned exiles who regarded it as their chief task to preserve their religion uncontaminated, a task that required the strict separation of the congregation both from all foreign peoples (Ezra x. 11; Neh. ix. 2) and from the Jewish inhabitants of Palestine who did not strictly observe the Law (Ezra vi. 22; Neh. x. 29). This separation was especially difficult to maintain when the victorious campaign of Alexander the Great had linked the East to the West... The Greek language became a common language for nearer Asia, and with the language went Greek culture, Greek art, and Greek thought... The Hellenic influence pervaded everything, and even in the very strongholds of Judaism it modified the organization of the state, the laws, and public affairs, art, science, and industry, affecting even the ordinary things of life and the common associations of the people... The Jews thus became sharers in a world-culture if not in a **world-empire** [emphasis added; their words, not ours].

> It was a denationalizing influence from the strictly Jewish point of view; this was the principal reason for the dislike,

---

[53] *Encyclopaedia Biblica*, Vol. I, p. 186.
[54] HELLENISM, By: Carl Siegfried, Richard Gottheil; https://jewishencyclopedia.com/articles/7535-hellenism.

which many Jewish teachers felt for things Hellenic… By the introduction of Grecian art, a door was opened to debauchery and riotous living; and though Judaism was hardly menaced by the introduction of direct idolatry, the connection of this culture with sublimated Greek polytheism became a real danger to the Jewish religion. This well-grounded fear inspired the rise of the Hasidæans and explains the change of sentiment on the part of the Rabbis toward the use of the Greek language (see Greek Language and the Jews). For this reason, the Hellenists are called υἱοὶ παράνομοι ("wicked men"; I Macc. i. 11), or ἄνδρες ἄνομοι καὶ ἀσεβεῖς ("wicked [unlawful] and ungodly men"; ib. vii. 5).

The work commenced by Alexander the Great was furthered by the first Ptolemies and Seleucids, who treated their Jewish subjects with much benevolence, though even at this time the high priest Onias III. fought bravely against the introduction of Hellenism. But the high-priestly family was divided owing to the intrigues of the Tobiads, especially of Joseph; and the high priests, instead of defending their patrimony, degraded it. Of such a kind were Menelaus and Jason, the latter of whom is said to have sent contributions to Hercules' games at Tyre, and to have built an arena in Jerusalem, which the priests were wont to frequent in place of the Temple (II Macc. iv. 13, 19)… The Hasmoneans Aristobulus and John Hyrcanus leaned also to the Hellenists.[55] But it was especially with the advent of the Idumean Herod and his dynasty that Hellenism once more threatened to overwhelm Jewish culture.

To summarize, at the beginning of the Second Temple period, the Jews returning from exile had determined to keep the Law. But doing so was difficult, and became even harder due to increased international contact and the appeal of the modern Grecian lifestyle.

The Jews rationalized they could maintain their identity as Jews by professing the one God—the Holy One of Israel—and rejecting the pantheon of Greek gods. The Hellenists were not strict in their

---

[55] See https://en.wikipedia.org/wiki/Hellenistic_Judaism#Individual_Hellenized_Jews for an extensive list of Hellenist High Priests, officials, and influencers.

observance of the Law and seem to have justified this laxity by emphasizing their monotheism.

When Paul and Barnabas went to Antioch, what they encountered was a culture predisposed to disenchantment with strict adherence to the Law. This understanding of the Hellenist mindset also explains why the Antiochian Christians were so disturbed to be confronted by the "Christian Traditionalist," presumably sent by the Jerusalem Church.[56]

Most remarkably, as the Christian Movement expanded, the Hellenistic sect of Judaism dissipated—apparently, the vast majority of those with a Hellenistic attitude toward the Law were absorbed quite easily into the Church. The former polarization between the Traditionalists and the Hellenists also shifted during this transition into the present-day antagonism between the Jews and Christians—those who keep the Law, and those who we might say, "distance themselves from the Law."

IGNATIUS OF ANTIOCH

The Antiochian/Hellenistic (anti-Semitic) stance toward the Law was codified by the Church in the early part of the second century through the letters of Ignatius, the bishop of Antioch. It should be noted that around this same time, the heretic, Marcion, was also involved in the task of proving that Christianity and Judaism—grace and law— were mutually exclusive, and that they do not even proceed from the same deity. Dr. Hamp has written extensively on Marcionism's continued detrimental effects on Christianity, despite the fact that Marcion was labeled a heretic by the Church![57] Ignatius, on the other hand, was sainted as a Christian martyr and his letters—practically canonized. The proclamations of Ignatius, who was considered to be one of the Apostolic Fathers, form the basis of what should properly be called, "Hellenistic Christianity."

---

[56] Acts 15:1: "And certain men came down from Judea and taught the brethren, 'Unless you are circumcised according to the custom of Moses, you cannot be saved.'"

[57] For further study see: *Haunted Theology and the Ghost of Marcion* by Dr. Douglas Hamp.

Figure 30 Ignatius of Antioch.[58]

Ignatius was a bishop of Antioch, said to be appointed by Peter and according to tradition was the successor to Evodius. Tradition also holds that Ignatius was a friend of Polycarp and that both young men had been disciples of John the Apostle. It is also supposed that Ignatius was one of the children Jesus took in His arms and blessed. Add, then, to these accolades a martyr's death and it is obvious why so much weight was placed on the opinions of Ignatius. Quotes from the letters written by Ignatius while purportedly being extradited to Rome for execution are presented below, followed by commentary.

---

[58] Neapolitan School of Painting, possibly Cesare Fracanzano (1605-1651) https://commons.wikimedia.org/wiki/File:Ignatius_of_Antiochie.jpg

Ignatius to the Magnesians, Ch. 8[59]:

1 Be not seduced by strange doctrines nor by antiquated fables, which are profitless.
For if even unto this day we live after the manner of Judaism, we avow that we have not received grace:
2 for the divine prophets lived after Christ Jesus. For this cause also they were persecuted, being inspired by His grace to the end that they which are disobedient might be fully persuaded that there is one God who manifested Himself through Jesus Christ His Son, who is His Word that proceeded from silence, who in all things was well-pleasing unto Him that sent Him.

Verse 1 clearly juxtaposes Judaism with grace, implying that traditional Judaism—keeping the Law—is prima facia evidence that an individual has not received (saving) grace. Verse 2 begins by stating that the prophets lived (after the manner) of Jesus, that is by grace rather than by obedience to the Law. This is simply absurd on several levels. First, Jesus obeyed the Law to the extent that He could ask: "Which of you convicts Me of sin?" (Jn. 8:46). Furthermore, the prophets kept the law themselves. Secondly, Ignatius redirects "obedience" away from meaning "obedience to the Law" and defines the meaning of obedience as the belief that there is only one God—the very ploy of the Hellenistic Jews. Verse 2 ends with a true statement—that the Son was well-pleasing to the Father. But ending these phrases with a true statement does not somehow make the rest of the content true.

Ignatius to the Magnesians, Ch. 9

1 If then those who had walked in ancient practices attained unto newness of hope, no longer observing sabbaths but fashioning their lives after the Lord's day, on which our life also arose through Him and through His death which some men deny – a mystery whereby we attained unto belief, and for this cause we endure patiently, that we may be found disciples of Jesus Christ our only teacher --
2 if this be so, how shall we be able to live apart from Him? seeing that even the prophets, being His disciples, were expecting Him as their teacher through the Spirit. And for this

---

[59] *IGNATIUS to the Magnesians, Apostolic Fathers*, Lightfoot & Harmer, 1891 translation.

cause He whom they rightly awaited, when He came, raised them from the dead.

These are some mighty big "ifs." The assumption presented by Ignatius is that because God's "ancient" Elect were looking forward to participating in Christ's resurrection, they therefore, to that extent, were "no longer observing sabbaths." He thereby implies that the saints of old were, at least, disobedient to the Law in their hearts. Seriously? Yet the Church did take this notion seriously. Moreover, Ignatius imposed this hypothetical on his hearers by threatening that those who wish to participate in the life of Christ must, likewise, forsake the sabbath and honor "the Lord's day."

At this point we should wonder: To what degree had the Antiochian Hellenist already ceased to comply with the third commandment? This doctrinal position seems to roll off the tongue at the beginning of the second century—perhaps shortly after John's death. It is far more likely that the Hellenized Church did not fall far from the tree of the Hellenistic Jewish community. The whole gist of Hellenism was, after all, adapting to the customs of the international community. As observed by historian Emil Schürer: "They who then wanted to affect anything in the political world must of necessity stand on a more or less friendly footing with Hellenism."[60]

Ignatius to the Magnesians, Ch. 10

1 Therefore let us not be insensible to His goodness. For if He should imitate us according to our deeds, we are lost. For this cause, seeing that we are become His disciples, let us learn to live as beseemeth Christianity. For whoso is called by another name besides this, is not of God.

Here we must interject between stanzas what is implied by Ignatius, but not stated outright—that those who are called "Jews" instead of "Christians" would not be "of God."

2 Therefore put away the vile leaven which hath waxed stale and sour, and betake yourselves to the new leaven, which is

---

[60] Shurer, *A History of the Jewish People in the Time of Christ*, Div. 2, Vol. 2, P. 40.

Jesus Christ. Be ye salted in Him, that none among you grow putrid, seeing that by your savour ye shall be proved.
3 It is monstrous to talk of Jesus Christ and to practise Judaism. For Christianity did not believe in Judaism, but Judaism in Christianity, wherein every tongue believed and was gathered together unto God.

Verse 3 begins by making it an abomination to speak of Messiah (who is the Lord—Acts 2:36) and, at the same time, to follow the Lord's instructions. Whereas, the inverse of this statement is actually true. It is monstrous to speak of Jesus Christ while *not* obeying His commandments.

Next, Ignatius anthropomorphizes Judaism and Christianity and asserts, "Christianity did not believe in Judaism." On the contrary, in Paul's own words: "But this I confess to you, that according to the Way which they call a sect, so I worship the God of my fathers, **believing all things which are written in the Law and in the Prophets**" (Acts 24:14, emphasis added). Indeed, Christian salvation is attained by the confession that Jesus is the same "LORD"—Gr. "Kurios"—of the Old Testament (Acts 10:9-10). Therefore, Christians believed in the Holy One of Israel and Jews continued to believe in the Holy One of Israel. And certainly, the words of the Lord are the final authority on this doctrine:

"Do not think that I came to destroy the Law or the Prophets. **I did not come to destroy** but to fulfill. For assuredly, I say to you, till heaven and earth pass away, one jot or one tittle will by no means pass from the law till all is fulfilled. Whoever therefore breaks one of the least of these commandments, and teaches men so, shall be called least in the kingdom of heaven; but whoever does and teaches them, he shall be called great in the kingdom of heaven. For I say to you, that unless your righteousness exceeds the righteousness of the scribes and Pharisees, you will by no means enter the kingdom of heaven" (Matt. 5:17-20).

Jesus' only criticism of the Jews of His day concerning obedience to the Law was that it should be carried out with the love of God, and not neglect or replace the love of God.

Ignatius' blatantly blind and baseless antagonism toward the Jews stemmed from nothing, more nor less, than from the Hellenistic determination that Jewish Traditionalism opposed the will of God; while the Hellenistic—watered down, so to speak—approach to obeying God's laws was the ordained method that should be adopted by the Church.

Judah's internal strife during the Second Temple period was simply the result of the God-fearing Jews' apprehension that further exile could only be avoided by obeying God's laws. From the "Set Apart"— who became the Pharisees, to the Traditionalists, and finally, the Zealots, all of these movements were established to promote the pure observance and practice of God's precepts. The Hellenists had determined that God's laws were a burden, and had preferred, rather, to mingle with nations. In most cases, international forces were brought into the three major conflicts listed above by those who opposed the religious purists. And, in turn, the liberal factions compromised their faith by bending to the norms of the current world empire; be it Persian, Greek, Syrian, or Roman.

ON KEEPING THE PASSOVER

The following quotations should be self-explanatory. These precious early writings prove that the Apostles and their immediate appointees—the first overseers and pastors—did, in fact keep the Passover as required by the Law of God. Yes, the Early Church, not just in Judea but in the Asian churches of modern day Turkey, kept the Law. (Emphasis added.)

Eusebius, Church History, Book V.

Chapter 23. The Question then agitated concerning the Passover.

> 1. A question of no small importance arose at that time. For the parishes of all Asia, as from an older tradition, held that the fourteenth day of the moon, on which day the Jews were commanded to sacrifice the lamb, should be observed as the feast of the Saviour's Passover. It was therefore necessary to end their fast on that day, whatever day of the week it should happen to be.

Chapter 24:

1. But the bishops of Asia, led by Polycrates, decided to hold to the old custom **handed down to them**. He himself, in a letter which he addressed to Victor and the church of Rome, set forth in the following words the tradition which had come down to him:

2. **We observe the exact day**; neither adding, nor taking away. For in Asia also **great lights have fallen asleep**, which shall rise again on the day of the Lord's coming, when he shall come with glory from heaven, and shall seek out all the saints. **Among these are Philip**, one of the twelve apostles, who fell asleep in Hierapolis; and his two aged virgin daughters, and another daughter, who lived in the Holy Spirit and now rests at Ephesus; and, moreover, **John**, who was both a witness and a teacher, who reclined upon the bosom of the Lord, and, being a priest, wore the sacerdotal plate.

3. He fell asleep at Ephesus.

4. And **Polycarp** in Smyrna, who was a bishop and martyr...

6. **All these observed the fourteenth day of the passover <u>according to the Gospel</u>, deviating in no respect, but following the rule of faith**. And I also, **Polycrates**, the least of you all, do according to the tradition of my relatives, some of whom I have closely followed. For seven of my relatives were bishops; and I am the eighth. And my relatives always observed the day when the people put away the leaven.

7. I, therefore, brethren, who have lived sixty-five years in the Lord, and have met with the **brethren throughout the world**, and have **gone through every Holy Scripture**, am not affrighted by terrifying words. For those greater than I have said 'We ought to obey God rather than man.' Acts 5:29.

From *Against Heresies*, Book III, Ch. 2:4:

Polycarp also was not only instructed by apostles, and conversed with many who had seen Christ, but was also, by apostles in Asia, appointed bishop of the Church in Smyrna, whom I [Irenaeus] also saw in my early youth, for he tarried [on earth] a very long time, and, when a very old man, gloriously and most nobly suffering martyrdom, departed this life, **having <u>always</u> taught the things which he had learned from the apostles, and which the Church has handed down, and <u>which alone are true</u>.** To these things all the Asiatic Churches testify, as do also those men who have succeeded Polycarp down to the present time.

Chapter 9: Did Judah Have Religion or Relationship?

The question of whether the Old Testament saints actually knew God and understood the Scriptures would seem odd to many. But those with a Dispensation Theology background—and many born-again believers, in general—have assumed that since they themselves did not know God or comprehend His Word before they received the Holy Spirit, neither could the saints of old have truly connected with God. There is a fair amount of justification for such thinking based several New Testament passages, which indicate that neither the Holy Spirit, nor the comprehension of Scripture, was given until Jesus had come and finished His ministry.

How Veiled Were the Scriptures?

Before looking into these passages, recall from previous chapters that God has always maintained a "remnant." And just as there are, what have been called, nominal Christians—members belonging to a church who have not experienced repentance and regeneration—there have likewise been those belonging to Abraham who have not had the faith of Abraham. Within the national context, such children of Israel might be deemed as the "Nominal Elect." These were the ones addressed by Moses when he said: "But to this day the LORD has not given you a mind that understands or eyes that see or ears that hear" (Deut. 29:4); and, as restated by Isaiah: "Be ever hearing, but never understanding; be ever seeing, but never perceiving" (Isa. 6:9).

These verses should not be taken to mean that no one understood, that no one perceived; or that God had rendered His people incapable communicating with Him. Yes, He does hide His face (because of man's disobedience—Isa. 59), but never His Word—Isa. 55:10-11: "For as the rain comes down, and the snow from heaven, and do not return there, but water the earth, and make it bring forth and bud, that it may give seed to the sower and bread to the eater, so shall My word be that goes forth from My mouth; it shall not return to Me void, but it shall accomplish what I please, and it shall prosper in the thing for which I sent it."

Now, let's look at two passages in the Gospel of John:

7:38 "He who believes in Me, as the Scripture has said, out of his heart will flow rivers of living water." 39 But this He spoke concerning the Spirit, whom those believing in Him would receive; for the Holy Spirit was not yet given, because Jesus was not yet glorified.

20:21 So Jesus said to them again, "Peace to you! As the Father has sent Me, I also send you." 22 And when He had said this, He breathed on them, and said to them, "Receive the Holy Spirit."

These verses from John (above) are often linked to Luke 24:45 (below) to imply that nobody can comprehend any scriptures, apart from the indwelling Spirit. But is that really what the Luke passage says?

Luke 24:

44 Then He said to them, "These are the words which I spoke to you while I was still with you, that all things must be fulfilled which were written in the Law of Moses and the Prophets and the Psalms concerning Me." 45 And He opened their understanding, that they might comprehend the Scriptures.

Jesus was quite specific that the scriptures He was enlightening the Disciples about were those passages concerning Himself—passages relating to the ministry of the Messiah. Earlier in chapter 24, Luke restated the account of the two disciples Jesus met on the road to Emmaus: "And beginning at Moses and all the Prophets, He expounded to them in all the Scriptures the things concerning Himself." (v. 27). These formerly concealed passages related to Jesus' sacrificial, vicarious, death and resurrection, which the Disciples previously did not understand and were afraid to ask Him about (Mark 9:32).

These passages must also be compared to the outpouring of the Holy Spirit on the Day of Pentecost as recorded in Acts Ch. 2: "And they were all filled with the Holy Spirit and began to speak with other tongues, as the Spirit gave them utterance... Therefore being exalted to the right hand of God, and having received from the Father the promise of the Holy Spirit, He poured out this which you now see and hear" (vss. 4, 33).

This outpouring had the effect of broadening the work of the Spirit beyond the scope of the Old Testament. There the Spirit had typically been "poured out" on kings, judges, and prophets, but was now to be poured out on "all flesh." Peter quoted Joel as follows:

17 And it shall come to pass in the last days, says God,
That I will pour out of My Spirit on all flesh;
Your sons and your daughters shall prophesy,
Your young men shall see visions,
Your old men shall dream dreams.
18 And on My menservants and on My maidservants
I will pour out My Spirit in those days;
And they shall prophesy.

Nevertheless, we find nowhere in any list of the "gifts of the Spirit" the ability to understand the Scriptures. The Bible speaks understandably any time the reader knows God and believes that the Bible is in fact the Word of God. That the faithful of old believed in the Word of God is most thoroughly certified by Psalm 119. Regarding the knowledge of God, He speaks through the prophet: "Let not the wise man boast in his wisdom, let not the mighty man boast in his might, let not the rich man boast in his riches, but let him who boasts boast in this, that he understands and knows me, that I am the Lord who practices steadfast love, justice, and righteousness in the earth. For in these things I delight, declares the Lord" (Jer. 9:24-25 ESV). Indeed, God also gave the assurance, "you will seek Me and find Me, when you search for Me with all your heart" (Jer. 29:13). God made Himself knowable and was known by His people—the faithful of the Land.

Why is this conversation necessary? Because there are many Christians who think the Old Testament was the result of automatic writing. "Automatic writing is the process or product of writing without using the conscious mind."[61] In other words, many believe—though they may not say it in so many words—that the Old Testament was written "in blindness," only to be understood after the time of Christ.

---

[61] www.newworldencyclopedia.org/entry/Automatic_writing.

Christians have been taught that until the Holy Spirit was "sent," the writers and readers, lacking the essential relationship with God, could not appreciate what they were writing, or what was being read. Christians who have adopted this "dead letter theology" might envision the boy Jesus listening on Sabbaths to passages that He knew were about Himself; but they relegate the rest of mankind—and especially the Jews—to the camp of those to whom the Scriptures were veiled.

SEEING, DID JUDAH PERCEIVE?

Yet, the Old Testament saints did understand and trust God's Word—some to the death as recorded in the "Hall of Faith" (Hebrews Ch. 11)—and they did, most personally, know their God. Furthermore, this knowledge of God was still active among the faithful of Judah at the time of Christ. We know this by examining what Jesus told the "woman at the well" (John Ch. 4). In that dialogue, both people are portrayed as representatives of two distinct ethnicities, Samaritans and Jews. These stereotypes are clearly established in the ninth verse: "Then the woman of Samaria said to Him, "How is it that You, being a Jew, ask a drink from me, a Samaritan woman?" For Jews have no dealings with Samaritans.""

Later in their conversation, "Jesus said to her, 'Woman, believe Me, the hour is coming when you will neither on this mountain, nor in Jerusalem, worship the Father. You worship what you do not know; **we know** (οἴδαμεν [*oidamen*]) what we worship, for salvation is of the Jews'" (Jn. 4:21-22, emphasis added).

When Jesus said, "we know what we worship," he was speaking on behalf of the Jews (Judah). Jesus' choice of words for "know" is also of great significance.[62] John could have chosen to use the Greek word, "gnosis" in his gospel with the meanings: understanding, knowledge, or intelligence. Or he could have used, "epistamai": to be acquainted with, to know. John, however, used the first person plural form of the Greek word derived from, "*eidó*."

---

[62] It is likely that Jesus was speaking to the Samaritan woman in Greek since Samaria was highly Hellenized. Nevertheless, we must assume that John used the most appropriate translation, if otherwise.

According to Thayer's Greek Lexicon, the word *eidó* (Strong's NT 1492) has the meanings:

1. to perceive (with the eyes; Latin conspicere, German erblicken)...
2. like the Latin video, to perceive by any of the senses: Matthew 27:54; Mark 15:39; Luke 17:15...

This is, then, most compelling; because Jesus was asserting that, unlike the Israelites who were "ever seeing, but never perceiving," the faithful Jews of Jesus' day were, in fact, perceiving what they were worshipping. Jesus was specifically contrasting the empty religion of the heathen Gentiles/Nations with the relationship, the knowledge of God, being experienced by the Jews. But then Jesus goes over the top and states outright that salvation is of the Jews. Remember Paul's reference to Judah—the Olive Tree; how all of the branches, natural and wild, are supported by the root of Judah and thereby enjoy the same "fatness."

Now, to be clear, we are not suggesting that Judah should be the object of worship. Indeed, the sincere Jew of Jesus' day did not worship themselves, but God. Nor are we suggesting, as the Judaizers of Acts Ch. 15, that one must become a Jew to be saved. The authors conscientiously strive "not to think beyond what is written" (1 Cor. 4:6), but rather to faithfully convey what *is* written. For truly, salvation is "of" (Gr. *ek*—out of) the Jews. The fact that the Son of David is Savior has been recognized even among the Jewish rabbis:

"Thus Judah profited, because from him came forth Perez and Hezron from whom are descended David and the Messiah-King, he who will save Israel. Behold how great the difficulties the Holy One indeed gave until he was to raise up the Messiah-King from Judah, he of whom it is written, "And the spirit of the Lord will be upon him."[63]

Continuing to draw from John's gospel, there we find that Jesus expected Nicodemus, as a teacher of Israel, to know and understand what Jesus had said regarding being reborn of the Spirit:

---

[63] Midrash Tanhuma, Bereshit va-Yeshev. Isaiah 61:1-3.

Jesus answered, "Most assuredly, I say to you, unless one is born of water and the Spirit, he cannot enter the kingdom of God. That which is born of the flesh is flesh, and that which is born of the Spirit is spirit. Do not marvel that I said to you, 'You must be born again.' The wind blows where it wishes, and you hear the sound of it, but cannot tell where it comes from and where it goes. So is everyone who is born of the Spirit."

Nicodemus answered and said to Him, "How can these things be?"

Jesus answered and said to him, "Are you the teacher of Israel, and do not know these things? Most assuredly, I say to you, We speak what We know and testify what We have seen, and you do not receive Our witness. If I have told you earthly things and you do not believe, how will you believe if I tell you heavenly things? (John 3:5-12).

When Jesus said, "We speak what We know...," some Bible commentators have assumed by the interjection of the plural in this one verse that Jesus was speaking on behalf of the Godhead, known as the "pluralis majestaticus." It is obvious that the publishers of the NKJV, quoted above, have also made this assumption because no such capitalization is found among the Greek source texts. Therefore, many Bible commentaries on this verse insist the use of the plural indicates that Jesus was including Himself along with others who were also spiritually enlightened.[64]

---

[64] *Ellicott's Commentary for English Readers*: (11) Once again the "Verily, verily" of deeper truth. "We speak that we do know" is in sharp contrast to their formal teaching of matters external to the truth. The plural is not usual in the language of Christ, and the immediate passage to the singular forbids us to accept the usual grammatical explanation that it is the plural of majesty. He apparently joins others with Himself,— those who have spoken and known and testified, and whose testimony has been rejected by the Jews. We have to think of him whose life-work was to bear witness of the Light (John 1:8), and of the band of disciples who form a little school round their Master, and who in Jerusalem, as in Galilee, testified of Him; and it may even be that in the house and presence of one of that band this conversation took place (comp. John 3:2). They knew the power of the new life, and had been baptised of water and of spirit. In their measure and degree, as He in fulness, they spake what they knew, and testified what they had seen. (Comp. John 15:27.)

These commentaries—Ellicott, Benson, Vincent, and Gill among others—each offer different explanations as to why anyone other than Jesus would have had the spiritual insight to "know" these things. Some look to the anointing of John the Baptist as a prophet. Others suggest the Holy Spirit was working in the Disciples and their follows, which is completely inconsistent with many of their own teachings, that the Spirit was absent until Jesus was glorified. What they are all overlooking is the presence of a "perceiving" and faithful remnant within the House of Judah who *were* speaking about, knowing, and witnessing the fulfillment of Messianic prophecy.

Yes, there was an awakened element of Judah, men and women like Simeon, who was "just and devout, waiting for the Consolation of Israel, and the Holy Spirit was upon him"—before the cross! John 3:11 even applies the same Greek word, *oidamen* that was used in Jesus' conversation with the Samaritan woman in John 4:22, implying "we [Jews] know [perceive] what we worship—or rather, who we worship—"because salvation is of the Jews." In other words, "that is why we Jews know all about these things."

Benson Commentary: John 3:11. We speak that we do know — I, and all that truly believe in me. Or, he may refer to the testimony that was given to the truth of his doctrine by John the Baptist, and to the preaching also of his own disciples, who all concurred in testifying the same things, the certainty of which they were assured of by the illuminating influences of the Holy Spirit, and by their own experience, while it was known to Christ by his omniscience, and by the intimate acquaintance that he had with all the counsels of his Father.

Vincent's Word Studies: After the use of the singular number in John 3:3, John 3:5, John 3:7, John 3:12, the plural here is noteworthy. It is not merely rhetorical - "a plural of majesty" - but is explained by John 3:8, "every one that is born of the Spirit."

Gill's Exposition of the Entire Bible: Verily, verily, I say unto thee, we speak that we do know... Meaning either himself, and John the Baptist his forerunner, who preached the same doctrine of regeneration, internal sanctification, and evangelical repentance, as well as outward reformation, as necessary to entrance into the kingdom of heaven, or the Gospel dispensation, he declared was just at hand; or his disciples with himself, who were now with him, and whom he had called to preach the same truths he himself did; or the prophets of the Old Testament, who agreed with him in these things.

Assuming that Jesus was speaking as a Jew, on behalf of the Jews, we can then understand why He spoke to Nicodemus in the plural: "we [Jews] speak what we [Jews] know and testify what we [Jews] have seen, and you do not receive our witness." Considering this interpretation of the verse, it makes perfect sense why Jesus would challenge Nicodemus asking, "Are you the teacher of Israel and do not know these things?" because Nicodemus *should* have known these things, because "we"—the faithful remnant of Judah—*do* know these things!

CHAPTER 10: THE SALVATION OF NATIONAL JUDAH

"Alas! For that day is great, that none is like it; And it is the time of Jacob's trouble [tribulation צָרָה]*, But he shall be saved out of it"*
(Jer 30:7).

National Israel—that is, the House of Israel—lost its nation-state identity. It was dissolved long before the time of Christ. That is why Jesus did not say that He was sent to the House of Israel—which had been a kingdom of ten tribes—but that He wasn't sent except to "the lost sheep of the House of Israel"—the individual sheep who had been scattered. But, as has been documented throughout this book, Judah retained—and retains—its national identity. Scripture also bears witness to the fact that national Judah remained in good standing under the Sinaitic Covenant though the Second Temple period. However, at Jesus' second coming, national Judah will at last join into the New Covenant. A snapshot of the events at the end of this Age is given in Psalms 102:13-16:

> You will arise and have mercy on Zion;
> For the time to favor her,
> Yes, the set time, has come.
> For Your servants take pleasure in her stones,
> And show favor to her dust.
> So the nations shall fear the name of the Lord,
> And all the kings of the earth Your glory.
> For the Lord shall build up Zion;
> He shall appear in His glory.

JUDAH'S TRIBULATION

There is a time within the seasons under the Father's authority (Acts 1:7) when Jesus will appear in His glory. At that time, the nations and their kings will come to fear the glory of God—specifically because of the way in which He will act on behalf of Zion. God will favor Jerusalem and Judea. One might say that God will do them a favor—a miraculous sign of grace that will astound the kings of the earth. This supernatural deliverance will come at the time spoken of in Revelation 16:13-14:

And I saw three unclean spirits like frogs coming out of the mouth of the dragon, out of the mouth of the beast, and out of the mouth of the false prophet. For they are spirits of demons, performing signs, which go out to the kings of the earth and of the whole world, to gather them to the battle of that great day of God Almighty.

This prophesied end-times battle is also described in Ezekiel 38 (Excerpts):

3 'Thus says the Lord God: "Behold, I am against you, O Gog, the prince of Rosh, Meshech, and Tubal… 8 After many days you will be visited. In the latter years you will come into the land of **those brought back from the sword** and gathered from many people on the mountains of Israel, which had long been desolate; they were brought out of the nations, and now all of them dwell safely.

10 'Thus says the Lord God: "On that day it shall come to pass that thoughts will arise in your mind, and you will make an evil plan: 11 You will say, 'I will go up against a land of unwalled villages; I will go to a peaceful people, who dwell safely, all of them dwelling without walls, and having neither bars nor gates'—14 "Therefore, son of man, prophesy and say to Gog, 'Thus says the Lord God: "On that day when My people Israel dwell safely, will you not know it? 15 Then you will come from your place out of the far north, you and many peoples with you, all of them riding on horses, a great company and a mighty army. 16 You will come up against My people Israel like a cloud, to cover the land. It will be in the latter days that I will bring you against My land, **so that the nations may know Me, when I am hallowed in you**, O Gog, before their eyes." [God will be hallowed because of the miracle about to be performed].

Satan will be making "war against the saints, and prevailing against them" (Dan. 7:21). His unstoppable army is marching "when the power of the holy people has been completely shattered" (Dan. 12:7). The Beast (Gog) will not realize God is setting a trap for him. He thinks he is invincible because he holds the contract of Death and Sheol (Isa. 28:18). God will save His people.

But he cannot come until the national Jewish leadership (in Jerusalem) invites him back. That God's arm of salvation would come only after repentance was prophesied by Hosea: "I will return again to My place till they acknowledge their offense. Then they will seek My face; In their affliction [tribulation צָרָה], they will earnestly seek Me" (Hos. 5:15).

THE REJECTED CORNERSTONE

The only way out of this predicament is for the modern state of Israel to seek one who can disable and annul the covenant. But who is there? There will no one on earth that can do this. But God provided the key to this dilemma in the rejected cornerstone:

Thus says the Lord GOD: "Behold, I lay in Zion a **stone** for a foundation, A tried stone, a precious **cornerstone**, a sure foundation; Whoever believes will not act hastily" (Isa. 28:16).

This is the same language as in Psalm 118:

The **stone** which the builders rejected Has become the chief **cornerstone** (Ps. 118:22). This was the LORD's doing; It is marvelous in our eyes (Ps. 118:23).

The stone which the builders rejected is pivotal in understanding Israel's salvation. Jesus specifically directed the passage of Psalms against the national Jewish leadership (in Jerusalem) and consequently the implications of Isaiah 28 as well.

"Have you not even read this Scripture: 'The **stone** which the builders rejected Has become the chief **cornerstone** (Mark 12:10). This was the LORD's doing, And it is marvelous in our eyes'?" (Mark 12:11) And they sought to lay hands on Him, but feared the multitude, for they knew He had spoken the parable against them (Mark 12:12).

Jesus was saying, "I am that stone." The national Jewish leadership of Jerusalem, of the house of Judah, missed that Jesus was that stone. Nevertheless, it says, "This was the Lord's doing." We cannot overlook that! One of the saddest teachings over the last 2000 years is that the Jews killed Jesus and therefore, they deserve His wrath. We do not fully understand how it was God's doing but it was.

We must understand that when Jesus said, "O Jerusalem, Jerusalem…How often I wanted to gather your children together… but you were not willing!" (Matt. 23:37), He was not talking about the general populous of Judah. In fact, the people joyously welcomed Jesus.

The masses of Jerusalem did accept Jesus as their king. On the first day of the week before Passover, which we often call Palm Sunday, Jesus instructed His disciples to go and fetch a young donkey, which he then rode into Jerusalem, in the same fashion that David told his servants to "have Solomon my son ride on my own mule, and take him down to Gihon. (1 Kgs. 1:33). By having His disciples borrow a donkey for this occasion, Jesus orchestrated and broadcast that He was the rightful king in the line of David, and the promised Messiah.

> "Rejoice greatly, O daughter of Zion! Shout, O daughter of Jerusalem! Behold, your King is coming to you; He is just and having salvation, Lowly and riding on a donkey, A colt, the foal of a donkey" (Zech. 9:9).

The people even spoke the right words, the anointed words that the ruling authorities of Judah should have spoken: "Blessed is He who comes in the name of the Lord."

> The next day a great multitude that had come to the feast, when they heard that Jesus was coming to Jerusalem, took branches of palm trees and went out to meet Him, and cried out: "[הוֹשִׁיעָה Hoshianna]! "Blessed is He who comes in the name of the LORD!" [The King of Israel! The Messiah] (John 12:12).

Hoshianna is from the Hebrew root [ישע] yod-shin-'ayin means please save. It is the same root as the name Yeshua (Jesus) and Ye-shu-AH, salvation. As people who spoke Hebrew, they would have realized they were calling out his name. They also said *baruch haba b'shem Adonai*," acknowledging Yeshua as the king of Israel and Messiah—the consolation of Israel, the one they had been waiting for who would bring peace.

And when He had come into Jerusalem, all the city was moved, saying, "Who is this?" the multitudes said, "This is Jesus [Yeshua ישוע], the prophet from Nazareth of Galilee" (Matt. 21:10-11). Compare these events with what we see in Psalm 118:

> "I will praise You, For You have answered me, and have become my **salvation** [ישׁוּעָה Yeshu'ah] …The stone which the

builders rejected has become the chief cornerstone [פִּנָּה]. This was the LORD's doing; It is marvelous in our eyes…Save now, I pray, [הוֹשִׁיעָה Hoshianna] O LORD; Blessed is he who comes in the name of the LORD! We have blessed you from the house of the LORD… You are my God, and I will praise You; You are my God, I will exalt You" (Ps. 118:18-28).

JUDAH'S LEADERSHIP REJECTED JESUS

The national Jewish leadership who were in power refused to acknowledge him because he was a direct threat to their own power, a threat to their leadership. Jesus' heartfelt cry "O Jerusalem, Jerusalem," was directed toward the power, the seat of power, those that made decisions. Just like when we speak of Washington D.C., we are not talking about the taxicab drivers, fast food workers etc., but about the President, Congress, and the Supreme Court.

The leadership of Jerusalem, like in a parable Jesus told, "hated him…saying, 'We will not have this man to reign over us'" (Luke 19:14). Once they rejected Jesus by refusing to welcome Him in the name of the Lord, which is from Psalm 118, then the application of that Psalm was also withheld. The promise "The LORD is on my side; I will not fear. What can man do to me?" (Ps 118:6) no longer applied. As a result, Jesus pronounced, "See! Your house is left to you desolate" (Matt. 23:38). Isaiah had spoken of this conundrum—this conflict of acting out what was in the hearts of the peoples vs. submitting to the decision made by their authorities: "the leaders of this people cause them to err, and those who are led by them are destroyed" (Isa 9:16; see also Mic 3:5; Isa 3:12). The national Jewish leaders' decision was official national policy.

Gen. 49:10 records Jacob's prophetic blessing, "the **scepter shall not depart from Judah**, Nor a lawgiver from between his feet, Until Shiloh comes; And to Him shall be the obedience of the people." Judah is the one who gives the law by which Israel is to live until Shiloh comes, that is, Jesus, the one to whom it belongs.

When the leadership of Judah refused to recognize that the kingdom belongs to Jesus—that He is in fact, "THE KING OF THE JEWS," as was written above the cross— their national house, the House of Judah, was made desolate until such time as they should officially and nationally welcome him. Therefore, Jesus said, "For I tell you, you will not see me from now until [απ αρτι εως *ap arti eos*] you say, 'Blessed is the one who comes in the name of the Lord!'" (Matt. 23:39 NET).

Those three words "from now until" [απ αρτι εως, *ap arti eos*] are Jesus' ultimatum: Your house is desolate from now—the moment you rejected me—until the time you welcome me in the name of the Lord. These are the words Jesus is waiting for:

> This is the day the LORD has made; We will rejoice and be glad in it (Ps. 118:24). Save now, I pray, O LORD; O LORD, I pray, send now prosperity (Ps. 118:25). Blessed is he who comes in the name of the LORD! We have blessed you from the house of the LORD (Ps. 118:26).

THE RESTORATION OF ALL THINGS

After the ascension of Jesus, Peter said to his brethren, "I know that you did it [killed Jesus] in ignorance, as did also your rulers" (Acts 3:17). He calls on them to repent so that the times of refreshing may come. "…Repent therefore and be converted, that your sins may be blotted out, so that times of refreshing may come from the presence of the Lord, and that He may send Jesus Christ" (Acts 3:19-20). The phrase "times of refreshing" implies relief from difficult, distressful, or burdensome circumstances. According to the New English Translation Bible syntactical notes it is generally regarded as a reference to the Messianic Age being ushered in.

Peter followed this up by saying about Jesus, "whom heaven must receive until the times of restoration of all things" (Acts 3:21). In other words, "Repent, be converted so that Jesus *may* come; but until that time, heaven will receive him—until the right time." What is implied by correlating these verses? If you, (Judah, Jerusalem) will repent, (even in Peter's Day), then Jesus would come, which is exactly what Jesus was saying, "Until you repent and until you welcome me in the name of the LORD, you are not going to see me again. But when you do repent, then you will see me."

Peter also told the people, "You must obey him in everything he tells you," in Acts 3:22. Peter "spoke to the **rulers**, the **elders** and the

scribes and as well as the **high priest**, Caiaphas, John, and Alexander…" (Acts 4:6) who were attempting to quash the message:

> Then Peter, filled with the Holy Spirit, said to them, "**Rulers** of the people and elders of Israel: (Acts 4:8) "Jesus Christ of Nazareth, whom you crucified, whom God raised from the dead... (Acts 4:10) "is the '**stone** which was **rejected** by <u>you</u> **builders**… (Acts 4:11) "which has become the chief **cornerstone**.' (Acts 4:11) "Nor is there salvation [Yeshuah] in any other, for there is no other name under heaven given among men by which we must be saved" (Acts 4:12).

This passage also comes from Psalm 118:

> The LORD is my strength and song, And He has become my salvation [Yeshuah] (Ps. 118:14). I will praise You, for You have answered me, and have become my salvation [Yeshuah] (Ps 118:21).

Peter was saying, "You leaders of Jerusalem are the builders, and have rejected Jesus, the chief cornerstone." Peter makes it clear that salvation [Hebrew Yeshuah] is only found in Yeshua-Jesus. Therefore, Peter was saying there would be no national restoration until such a time as the builders, that is, the national Jewish leaders in Jerusalem, welcome him in the name of the Lord.

For Jesus to come back what must happen? The national leadership, the seat of authority now residing in Jerusalem, must receive Jesus in the name of the Lord. Even though many believers around the world and throughout the ages (both Jews and citizens of the commonwealth of Israel) have prayed, "Lord come back," this matter requires a national decree in Jerusalem by the ones who sit in that seat of authority to welcome Him back in the name of the Lord, just as Jesus said.

There will likely be a final meeting of the leaders of Jerusalem—probably the Sanhedrin or Knesset, (or whoever is left). They may be taking refuge in one of the many underground bunkers in Israel or in the tunnels under the old city. An overwhelming dread will hang over them as all the nations of the world, led by the Beast, are pressing down on Jerusalem to raze it to the ground and annihilate every last person. As they stare extinction in the face and acknowledge all their military strength is gone and they have no more ability to fight for their country or their lives they will pray and wonder why HaMashiach, Messiah is delayed. At that point, God will "pour out on the kingship of David and the population of Jerusalem a spirit of grace and supplication…" (Zech. 12:10 [NET2]) God will give them what they need, which is to look deep into their nation's soul and consider why Messiah has not come.

The Babylonian Talmud reveals a great deal as to why they think Messiah has not come. The rabbis considered the extent of human history to be analogous to a week, where each day represented one thousand years. Based on that understanding we read in Sanhedrin 97a,

> "Rabbi Kattina said: 'Six thousand years shall the world exist, and one [thousand], it shall be desolate,' as it is written, 'And YHVH alone shall be exalted in that day.' Abaye said: 'it will be desolate two [thousand],' as it is said, '**After two days will he revive us**: in the third day, he will raise us up, and we shall live in his sight.'"

In a Rabbinic footnote to this passage, they interpreted the **'two days'** in Hosea 6:2 to mean two thousand years. That means that after a period of two thousand years, and in the beginning of the next thousand years,[65] God would revive them so that they might live in his sight. The passage continues with the Tanna debe Eliyyahu who taught on the coming of Messiah within the six thousand plus one thousand year "week":

---

[65] "It has been taught in accordance with Rabbi Kattina: Just as the seventh year is one year of release in seven, so is the world: one thousand years out of seven shall be fallow, as it is written, 'And YHVH alone shall be exalted in that day,' …and it is also said, "For a thousand years in your sight are but as yesterday when it is past.'" [Rabbinic Footnote: Ps XC, 4; thus 'day' in the preceding verses means a thousand years.]

The world is to exist six thousand years. In the **first two thousand** there was **desolation**; two thousand years the **Torah flourished**; and the next two thousand years is the **Messianic era**.

The first two thousand years of "desolation" include the fall of Adam and Eve, the Nephilim and the flood followed by the tower of Babel, (Genesis 1-11). The next two thousand years in which Torah flourished, began with Abraham and then of course Moses on down till the first century (Genesis 12-Malachi). According to the Hebrew calendar, which begins with the year of creation, Abraham was born 1,948 years after creation (anno mundi). The date of Abraham receiving the covenant in Genesis 15 was given 2,018 years anno mundi. For reference, 2021 on the Gregorian calendar corresponds to 5781 on the Hebrew / Jewish (anno mundi) calendar. That means the last two thousand years of the Messianic era, in which Messiah comes and the war of Gog & Magog takes place, began around the first century on the Gregorian calendar, around the time of Jesus. According to a rabbinic footnote in the text, Messiah will come within that period. In other words, 1st 2000 Desolation + 2nd 2000 Torah Flourished + 3rd 2000 the Messianic Age.

The Talmud continues the discussion talking about the minimum time they calculated the world had to exist before Messiah would come.

Elijah said to Rab Judah, the brother of R. Salia the pious: 'The world shall exist not less than eighty-five jubilees…'Before that, do not expect him; afterwards thou mayest await him.'[66]

In other words, there would be a minimum of 85 Jubilees before Messiah would come. A Jubilee is calculated at either 49 or 50 years. If 49, then he would come after 4165 years or if 50 years, then he would come 4250 years after creation. In another text, a similar calculation is made based on "a scroll written in Hebrew in Assyrian characters" which had been discovered by a Jewish man "amongst the Roman archives."[67]

---

[66] http://www.come-and-hear.com/sanhedrin/sanhedrin_97.html
[67] Ibid.

In it is stated that four thousand, two hundred and thirty-one years after the creation the world will be **orphaned**. [As to the years following,] some of them will be…in the war of Gog and Magog, and the remaining [period] will be the Messianic era.[68]

Based on these texts from the Babylonian Talmud, the Messiah should have come sometime around the first century on the Gregorian calendar. The text continues in Sanhedrin 97b, "but through **our many iniquities** all these years have been lost." Then the footnote states bluntly, "**He should have come** at the beginning of the last two thousand years; the **delay is due to our sins**."[69]

According to their own texts—without the prompting of any Christian texts—the Jewish sages already have the answer but simply cannot see it. It is like when people come to ask for advice and after they have shared their story, the answer occurs to them without the advice of the counselor. Eventually, based on their own texts, they will realize their Messiah was expected to come four thousand years after creation and then shortly thereafter the world "would be orphaned." When they ask themselves why Messiah has not come, and yet "should have come at the beginning of the last two thousand years," the answer will be in the same text: "the delay is due to our sins."[70] Their text told them the world would be orphaned. Then they will discover Jesus' words; who said to his disciples "Let not your heart be troubled...I will not leave you orphans; I will come to you" (John 14:1, 18).

GRACE AND SUPPLICATION

The spirit of grace and supplication will then cause the national Jewish leadership in Jerusalem to realize not all hope is lost; they will look to the only one who can save them. "I will pour out on the kingship of David and the population of **Jerusalem** a spirit of grace and supplication so that **they will look to** [אל el] me, the one they have pierced" (Zech. 12:10 [NET2]).

---

[68] Ibid.
[69] The Babylonian Talmud: Mas. Sanhedrin 97a and b (Soncino Press)
[70] The Babylonian Talmud: Mas. Sanhedrin 97a and b (Soncino Press)

The preposition *el* [אל el] (Greek pros) means "to or toward" and not *al* which means "upon, over, above." Sadly, based on that unfortunate translation, commentators have implied Jesus is returning to destroy the inhabitants of Jerusalem and when they look "upon" him they will cry, "Oh no!! Here comes Jesus, we are in trouble!" This false teaching is the essence of Preterism which posits that Jesus came back on the dust clouds of the Roman army to destroy the Jews. That is **not** what the Bible teaches. Jesus is not coming to destroy Israel but to save her.[71]

The Septuagint of Zech. 12:10 reads (*epiblepsontai pros me*), "they will look to me/toward me," which is the same preposition we find in "In the beginning was the Word, and the Word was with [pros] God," (John 1:1). Pros means facing or toward; it is a relationship word. In a beautiful relationship, the Logos (Jesus) and the Father are looking at each other. The use of this preposition implies they will look to him as a little baby looks to his mother or father to give him sustenance, clothing, and protection. They will finally look to Jesus to save them. Suddenly, many texts will flood into their minds, and they will have their "aha" moment. Something like this passage from Numbers Rabbah might come to mind:

> When King Solomon speaks of his 'beloved,' he usually means Israel the nation. In one instance, he compares his beloved to a roe, and therein he refers to a feature, which marks alike **Moses** and the **Messiah**, the **two redeemers of Israel**. Just as a roe comes within the range of man's vision only to disappear from sight and then appear again, so it is with these redeemers.
>
> **Moses appeared** to the Israelites, **then disappeared**, and eventually **appeared once more**, and the same peculiarity we have in connection with **Messiah**; He will **appear, disappear, and appear**.[72]

---

[71] For behold, the LORD comes out of His place To punish the inhabitants of the earth for their iniquity... (Isa. 26:21). "Then the LORD will go forth and fight against those nations, As He fights in the day of battle." (Zech. 14:3).

[72] Numb. Rabba 11.

God will pour out his spirit of grace and supplication so that they can look to Yeshua for the first time in their collective history. In their distress they may reconsider the long-neglected words of Isaiah Ch. 53:

> My servant grew up in the LORD's presence like a tender green shoot, sprouting from a root in dry and sterile ground. There was nothing beautiful or majestic about his appearance, nothing to attract us to him (Isa. 53:2). He was despised and rejected – a man of sorrows, acquainted with bitterest grief. We turned our backs on him and looked the other way when he went by. He was despised, and we did not care (Isa. 53:3). Yet it was our weaknesses he carried; it was our sorrows that weighed him down. And we thought his troubles were a punishment from God for his own sins! (Isa. 53:4) But he was wounded and crushed for our sins. He was beaten that we might have peace. He was whipped, and we were healed! (Isa. 53:5).

> All of us have strayed away like sheep. We have left God's paths to follow our own. Yet, the LORD laid on him the guilt and sins of us all (Isa. 53:6). He was oppressed and treated harshly, yet he never said a word. He was led as a lamb to the slaughter. And as a sheep is silent before the shearers, he did not open his mouth (Isa. 53:7). From prison and trial, they led him away to his death. But who among the people realized that he was dying for their sins--that he was suffering their punishment? (Isa. 53:8).

The painful reality of their rejection of HaMashiach, the only one that can save them, will truly sink in. They will contemplate how the one they had pinned their hopes on for thousands of years was the chief cornerstone that the builders, their leaders, had rejected and who, though he had done no wrong, was whipped and sent to his death on a cross like a criminal and was put in a rich man's grave (Isa. 53:8, 9).

> They will mourn for Him as one mourns for his only son, and grieve for Him as one grieves for a firstborn. (Zech. 12:10) "In that day there shall be a great mourning in Jerusalem... (Zech. 12:11) "all the families that remain, every family by itself, and their wives by themselves (Zech. 12:14).

The leaders will consider how the masses said "*Baruch Haba B'shem Adonai,*" but their leaders at the time said, "Crucify him." They will weep, and for the first time ever, the national Jewish leadership in Jerusalem will acknowledge their offense and that will be the key to Messiah's second coming.

With a thorough understanding of this future event, it becomes clear that the ascension was not only a testimony of Christ's righteousness (Jn. 16:10), but a fulfillment of Hosea's prophecy: "I will return again to My place [heaven—the Father's right hand] till they acknowledge their offense. Then they will seek My face; In their affliction [tribulation] they will earnestly seek Me" (Hos. 5:15).

Realizing that it was calling on God's name—not their own strength—that had saved them, they will recite Psalms 118:10-14 (NIV):

All the nations surrounded me,
   but in the name of the Lord I cut them down.
They surrounded me on every side,
   but in the name of the Lord I cut them down.
They swarmed around me like bees, but they were consumed as quickly as burning thorns;
   in the name of the Lord I cut them down.
I was pushed back and about to fall,
   but the Lord helped me.
The Lord is my strength and my defense;
   he has become my salvation.

Thus, with all their heart they will call upon Jesus to save them. They will shout and join the throngs of people who welcomed Jesus at his first coming by saying "Please save [Hoshianna], I pray, O LORD; O LORD, I pray, send now prosperity. Blessed is he who comes in the name of the LORD" "*Baruch Haba B'shem Adonai*," (Ps. 118:25-26); come Yeshua, "we welcome you in the name of Yehovah. Just as they anticipated in the Babylonian Talmud, their confession will bring them to say:

Come, and let us return to the LORD; For He has torn, but He will heal us; He has stricken, but He will bind us up. (Hos. 6:1) After two days He will revive us; On the third day He will raise us up, That we may live in His sight. (Hos. 6:2)

Thomas Constable points out that "Corporate Israel has never prayed like this. The fulfillment must still be future, at the beginning of Christ's millennial reign."[73]

THE COVENANT WITH DEATH

A discussion of the end times is beyond the scope of this book, however, Isaiah prophecies that the national Jewish leadership in Jerusalem, "Who **rule** this people who are in **Jerusalem**, (Isa. 28:14) will one day make "a **covenant** with **death**, And with **Sheol**..." (Isa. 28:15) and God states: "Your covenant with death will be annulled, And your agreement with Sheol will not stand" (Isa. 28:18).

This raises the question of how can God simply "annul" their covenant? God cannot just snap his fingers and change things willy-nilly. Satan is counting on him to act righteously. So, there must be a legal mechanism for the annulment to happen. The beautiful thing is that there is such a mechanism. In a nutshell, the "old covenant" was a marriage contract that God and Israel entered into at Sinai.

> I spread My wing over you and covered your nakedness. Yes, I swore an oath to you and entered into a **covenant** with you, and you became Mine," says the Lord GOD. (Ezek. 16:8)

> The covenant that I made with their fathers in the day that I took them by the hand to lead them out of the land of Egypt, My covenant which they broke, though I was a **husband** to them, says the LORD. (Jer. 31:32)

God divorced the northern kingdom of Israel because of their adultery: "Then I saw that for all the causes for which backsliding Israel had committed **adultery**, I had **put her away and given her a certificate of divorce**; yet her treacherous sister Judah did not fear, but went and played the harlot also" (Jer. 3:8). God did not divorce Judah "for the sake of My servant David, and for the sake of Jerusalem, the city which I have chosen out of all the tribes of Israel" (1Kgs. 11:32). Paul explained how the old marriage (old covenant) is annulled by the death of the husband (covered in previous chapters).

---

[73] The Expository Notes of Dr. Thomas L. Constable, 2009

The national Jewish leadership in Jerusalem will enter the covenant of death and Sheol still under the old marriage covenant with its stains of adultery and infidelity. By welcoming Jesus in the name of the Lord, they recognize him as the husband who died and "the one they pierced" (Zech. 12:10). Paul says because of that "you also have become dead to the law [of the husband] through the body of Christ" (Rom 7:4).

When they become dead through belief in Jesus, then all contracts they made corporately, die with them; and so their covenant with Death is annulled, like it never was. Isaiah speaks of this time when Jesus comes (Isa 4:2), and purges the blood of Jerusalem:

> And it shall come to pass that he who is **left** in Zion and remains in **Jerusalem** will be called **holy**–everyone who is recorded among the living in Jerusalem. (Isa 4:3) When the Lord has washed away the filth of the daughters of Zion, and purged the blood of Jerusalem from her midst, by the spirit of judgment and by the spirit of burning. (Isa 4:4).

God also specifically states he will ransom Ephraim (the house of Israel) from Sheol and Death, the same duo with which the leaders of Jerusalem make a deal:

> The iniquity of Ephraim is bound up; his sin is kept in store (Hos. 13:12). Shall I ransom them from the power of Sheol [שְׁאוֹל]? Shall I redeem them from Death? O Death [מָוֶת Mavet], where are your plagues? O Sheol, where is your sting? Compassion is hidden from my eyes (Hos. 13:14).

Paul uses this passage to speak about the resurrection that and the transformation that will take place for God's faithful.

> In a moment, in the twinkling of an eye, at the last trumpet. For the trumpet will sound, and the dead will be raised incorruptible, and we shall be changed. (1 Cor. 15:52) For this corruptible must put on incorruption, and this mortal must put on immortality. (1 Cor. 15:53) So when this corruptible has put on incorruption, and this mortal has put on immortality, then shall be brought to pass the saying that is written: "**Death** is swallowed up in victory." (1 Cor. 15:54) "O Death, where is your sting? O **Hades**, where is your victory?" (1 Cor. 15:55)

Both passages provide supplemental proof that we are looking at the same duo predicted to reign over the last 3.5 years of this age and with whom the world will make a covenant. The confession of the Jerusalem leadership annuls their contract with Death and Sheol. Up until then "the same horn was making war against the saints, and prevailing against them" (Dan. 7:21) until the Ancient of Days came, and a judgment was made in favor of the saints" (Dan. 7:21-22).

Just as Jesus said that they would not see him "from now until you say, 'Blessed is the one who comes in the name of the Lord!'" (Matt. 23:39 NET) Nothing will change for the saints "until" and then the judgment is made for them as a result of what they confess. Jesus alluded to this shift as well when he said: "For then there will be great tribulation, such as has not been since the beginning of the world until this time, no, nor ever shall be. (Matt. 24:21) "And unless those days were shortened, no flesh would be saved; but for the elect's sake [δια δε τους εκλεκτους *dia de tous eklektos*] those days will be shortened" (Matt. 24:22).

If we know that the tribulation will be 1260 days long, how can the days be shortened?

When the word "Dia" is followed by an accusative (objective) case, according to BDAG[74] Lexicon, it means, "the reason why something happens, results, exists: because of, for the sake of."[75] Based on the Greek grammar, the saints are not passive recipients of an act of pity from God. Rather, those days will be shortened "as a result" of something the elect do. The elect will bring about the shortening of the days. What will they do? They will finally answer Jesus' challenge and welcome him in the name of the LORD; and say "*baruch haba b'shem Adonai*" (Matt. 23:39).

Their welcoming Jesus in the name of the Lord will set in motion his return! Just before that there seems to be a time of silence, "Be silent, all flesh, before the LORD; for He is aroused from His holy habitation" (Zech. 2:13). It is as if He were drawing a deep breath followed by: "The LORD also will roar from Zion, And utter His voice from Jerusalem; The heavens and earth will shake; But the LORD will be a shelter for His people, And the strength of the children of Israel" (Joel 3:16). Their welcoming of Jesus, the stone they rejected, will also correspond to his gathering of all who were scattered of the house of Israel into the nations centuries before and also of the house of Judah that was likewise scattered after their national rejection of Jesus.

CHAPTER 11: SCATTERED JUDAH AT THE TIME OF CHRIST

---

[74] Third edition of Baur's Lexicon by contributors Bauer–Arndt–Gingrich–Danker (BDAG). University of Chicago Press, 2001.

[75] hated because of the name Mt 10:22; persecution arises because of teaching 13:21; because of unbelief vs. 58; because of a tradition 15:3; (BDAG)

very land and every sea was filled with the Jewish people.[76]

"Strabo, speaking of the time of Sulla, says (about 85 B.C.), that **the Jewish people had already come into every city**, and that it was not easy to find a place in the world which had not received this race, and was not occupied by them." Judah, like Israel, was in fact scattered among the nations; but after the Captivity, their sojourning was not a result of God's punishment but a matter of choice. What had been learned through Israel's bondage in Egypt and Judah's 70 years in Babylon was that the Jews could maintain their identity and their faith apart from the Land and the Temple. The faith of the Fathers proved to be portable, as in the days of the Tabernacle in the wilderness. Why is it important to know how remotely many of the Jews had settled? It has to do with understanding the conundrum between personal faith and submission to the authority of the national leaders as discussed in the previous chapter.

Formerly in this book, it was noted that some Jews in Ephesus had only known about the baptism of John at the time of Paul's second missionary journey. Now consider that at the end of Paul's life—estimated to be about 65 years—some Jews in Rome still did not know that their Jewish rulers had spoken against Paul:

> Then they said to him, "We neither received letters from Judea concerning you, nor have any of the brethren who came reported or spoken any evil of you. But we desire to hear from you what you think; for concerning this sect, we know that it is spoken against everywhere" (Acts 28:21-22).

These men did acknowledge that Christianity was considered a heretical sect, but they did not have any knowledge of Jesus, His ministry, or why their leaders had rejected Him. This is clearly indicated by the fact that they did not understand why everyone was speaking against "this sect." How long might it have been before the news of Messiah—His life, death, and resurrection—reached "every land and every sea?

---

[76] *Orac, Sibyll.* iii. 271.

To such isolated Jews, of whom perhaps several generations had passed since the cross, their relationship with God had not changed—as far as they knew. With a better knowledge of the historical backdrop of the Jewish people, it becomes easier to understand the "chronic hesitation" to make a positive response to Jesus on the individual level, which has persisted over the last 2,000 years.

THE JEWISH DIASPORA

It is easy to get the impression from reading the Bible, without reference to other sources, that the Jews at the time of Jesus were located primarily in Judea and Babylon—with a few communities sprinkled around the areas visited by Paul. With this limited understanding, a person might naturally assume that all of the Jews heard the reports about Jesus' ministry and His rejection by their leaders rather quickly. Once, however, the extent of the Jewish diaspora is discovered, it becomes clear that, logistically, the news from the homeland may have taken a very long time. Not long after the time of Paul's death, the Temple was destroyed. Such reports about the Temple would have taken precedence over all other events. Especially to those who still hadn't heard about Jesus.

What follows in the body of this chapter is substantially quoted from *A History of the Jewish People in the Time of Jesus Christ*[77] by researcher Emil Schürer. Schürer was aware of the distinction between the two houses of Israel, as the quoted citations will reveal, because from time to time, he mentions the location of the Ten Tribes and of the Samaritans.

> The history of the Jews during the times of Christ is not confined to the narrow limits of the Holy Land. Jewish communities of greater or less magnitude and importance had settled in almost all the countries of the then civilized world. These remained, on the one hand, in constant communication with the mother country, and on the other, in active intercourse with the non-Jewish world, and thus became of great importance both in respect of the internal development of Judaism and its influence upon other civilized nations.

---

[77] *A History of the Jewish People in the Time of Jesus Christ* by Emil Schürer. Charles Scribner's Sons, New York, 1896.

As noted above, news about Jesus of Nazareth and the sect called "the way" were not the major topics of communication among the Jewish network of communities. News of Judea's internal affairs and obviously, the destruction of the Temple, would have been of utmost importance.

The causes of this dispersion were of very different kinds. In former times the Assyrian and Babylonian conquerors of Israel violently deported large masses of the nation into their eastern provinces. This occurred again, though to a less extent, when Pompey, e.g., carried off hundreds of Jewish captives to Rome.

Of greater importance however were the voluntary emigrations of Jewish settlers during the Graeco-Roman period to the countries bordering on Palestine, and to all the chief towns of the then civilized world for the sake chiefly of trade. It was especially at the commencement of the Hellenistic period, that these migrations were most numerous.

The Hellenistic Jews did not maintain the strict separation between Jew and Gentile, which was the practice of the Traditionalists. However, even the Jew's in their interaction with Samaritans, from whom they distanced themselves in every other way, did allow the normal carrying on of commerce with even the Samaritans: "There were mutual recriminations between Jews and Samaritans, which led to strained relations and fierce condemnation, and yet, strange to say, the rabbis did not treat the land as "unclean" (Edersheim, *Life of Jesus the Messiah*, bk. 3, 100, 7); and consequently the Disciples [John 4:8] were not precluded from purchasing articles of food from the Samaritan village.[78]

The Diadochoi and their successors, for the sake of consolidating their kingdoms, promoted to the uttermost of their power the intermingling of the different nationalities, and consequently migrations from one province to another. [The Diadochoi were the rival generals, families, and friends of Alexander the Great, who fought for control over his empire after his death in 323 BCE. **The Wars of the Diadochi mark the beginning of the Hellenistic period.**][79]

---

[78] https://biblehub.com/commentaries/pulpit/john/4.htm
[79] https://en.wikipedia.org/wiki/Diadochi

They were also frequently in need of great masses of settlers for their newly founded towns. And in both of these interests, the rights of citizenship or other privileges were in many places granted, without further ceremony, to immigrants.

Attracted by these circumstances, large numbers of Jews were also induced to settle in other lands. Adverse events at home may have also contributed, and especially the exposed situation of Palestine, which in all complications between Egypt and Syria became the scene of war. This induced many thousands of Jews to emigrate to the neighbouring countries of Syria and Egypt, where, especially in the capitals of Antioch and Alexandria, and in all the newly founded Hellenistic cities, valuable privileges were bestowed upon them. They next resorted to Asia Minor, particularly the towns of the Ionic coast, as well as to all the more important ports and commercial cities of the Mediterranean Sea.

Figure 31. Greek settlements in western Asia Minor, Ionian area: dark grey.[80]

---

[80] After the battle of the Granicus most of the Ionian cities submitted to the rule of Alexander the Great and his Diadochi. As such Ionia enjoyed a great prosperity during the Hellenistic times. Source:
https://en.wikipedia.org/wiki/Ionia

About the same time (139-138 B.C.) the Roman Senate dispatched a circular in favour of the Jews to the kings of Egypt, Syria, Pergamos, Cappadocia and Parthia, and to a great number of provinces, towns and islands of the Mediterranean Sea (1 Macc. xv. 16-24). It may hence be safely inferred, that there was then already a greater or less number of Jews in all these lands.[81] Strabo, speaking of the time of Sulla, says (about 85 B.C.), that the Jewish people had already come into every city, and that it was not easy to find a place in the world which had not received this race, and was not occupied by them.[82] Josephus ' too[83] and Philo[84] express themselves incidentally in a similar manner.

The extent of the Jewish dispersion is most amply described in the epistle of Agrippa to Caligula, given by Philo. **Jerusalem—it is here said—is the capital not only of Judaea, but of most countries**, by reason of the colonies which it has sent out on fitting occasions into the neighbouring lands of Egypt, Phoenicia, Syria, Coelesyria, and the still more remote Pamphylia and Cilicia, into most parts of Asia as far as Bithynia, and into the most distant corners of Pontus; also, to Europe, Thessaly, Boeotia, Macedonia, Etolia, Attica, Argos, Corinth, and the most and best parts of Peloponnesus. And not only is the continent full of Jewish settlements, but also the more important islands, — Euboea, Cyprus, Crete, — to say nothing of the lands beyond the Euphrates. For all, with the exception of a small portion of Babylon and those satrapies which embrace the fertile land lying around it, have Jewish inhabitants.[85] The Acts of the Apostles also mention Jews and their associates from Parthia, Media, Elam, and Mesopotamia,

---

[81] Besides the kings of Egypt, Syria, Pergamos, Cappadocia and Parthia, there are also named in 1 Macc. xv. 16-24 : Sampsaine (Samsun on the Black Seal), Sparta, Sicyon (in Peloponnesus), the islands of Delos and Samos, the town of Gortyna in Crete, the country of Caria with the towns of Myndos, Halicarnassus and Cnidos, the islands of Cos and Rhodes, the country of Lycia with the town of Phasaelis. the country of Pamphylia with the town Side, the Phoenician town Aradus, and finally Cyprus and Cyrene.

[82] Strabo in Joseph. *Antt.* xiv. 7. 2

[83] Joseph. *Bell. Jud.* ii. 16. 4 (Bekker, p. 188. Jud. vii. 3. 3).

[84] Philo, *In Flaccum*, Sec. 7

[85] Philo, *Legat, ad Cajum*, Sec. 36, Mang, ii. 587.

from Cappadocia, Pontus and Asia, Phrygia and Pamphylia, Egypt and Cyrene, from Rome, Crete and Arabia (Acts ii 9-11).

In Mesopotamia, Media, and Babylonia lived the descendants of those members of the kingdom of the ten tribes and of the kingdom of Judah who had once been carried away thither by the Assyrians and Chaldeans.[86] The "ten tribes" never returned at all from captivity,[87] and even in the times of Akiba there were disputes as to whether they would ever do so.[88] Nor must the return of the tribes of Judah and Benjamin be conceived of as complete. Nay, these exiles subsequently received fresh accessions. For the Persian king Artaxerxes Ochus, on his return from his Egyptian campaign (about 340 B.C.), brought with him Jewish captives also, and planted them in Hyrcania on the Caspian Sea.[89]

These Jewish settlements may also have been increased by voluntary additions. From all these causes, **the Jews in those provinces were numbered, not by thousands, but by millions.**[90] Since they dwelt on the eastern borders of the Roman Empire, — till Trajan, as subjects of the Parthians, and subsequently as inhabitants of those eastern provinces which

---

[86] Comp. on the different deportations, Winer, *Realworterb.*, art. " Exil." On the localities, see note 14, below.

[87] Joseph. *Antt.* xi. 5. 2. 4 Ezra xiii. 39-47. Origen, *Epist. ad Africanum*, Sec. 14.

[88] *Sanhedrin* x. 3, *fin.* : "The ten tribes never return, for it is said of them (Deut. xxix. 27) : He will cast them into another land, as it is this day. As then this day departs and never returns, so too are they to depart and never return. As the day becomes dark and then again light, so will it one day be light again to the ten tribes with whom it was dark."

[89] Syncellus, ed. Diiidorf, i. 486.

[90] Joseph. *Antt.* xi. 5. 2; *Antt.* xv. 2. 2; On the history of the Babylonian Jews, comp, especially *Antt.* xviii. 9. Reference is sometimes at least made in the Mishna to the Jews of Babylonia and Media. See *Shekalim* iii. 4 (the half-shekel tax of Babylonia and Media) ; *Challa* iv. 11 (the first-born not accepted from Babylonia) ; *Joma* vi. 4 (the Babylonians plucked the wool of the scape-goat on the day of atonement) ; *Menachoth* xi. 7 (Babylonian priests) ; *Baba mezia* iv. 7, *Shabhath* vi. 6 (Median Jewesses) ; *Baba kamma* ix. 5 = *Baba mezia* iv. 7 (restitution for plundered property is binding as far as Media) ; *Shabbath* ii. 1, *Nasir* v. 4, *Baba bathra* v. 2 (Nahum the Mede). The Book of Tobit also proves that Jews dwelt in Media (Tob. i. 14, iii. 7, etc.).

could never be securely maintained by the Romans,[91] — their attitude was always of political importance to the empire. P. Petronius, legate of Syria, esteemed it dangerous in the year 40 B.C. to excite in them a hostile disposition towards Rome.[92]

During the Vespasian war the insurgents sought to incite their co-religionists beyond the Euphrates to hostilities against Rome.[93] It was a great peril for Trajan in his advance against the Parthians to be menaced in his rear by the insurrection of the Mesopotamian Jews. Josephus names the strong cities of **Nehardea and Nisibis**, the former on the Euphrates, the latter in its valley, as **the chief dwelling places of the Babylonian and Mesopotamian Jews.**[94] Both cities were in subsequent centuries chief scats of Talmudic Judaism, and are therefore frequently mentioned in the Babylonian Talmud.[95]

Josephus names Syria as the country in which was the largest percentage of Jewish inhabitants, and its capital, Antioch, was especially distinguished in this respect.[96]

---

[91] On the political history, see Marquardt, *Romische Staatsverwaltung*, vol. i. (1881) pp. 435-438.

[92] Philo, *Legat. ad Cajum*, Sec. 33, Mang. ii. 578.

[93] Joseph. *Bell. Jud.* vi. 6. 2 (p. 108, line 19 sq., ed. Bekker).

[94] Joseph. *Antt.* xviii. 9. 1 and 9, *fin.* OnNehardea see Pauly's *Real-Enc.* v. 375 sq. (*s.v.* Naarda). Ritter, *Erdkunde*, x. 146. Hamburger, *Real- Enc. für Bihel und Talmud*, ii. 852 sq. On Nisibis, Pauly's *Real-Enc.*
v. 659 sq. Ritter, *Erdkunde*, xi. 413 sqq. Nisibis was not on the Euphrates, as might appear from Josephus, but on the Mygdonius, an affluent of the Chaboras, which again is an affluent of the Euphrates. It formed the centre of the localities mentioned 2 Kings xvii. 6, xviii. 11, to which the members of the kingdom of the ten tribes were carried by the Assyrians (sec Gesenius' *Thesaurus*, and Winer's *Realwörterbuch* on the articles.
Halach, Habor, Gozan, Media; and the commentaries on 2 Kings xvii. 6, xviii. 11). Nehardea, on the other hand, lay further southward in Babylonia proper. Thus *around Nisibis were grouped the descendants of the ten tribes, and around Nehardea the descendants of the tribes of Benjamin and Judah*, increased in both instances by subsequent additions. For Rabbinical matter on the abode of the ten tribes, see Lightfoot, *Horae Hebr. in epist. 1 ad Corinthios*, addenda ad c. xiv. (*Opp.* ed. Roterodam. ii. 929-932) ; Hamburger, *Real-Enc.* ii. 1281 sqq. (art. "Zehn Stämme"). Comp, also 4 Ezra xiii. 39-47, and above, p. 170.

[95] See Berliner *Beiträge zur Geographic und Ethnographie Babyloniens im Talmud und Midrash* (Berlin 1884), pp. 47 sqq., 53 sq; *Jebamoth* xvi. 7.

[96] *Bell. Jud.* viL 3. 3.

Other cities of Syria also numbered their Jewish inhabitants by thousands; this was the case with Damascus, where, according to the statement of Josephus, 10,000 or (according to another passage) 18,000 Jews are said to have been assassinated at the time of the war.[97] Philo tells us of Asia also, as of Syria, that Jews dwelt in *large numbers in every city*.[98] Aristotle, during his sojourn in Asia Minor (348-345 B.C.), had a meeting with an educated Jew, who had come thither, who Clearchus, a disciple of Aristotle, gives in his book on sleep further particulars concerning this meeting.[99]

Antiochus the Great settled 2000 Jewish families from Mesopotamia and Babylonia in Phrygia and Lydia.[100] And to mention nothing else, the Roman edicts in favour of the Jews communicated by Josephus (*Antt.* xiv. 10, xvi. 6), and the entire history of the Apostle Paul, show how widely the Jews had spread over the whole of Asia Minor. The statement of Agrippa in his epistle cited above, that Jews had settled in Bithynia and in the most distant corners of Pontus,[101] is abundantly confirmed by the Jewish inscriptions in the Greek language found in the Crimea.[102]

---

[97] 10,000, *Bell. Jud.* ii. 20. 2. 18,000, *Bell. Jud.* vii. 8. 7 (p. 161, 27, ed. Bekker).

[98] 18 Philo, *ad Legat. Cajum*, Sec. 33, Mang. ii. 582.

[99] The account of Clearchus is preserved by Josephus, *contra Apionem*, i. 22 (p. 200 sq., ed. Bekker). Eusebius, *Praep. evang.* ix. 5, has the history from Josephus. Clemens Alexandrinus, *Strom*, i. 15. 70, also briefly notices
the matter. Comp. Muller, *Fragmenta Hist. Graec.* ii. 323 sq. Gutschmid, *Neue Beitrüge zur Geschichte des alten Orients* (1876), p. 77.

[100] *Antt.* xii. 3. 4.

[101] Philo, ed. Mang. ii. 587; Comp. also Acts xviii. 2 (Aquila, a Jew of Pontus).

[102] See a Jewish inscription from Pantikapaion (on the Cimmerian Bosphorus) of the year 377 aer. Bosp. = A.D. 81, in the *Corp. Inscr. Graec.* vol. ii. p. 1005 (addenda, n. 2114[bb]). Another from Anapa (also in the Crimea) of the year 338 aer. Bosp. = A.D. 42 in Stcphani, *Pererga archaeologica (Bulletin de l'Academie de St. Petersbourg,* vol. i. 1860, col. 244 sqq.). See also Caspari, *Quellen zur Geschichte des Taufsymbols,* iii. (1875) p. 269. The Hebrew inscriptions from the Crimea, some of which Chwolsen thought might be referred to even the first century after Christ (Chwolsen, *Achtzehn hebräische Grahschriften aus der Krim, Memoires de l'Academie imperial des sciences de St. Petersbourg,* vii.e Serie, vol. ix. 1866, No. 7), are much more modern, the dates which decide the question having been fabricated by Firkowitsch. See the proof in Strack (*A. Firkowitsch und seine Entdeckungen, ein Grabstein der hebräischen Grabschriften der Krim,* Leipzig 1876) and Harkavy (*Altjüdische*

But most important with regard to the history of civilization was the Jewish Dispersion in Egypt and especially in Alexandria.[103] Long before the time of Alexander the Great Jewish immigrants were already found there. Psammetichus I. is said to have had Jewish mercenaries in his army in his war against the Ethiopians, 650 B.C.[104] In the time of Jeremiah a large train of Jewish emigrants went into Egypt, for fear of the Chaldees and in opposition to the will of the prophet (Jer. xlii., xliii; for the occasion, see Jer. xli.). They settled in various parts of Egypt, in Migdol, Tahpanhes, Noph and Pathros (Jer. xliv.); and though many of them embraced the religion of Egypt and many were extirpated by war, still a remnant was left. A forcible deportation of Jewish colonists to Egypt is said to have taken place in the time of the Persian supremacy.[105] Their most flourishing period however does not begin till the time of Alexander the Great. As early as the foundation of Alexandria, Jewish settlers were attracted to it by the bestowal upon them of the rights of citizenship.[106] Large numbers of Jews afterwards came to Egypt chiefly under Ptolemy I. Lagos, some as prisoners of war and some as voluntary immigrants. They were employed by Ptolemy as mercenaries, especially for garrisoning fortified places.[107]

Denkmäler aus der Krim, Memoires de l'Acade'mie imperiale des sciences de St. Petersbourg, vii.e Serie, vol. xxiv. 1876, No. 1). The fact of the forgery was subsequently acknowledged to at least a limited extent by Chwolsen himself (in his *Corpus Inscriptionum Hebraicarum*, Petersburg 1882). Comp. also Kautzsch in the *Theol. Litztg.* 1883, p. 319 sqq.

[103] Comp. Citss, *De culoniis Judaeorum in Aegyptum terrasque cum Aegypto conjunctas post Mosen deductis*, P. I., Stuttg. 1832. Hamburger, *Real-Enc.* art. "Alexandrien." See other literature in Reuss, *Gesch. der heil. Schriften Alten Testaments*, Sec. 430.

[104] Aristeae, *epist.* ed. M. Schmidt, in Merx' *Archiv für wissenschaftl, Erforschung des A. T.* vol. i. p. 255 (Havercamp's *Josephus*, ii. 2. 104), enumerates the three following chief emigrations of Jews to Egypt, from Ptolemy I backwards. That Psammetichus had foreign mercenaries in his army is evidenced elsewhere also ; sec Cless, *De coloniis*, pp. 4-7, and Pauly's *Real-Enc.* vi. 1. 167 sq.

[105] Aristeas speaks of such a one in two passages ; see one in note 24, above; the other, ed. Schmidt, p. 260, Havercamp's *Josephus* ii. 2. 107. Comp, also Cless, *De coloniis*, pp. 11-13.

[106] *Apion.* ii. 4. *Antt.* xix. 5. 2.

[107] Hecateus in Joseph. *Apion.* i. 22 (ßekkcr, p. 203, lin. 31 sq.). Further particulars in the passage quoted note 24 from Aristeas, and Josephus, *Antt.* xii. 1.

In Alexandria a special quarter apart from the rest of the city was, in the times of the Diadochoi, assigned to the Jews, "that they might lead a purer life by mingling less with foreigners." [108] This Jewish quarter lay on the harbourless coast, in the neighbourhood of the royal palace, and therefore in the north-eastern part of the town. [109] This severance was not afterwards strictly maintained. For according to Philo there were **Jewish houses of prayer in all parts of the city**, [110] and many Jews dwelt scattered through all its quarters. [111] But even Philo says also, that of the five districts of the town, which were named after the first five letters of the alphabet, two were called "the Jewish," because they were chiefly inhabited by Jews. [112] The separation was however on the whole maintained, and we shall find the Jewish quarter still in the same place, viz. in the east of the town, in Philo's time. [113]

---

[108] *Bell. Jud.* ii. 18. 7; Strabo in Joseph. *Antt*, xiv. 7. 2; According to Joseph. *Apion.* ii. 4, it might appear as though Alexander the Great had assigned this special quarter to the Jews. But, according to the evidently more accurate statement in *Bell. Jud.* ii. 18. 7, this was first done by the Diadochoi. Comp. J. G. Müller, *Des Flavius Joseplius Schrift gegen den Apion* (1877), p. 239.

[109] Josephus, *c. Apion.* ii. 4, *init.* (cited from Apion); The great harbour of Alexandria, along which lay the greater part of the town, is bounded on the west by the island of Pharos and the mole connecting the island with the continent, on the east by the promontory of Lochias, which juts out from the mainland into the sea (see especially the plan in Kiepert, *Zur Topographie des alten Alexandria*, Berlin 1872; also M. Erdmann, *Zur Kunde der hellenistischen Städtegründungen, Strassburger Prog.* 1883, pp. 10-23). On the promontory of Lochias and in its neighbourhood lay the royal citadel, with the numerous buildings appertaining to it (Strabo, xvii. 1. 9, p. 794), which together made up a fifth of the town (Plinius, v. 10. 62 ; see in general Pauly's *Real-Enc.* i. 1. 739 sq.). Hence the Jewish quarter lay on the coast east of the promontory of Lochias.

[110] Philo, *Legat. ad Cajum*, Sec. 20, Mang. ii. 565.

[111] Philo, *In Flaccum*, Sec. 8, Mang. ii. 525. See the next note.

[112] Philo, *In Flaccum*, Sec. 8, Mang. ii. 525.The division of Alexandria into five districts and their appellation after the first five letters of the alphabet is also testified elsewhere. See Pseudo-Callisthenes, i. 32 (ed. Meusel in Fleckeisen's *Jahrbb. für class. Philol. Supplemental*, vol. v.); The second of these districts is mentioned in an inscription of the time of Antoninus Pius; (see Lumbroso in the *Annali dell' Instituto di corrisp. archeol.* 1875, p. 15; Bursian's *Jahresbericht*, f. 1874-75, vol ii. p. 305; Marquardt, *Römische Staatsverwaltung*, i. 1881, p. 455).

[113] Josephus expressly says, *c. Apion.* ii. 4, that the Jews did not subsequently relinquish the place occupied by them.

According to an incidental notice in Josephus, the Jews dwelt chiefly in the "so-called Delta" *i.e.* in the fourth district of the town.[114] Philo estimates the entire number of the Jewish inhabitants of Egypt at about a million in his days.[115]

The Jews of Alexandria and Egypt took, in conformity with their large numbers and importance, a prominent part in all the chief conflicts between the Jewish and the heathen world, in the great persecution under Caligula (see Sec. 17*c*) and in the insurrections in the times of Nero, Vespasian[116] and Trajan (see Sec. 21).[117] The very history of these conflicts is at the same time a proof of the continued importance of the Egyptian Jews in the Roman Period also.

But besides the Jews properly so called, there were also Samaritans dwelling in Egypt. Ptolemy I. Lagos, when he conquered Palestine, carried away with him many captives, not only from Judaea and Jerusalem, hut also "from Samaria and Mount Gerizim," and settled them in Egypt.[118] In the time of Ptolemy VI. Philometor the Jews and Samaritans are said to have brought their dispute, as to whether Jerusalem or Gerizim was the true place of worship, before the tribunal of the king.[119] Hadrian in his letter to Servianus says of the Samaritans in Egypt as well as of the Jews and Christians dwelling there, that they were all of them "astrologers, haruspices and quacks.[120]

The Jewish Dispersion penetrated from Egypt farther westward. It was very numerously represented in Cyrenaica. Ptolemy I. Lagos had already sent Jewish settlers thither.[121]

---

[114] *Bell. Jud.* ii. 18. 8.

[115] Philo, *In Flaccnm*, Sec. 6, Mang. ii. 523.

[116] *Bell. Jud* ii. 18. 7-8, vii. 10.

[117] Comp. on the Alexandrian persecutions of the Jews, the Rabbinical passages cited by Buxtorf, *Lex. Chald.* col. 99, *s.v.*

[118] Joseph. *Antt.* xii. 1.

[119] *Antt.* xiii. 3. 4. Comp. xii. 1, *fin.*

[120] *Vopisc. vita Saturnini*, c. 8 (in the *Scriptores historiae Augustae*) : nemo illic archisynagogus Judaeorum, nemo Samarites, nemo Christianorum presbyter non mathematicus, non haruspex, non aliptes.

[121] Joseph. *Apion.* ii. 4. Comp. on the history of Cyrenaica, Thrige, *Res Cyrenensium*, Hafniae 1828. Clinton, *Fasti Helleneci*, iii. 394-398. Marquardt, Römische Staatsverwaltung, i. (1881) pp. 457-464, and the literature

According to Strabo, the inhabitants of the city of Cyrene were in Sulla's time (about 85 B.C.) divided into four classes: 1. citizens, 2. agriculturists, 3. *Metoikoi* [resident foreigners], 4. Jews.[122] At that time the Jews were already playing a prominent part in the disturbances in Cyrene, which Lucullus had to allay during his accidental presence there.[123] The Jews at Cyrene seem to have been at all times quite specially disposed to insurrection. In the time of Vespasian the after-piece of the war was played out here,[124] and in the time of Trajan Cyrenaica was a main seat of the great Jewish revolt (see above, Sec. 21).[125] We may also safely assume, that Jewish settlements likewise existed still farther westward. Only single traces of such are however to be discovered with any certainty.[126]

---

there cited. On the geography, Forbiger, *Handb. der alten Geographie*, ii. 825-832.

[122] Strabo in Joseph. *Antt.* xiv. 7. 2.

[123] Strabo in Joseph. *Antt.* xiv. 7. 2. On the doings of Lucullus in Cyrene, see Plutarch. *Lucull.* 2. Marquardt, *Staatsverwaltung*, i. 459. His main object was to requisition ships for Sulla. But he had also internal disturbances to compose, the condition of Cyrene, which was not organized as a province till 74 B.C., being still very disordered.

[124] Joseph. *Bell. Jud.* vii. 11 ; *Vita*, 76.

[125] Comp. on the history of the Jews in Cyrene, 1 Macc. xv. 23 (also above, p. 221) ; *Antt.* xvi. 6. 1, 5; and the inscription of Berenike, *Corp. Inscr. Graec*, n. 5361. Jews of Cyrene are mentioned 2 Macc. ii. 23 (Jason of Cyrene), Matt, xxvii. 32 = Mark xv. 21 = Luke xxiii. 26 (Simon of Cyrene); Acts ii. 10 (Cyrenians at the feast of Pentecost at Jerusalem); Acts vi. 9 (synagogue of the Cyrenians in Jerusalem) ; Acts xi. 20 (Cyrenians come from Jerusalem to Antioch) ; Acts xiii. 1 (Lucius of Cyrene at Antioch).

[126] A Jewish inscription Pompejo Restuto Judeo at Citra, in Leon Renier, *Inscriptions de l'Algerie* (Paris 1855), n. 2072= *Corp. Inscr. Lat.* vol. viii. n. 7155. A pater sinagogae upon an inscription at Sitifis in Mauritania in Orelli-Henzen, *Inscr. Lat.* vol. iii. n. 6145 = *Corp. Inscr. Lat.* vol. viii. n. 8499. That there were Jews in Carthage in Tertullian's time appears from the commencement of his work, *adv. Judaeos*. Freidländer, *De Judaeorum coloniis* (Königsberg *Prog.* 1876), refers to a passage of Procopius (*De aedif.* vi. 2, ed. Dindorf, iii. 334).

The diffusion of the Jews in Greece is already evident from the history of the Apostle Paul, who found Jewish synagogues in Thessalonica, Beroea, Athens and Corinth (Acts xvii. 1, 10, 17, xviii. 4, 7). This is confirmed by the expressions of Agrippa in the above-mentioned epistle to Caligula.[127]

There were also Jews in almost all the islands of the Grecian Archipelago and the Mediterranean Sea, and in some of these in large numbers. In the epistle Euböa, Cyprus and Crete are decidedly mentioned.[128] And if we only know this expressly in a smaller measure of the smaller islands, the reason lies in the scantiness of our sources of information.[129]

In *Italy* Rome was the seat of a Jewish community numbered by thousands.[130] The first appearance of Jews in Rome dates from the time of the Maccabees. Judas Maccabaeus sent an embassy to the Senate to conclude an alliance with Rome, or, to speak more correctly, to obtain an assurance of its friendship and assistance (1 Macc. viii. 17-32).

His brother and successor Jonathan followed his example (1 Macc. xii. 1-4, xvi.). Of greater importance was the embassy,

---

[127] Comp, also *Corp. Inscr. Graec*, vol. iv. n. 9900 (a Jewish inscription at Athens), n. 9896 (at Patras in Achaia).

[128] Philo, *Legat. ad Cajum*, Sec. 36, Mang. ii. 587. Comp. on Cyprus, Acts xiii. 4 sqq. Joseph. *Antt*. 10. 4, and the history of the great insurrection under Trajan (Sec. 21, above); on Crete, Joseph. *Antt*. xvii. 12. 1; *Bell. Jud*. ii. 7. 1; *Vita*, 76.

[129] Comp. 1 Macc. xv. 23 (on this see above, p. 221. Delos, Samos, Cos and Rhodes are named). *Corp. Inscr. Graec*. n. 9894 (a Jewish inscription at Algina); Joseph. *Antt*. xvii. 12, 1; *Bell Jud*. ii. 7. 1 (Melos); *Antt*. xiv. 10. 8 (Paros); *Antt*. xiv. 10. 8 and 14 (Delos); *Antt*. xiv. 7. 2 and 10. 15 (Cos).

[130] Comp. on the Jews in Rome, Migliore, *Ad inscriptionem Flaviue Antoninae commentarius sive de antiquis Judaeis Italicis excrcitatio epigraphica* (MS. of the Vatican library, n. 9143, cited by Engeström). Auer, die Juden in *Rom unmittelbar vor und nach Christi Geburt* (Zeitschr. für die gesammte kathol. Theol. vol. iv. No. 1, 1852, pp. 56-105). Hausrath, *Neutestamentl. Zeitgesch.*, 2nd ed. iii. 383-392 (1st ed. iii, 71-81). Renan, *Paulus*, p. 131 sqq. Engeström, *Om Judarne i Rom under äldre tider och deras katakomber*, Upsala 1876. Huidekoper, *Judaism at Rome*, New York 1876. Schürer, *Die Gemeindeverfassung der Juden in Rom in der Kaiserzeit*, Leipzig 1879. Hamburger, *Real-Enc. für Bibel und Talmud*, Div. ii. pp. 1033-1037 (art. "Rom"). Hild, *Les juifs a Rome devant l'opinion et dans la litterature (Revue des etudes juives*, vol. viii. 1884, pp. 1-37, and continuation). Hudson, *History of the Jews in Rome*, 2nd ed. London 1884 (394 pp.). The works and articles of Levy, Garrucci and others on the inscriptions of the Jewish catacombs in Rome (see above, Sec. 2).

which Simon the third of the Maccabaean brothers sent to Rome in the year 140-139 B.C. It effected an actual offensive and defensive alliance with the Romans (1 Macc. xiv. 24, xv. 15-24).

During their prolonged sojourn at Rome the envoys or their retinue seem also to have attempted a religious propaganda. For it is this that is alluded to in the certainly somewhat confused notice in Valerius Maximus, i. 3. 2.[131] Jupiter Zabazius is indeed a Phrygian deity.[132] Since however *Judaeos* is certified by the text, his appellation in our passage undoubtedly rests upon a confusion of the Jewish *Sabaoth (Zebaoth)* with *Sabazius* (Zebaoth is indeed not a proper name. The Hebrew Jahveh Zebaoth having however been rendered by the LXX. especially in Isaiah).[133]

The event, here related, happened however (according to the immediately preceding words in Valerius Maximus) during the consulate of Popilius Laenas and L. Calpurnius Piso (B.C. 139),

---

[131] There is a large hiatus in the first book of the text of Valerius Maximus. Two extracts from his works, which have been preserved to us, that of Julius Paris and that of Januarius Nepotianus (both given by Mai, *Scriptorum vclerum nova collectio*, iii. 3, 1828) help to fill it up. (For the hiatus, see also Kempt's edition of Valerius Maximus, 1854.) The passage with which we are concerned is given above, according to the extract of Paris. In the extract of Nepotianus this same passage runs as follows : Judaeos quoque, qui Romanis tradere sacra sua conati erant, idem

Hippalus urbe exterminavit ; arasque privatas e publicis locis abiecit. Since then both summarizers have the word *Judaeos*, it must without doubt have existed in Valerius Maximus. It is wanting only in the printed common text derived from a bad transcript from Paris, which I followed in the first edition of this book.

[132] Comp. on Sabazius, Georgii in Pauly's *Real-Enc.* vii. 1, 615-621. Lenormant in the *Revue archeologique* , new series, vol. xxviii. 1874, pp. 300 sqq., 380 sqq., xxix. 1875, p. 43 sqq. On his worship in Rome, Marquardt, *Römische Staatsverwaltung*, iii. 1878, p. 80 sq.; *Corp. Inscr.* Lat. vol. vi. n. 429, 430. Cicero already knows of the Sabazia (De natura deorum, iii. 23. 58).

[133] See *Orac. Sibyll.* i. 304, 316, ii. 240, xii. 132 (ed. Friedlieb, x. 132). Celsus in Origen, c. *Cels.* i. 24, v. 41, 45. The Gnostics in Irenaeus, i. 30. 5; Origen, c. *Cels.* vi. 31, 32; Epiphanius, *haer.* xxvi. 10, xl. 2. Many Gnostics (see Baudissin, *Studien zur semitischen Religionsgeschichte*, No. 1, 1870, p. 187 sqq.); Origen himself, *Exhortatio ad martyrium*, c. 46; Hieronymius, *epist.* 25 *ad Marcellam de decem nominibus Dei (Opp.* ed. Vallarsi, i. 130). Also in similar anonymous treatises on the names of God (Hieronymi *Opp.* ed. Vallarsi, iii. 749 sq. Legarde, *Onomastica sacra*, pp. 160, 205 sq.). The Hebrew Sabbath is certainly out of the question, as it is not possible to see how that could be understood as the name of the Deity.

i.e. exactly at the time of Simon's embassy, to which it is most probably to be referred. It may also be inferred from it, that no Jews then dwelt permanently in Rome.

The settlement there of a great number of Jews dates only from the time of Pompey. After his conquest of Jerusalem in the year 63 B.C., he brought numerous Jewish prisoners of war with him to Rome. They were then sold as slaves; but many of them were soon set at liberty, their strict adherence to their Jewish customs being inconvenient to their masters. Endowed with the privileges of Roman citizenship, they settled beyond the Tiber and formed an independent Jewish community.[134] From that time onwards the Jewish colony in Trastevere formed no unimportant factor in Roman life. When Cicero, in the year 59 B.C., made his oration in defense of Flaccus, we find many Jews present among the auditors.[135]

At the death of Caesar, the great protector of the Jews, a multitude of the latter made lamentation at his bier during whole nights.[136] In the time of Augustus they were already numbered by thousands. Josephus at least tells us that 8000 Roman Jews joined the deputation which came from Palestine to Rome in the year 4 B.C.[137] In the time of Tiberius repressive measures commenced. According to Josephus, the whole Jewish population was banished from Rome A.D. 19, because a few Jews had swindled a noble female proselyte named Fulvia of large sums of money under the pretext of sending them to the temple at Jerusalem.[138]

Four thousand Jews capable of bearing arms were on this account deported to Sardinia to fight against the brigands in that island; the rest were banished from the city. Such are the

---

[134] Philo, *Legat. ad Cajum*, Sec. 23, Mang. ii. 568.
[135] Cicero, *pro Flacco*, 28.
[136] Sueton. *Caesar*, 84.
[137] *Antt.* xvii. 11. 1; *Bell. Jud.* ii. 6. 1.
[138] *Antt.* xviii. 3. 5.

accounts of Tacitus,[139] Suetonius,[140] and Josephus,[141] whose statements essentially agree. According to the contemporary narrative of Philo, these measures were chiefly carried out by the then powerful Sejanus.[142]

After his overthrow, A.D. 31, Tiberius perceived that the Jews had been slandered without cause by Sejanus, and commanded the authorities in all places not to molest the Jews, nor to prevent the practice of their customs.[143] It may here be assumed that a return to Rome was also allowed them; and this explains the fact that Philo should, so early as the time of Caligula, again take for granted the existence of the Jewish community.

The reign of Claudius began with a general Edict of Toleration in favour of the Jews.[144] But this emperor also subsequently found himself obliged to take measures against them. According to the short accounts in the Acts and Suetonius, an actual expulsion of the Jews took place under Claudius.[145]

According however to the evidently more accurate account of Dio Cassius, Claudius only prohibited the assemblies of the Jews, because their expulsion could not be carried out without

---

[139] Annal. ii. 85.

[140] *Vita Tiber.* 36.

[141] Josephus (*Antt.* xviii. 3. 5) says expressly, that 4000 Jews were chosen for military service and sent to Sardinia. Tacitus gives the same number, but speaks of Egyptians and Jews. According to Tacitus, the rest had been expelled from Italy; according to Josephus, only from Rome. Suetonius agrees more with Josephus. On the chronology, comp. Volkmar, *Die Religionsverfolgung unter Kaiser Tiberius und die Chronologie des Fl. Josephus in der Pilatus Periode (Jahrbb. für prot. Theol.* 1885, pp. 136-143). Volkmar correctly concludes, that Josephus (*Antt.* xviii. 3. 5) means the same expulsion of Jews as Tacitus, and that it took place (according to the narrative of Tacitus) A.D. 19.

[142] Euseb. *Chron. ad ann. Abr.* 2050 (ed. Schoene, ii. 150), from the Armenian. Syncellus, ed. Dindorf, i. 621; Hieronymus, *Chron.* (in Euseb. *Chron.* ed. Schoene, ii. 151). The same information, according to the same work of Philo, is also found in Euseb. *Hist. eccl.* ii 5.

[143] Philo, *Legat. ad Cajum*, Sec. 24, ed. Mang. ii. 569.

[144] Joseph. *Antt.* xix. 5. 2, 3.

[145] Acts xviii. 2. Tüfin;. Sueton.

great tumult.[146] This prohibition was indeed equal to a prohibition of the free exercise of their religion, and would certainly have the result of inducing many to leave the city. Its date cannot be accurately determined; it was probably promulgated in the later times of Claudius.[147]

From the words of Suetonius, it might indeed be inferred that it was occasioned by the disturbances, which arose within

---

[146] 'Dio Cass. lx. 6; In Dio Cassius this notice stands at the beginning of the reign of Claudius, while the measure related in the Acts of the Apostles probably took place much later (see note 68). Dio Cassius however is not here giving as yet a chronological narrative, but only describing the general characteristics of Claudius (this to me seems certain notwithstanding the remarks to the contrary of H. Lehmann, *Studien zur Gesch. des apost. Zeitalters*, pp. 2-4. Dio passes over not to a chronological narrative, but to a description of the good side of Claudius). It is not credible that an unfavourable edict against the Jews should be carried into effect in the early days of Claudius, who was just then issuing an edict for their toleration. The edict therefore mentioned by Dio Cassius is most probably identical with that of Suetonius. For it would indeed be strange if one should mention the former and the other the latter. The expulit of Suetonius must be understood according to the analogy of Suetonius. The expulsion was indeed contemplated, but when it was perceived that it would encounter difficulties, it was abandoned. This also explains the silence of Tacitus and Josephus.

[147] The year might be accurately determined if this edict were identical with that mentioned by Tacitus of the year 52. Tac. *Annal*, xii. 52. But the *mathematici* cannot possibly mean the Jewish community at Rome. In the Chronicle of Eusebius and Jerome the expulsion of the Jews by Claudius is not mentioned. Orosius alone, vii. 6. 15 (ed. Zangemeister, 1882), gives a precise date for this edict: Anno ejusdem nono expulsos per Claudium Urbe Judaeos Josephus refert. Since however Josephus makes no mention at all of the matter, the statement is certainly incorrect with respect to authority and therefore probably unreliable with respect to matter. It is moreover probable, from the connection of the Acts of the Apostles (observe the Greek in Acts xviii. 2), that the edict was issued about A.D. 50-52. Comp. in general. Anger, *De temporum in actis apostolorum ratione* (1833), p. 116 sqq. Wieseler, *Chronologie des apostol. Zeitalters*, pp. 120-128. Winer, *RWB*. i. 231 sq. (art. "Claudius"). H. Lehmann, *Studien zur Geschichte des apostolischen Zeitalters* (1856), pp. 1-9. Lewin, *Fasti Sacri* (London 1865), n. 1773, 1774. Keim, art. " Claudius," in Schenkel's *Bibellex*.

Judaism in consequence of the preaching of Christ.[148] This edict of Claudius had also but transient consequences. Such measures were not capable of extirpating the firmly rooted Jewish community, or of even permanently weakening it. It was already, chiefly by means of its numerous proselytes, too much intertwined with Roman life for its complete suppression to be successful. The Jews, when expelled from the city, emigrated to the neighbourhood, perhaps to Aricia,[149] soon to return thence to their old abodes. Their history in Rome may be summed up in the words of Dio Cassius: **Often suppressed, they nevertheless mightily increased, so that they achieved even the free exercise of their customs.**[150]

The aristocratic Roman indeed looked down upon them with contempt. But the numerous lampoons of the satirists are just so many evidences of the notice they attracted in Roman society.[151] Even from the time of Augustus, direct relations of Jews to the imperial court are not lacking; nay, in the reign of Nero, the Empress Poppaea seems herself to have been inclined to Judaism.[152]

---

[148] On Chrestus = Cristus, see Hug, *Einl. in das N. T.* (4th ed.) ii 335. Credner, *Einl. in das N. T.* p. 381. Hilgenfeld, *Einl. in das N. T.* p. 303 sq. Huidekoper, *Judaism at Rome*, p. 220 sq.

[149] This is intimated by the scholiast on Juvenal, iv. 117: qui ud portam Aricinam sive ad clivum mendicaret inter Judaeos, qui ad Ariciam transierant ex Urbe missi.

[150] Die Cass, xxxvii. 17.

[151] On the social position of the Jews in Rome, see the literature cited above, note 52, especially Hausrath, *Neutestamentl. Zeitgesch.* 2nd ed. iii. 383-392.

[152] The Greek names borne by two Jewish communities in Rome (see below, No. 2), point to the relations of Jews to Augustus and Agrippa. The Empress Livia had a Jewish female slave of the name of Akme (Joseph. *Antt.* xvii. 5. 7; *Bell. Jud.* i. 32. 6, 33. 7). Upon an inscription of the time of Claudius, a [Cl]audia Aster [Hi]erosoly mitana [ca]ptiva, evidently a Jewish female slave of Claudius, is mentioned (Orelli-Henzen, *Inscr. Lat.* n. 5302 = Mommsen, *Inscr. Regni Neap.* n. 6467 = *Corp. Inscr. Lat.* vol. x. n. 1971). We find a Jewish comedian Alityrus at the court of Nero (Joseph. *Vita*, 3). Tacitus, *Annal.* xvi. 6, remarks of her, that after her death she was not burnt according to Roman custom, but embalmed "after the fashion of foreign kings." The Jewish historian Josephus lived in Rome under Vespasian, Titus, and Domitian, honoured and assisted by the kindness of all three emperors (Joseph. *Vita*, 76). In the person of Domitian's cousin Flavius Clemens, not Judaism indeed, but Christianity, which proceeded from Judaism, penetrated even the imperial family (for so are Dio Cass. lxvii. 14, and Sueton. *Domit.* 15, now universally and correctly understood). Of later date may perhaps be mentioned also the Jewish playfellow (conlusor) of

By degrees they spread farther in the city also. The quarter in Trastevere was no longer their only one. We find them subsequently in the Campus Martius, and in the midst of the Roman commercial world in the Subura. Juvenal jests at the fact, that the sacred grove of Egeria, before the Porta Capeno, was leased to Jews and swarmed with Jewish beggars (*Sat.* iii. 12-16). The settlement of Jews in various quarters of the town, and their continued prosperity down to the later imperial times, are also especially evidenced by Jewish burying-grounds, some of them the discovery of recent times.

Of these, the five following are now known:[153] (1) A somewhat insignificant cemetery before the Porta Portuensis, discovered by Bosio in the year 1602. This was certainly the burial-place of the Jews in Trastevere.

The knowledge of the locality was afterwards lost, and all efforts for its re-discovery have hitherto been unsuccessful.[154] (2) A large cemetery, discovered in the beginning of the sixth decade of this century, on the Via Appia in the Vigna Randanini

Caracalla (Spartian. *Caracalla*, 1 ; also Gorres, Zeitschr. f. Wissenschaftl. Theol. 1884, p. 147 sqq.). We must remember too the active relations of Herod and his dynasty with Augustus and his successors. Most of Herod's sons were brought up at Rome. Agrippa I. spent the greater part of his life in Rome, remaining there till his nomination as king; as a boy he was on terms of friendship with Drusus, the son of Tiberius (Joseph. *Antt.* xviii. 6. 1), and afterwards with Caligula. The intimate relations of Agrippa II. and Berenice with Vespasian and Titus are well known; and lastly, it is worthy of remark how frequently the Gentile names of emperors are found among Jewish names upon inscriptions. The following occur, and that in tolerably large numbers: Julius, Claudius, Flavius, Aelius, Aurelius, Valerius. Even though these names may frequently refer not to the old families, but to later emperors (Constantine the Great's full name *e.g.* being C. Flavius Valerius Aurelius Claudius Const.), still they certainly prove a close relation of the Jews to the emperors. Comp. also Harnack's article on the Christians at the imperial court (*Princeton Review*, July 1878, pp. 239-280).

[153] Comp. the summary in Kraus, *Roma Sotterranea* (1st. ed. 1873), p. 489 sq.; and in Caspari, *Quellen zur Gesch. des Taufsymbols*, iii. 1875, p. 271 sq.

[154] Garrucci, *Cimitero degli antichi Ebrei*, p. 3.

(somewhat farther out than the catacomb of Callistus). To it we owe our acquaintance with a large number of Romano-Jewish inscriptions.[155] (3) In the year 1867 (or 1866) a Jewish cemetery, of which de Rossi gives a short account, was discovered in the vineyard of Count Cimarra, also on the Via Appia, nearly opposite the catacomb of Callistus.[156] (4) A Jewish cemetery on the Via Labicana, therefore in the neighbourhood of the Esquinal and Viminal, of perhaps the date of the Antonines, was pointed out by Marucchi in the year 1883.[157] (5) There was also in Porto (at the mouth of the Tiber) a Jewish cemetery, from which are derived many of the Jewish epitaphs with which we have for a long time been acquainted.[158] The antiquity of this cemetery, and of the inscriptions contained in it, can only be approximately determined. They may date chiefly from the second to the fourth centuries after Christ.

Besides Jews properly so called, there were in Rome (as in Alexandria) Samaritans also. A Samaritan of the name of Thallus, a freedman of the Emperor Tiberius, once lent a large sum to Agrippa I, in Rome.[159] The existence of a Samaritan community in Rome, in the time of the Ostrogoth king

---

[155] Comp. Garrucci, *Cimitero degli antichi Ebrei scoperto recentemente in Vigna Randanini*, Rome 1862. The same, *Dissertazioni archeologiche di vario argomento*, vol. ii. Roma 1865, pp. 150-192. On the situation of the cemetery, see the plan in De Rossi, *Bulletino di Archeologia cristiana* (1st series), vol. v. 1867, p. 3, and the explanation, p. 16.

[156] De Rossi, *Bullettino*, v. 16.

[157] Marucchi in de Rossi's *Bullettino*, 1883, p. 79 sq.

[158] See de Rossi, *Bulletino*, iv. 1866, p. 40. The inscriptions known down to the year 1850 are collected in *Corp. Inscr. Graec.* vol. iv. n. 9901 9926. Comp. the literature on the inscriptions, Sec. 2, above.

[159] Joseph. *Antt.* xviii. 6. 4.

Theodoric, is evidenced by a letter of this king to the knight Arigernus, which is embodied in the collection of letters of Cassiodorus.[160] That the Samaritans were by no means without importance in the Roman Empire in later imperial times, is shown by the frequent reference to them in imperial legislation.[161]

After the Jewish community in Rome, that of Puteoli (Dikäarchia) is presumably the most ancient in Italy. In this chief trading port of Italy with the East, we find Jews so early as B.C. 4, immediately after the death of Herod the Great.[162] Their presence cannot be pointed out in other parts of Italy till later imperial times; this does not however permit any negative inference as to the date of their settlement.[163]

Much material in the way of inscriptions has recently been furnished especially by the discovery of the catacomb of *Venosa* (Venusia in Apulia, the birthplace of Horace). Its inscriptions in Greek, Latin and Hebrew are, according to Mommsen's judgment, of the sixth century after Christ.[164] We

---

[160] Cassiodor. *Variarum*, iii. 45.

[161] *Codex Theodosianus* (ed. Haenel), xiii. 5. 18, xvi. 8. 16, u. 28. *Novell. Justin.* 129, u. 144.

[162] Joseph. *Antt.* xvii. 12. 1; *Bell. Jud.* ii. 7. 1. There was also a Christian church here so early as A.D. 61 (Acts xxviii. 13, 14).

[163] See the information in Friedländer, *Darstellungen aus der Sittengeschichte Roms*, vol. iii. (1871) pp. 511, 512. The same, *De Judaeorum* DIV. II. VOL. II. Q *coloniis* (Königsberg *Progr.* 1876), pp. 1, 2. Renan, *L'Antichrist* (1873), p. 8. For Lower Italy, also Ascoli, *Iscrizioni* (1880), pp. 33-38. The places in which they are found are especially the following: Genoa (Cassiodor. *Variar.* ii. 27), Milan (Cassiodor. *Variar.* v. 37), Brescia (inscription, *Corp. Inscr. Lat.* vol. v. n. 4411), Aquileia (Roman inscription in Garrucci, *Cimitero*, p. 62), Bologna (Ambrosius, *Exhortatio virginitatis*, c. 1), Ravenna (*Anonymus Valesii* cc. 81-82, in the appendix to most editions of Ammianus Marcellinus), Capua (inscription in Mommsen, *Inscr. Regni Neap.* 3657 = *Corp. Inscr. Lat.* vol. x. n. 3905), Naples (*Procop. Bell. Gotth.* i. 8 and 10, ed. Dindorf, vol. ii. pp. 44 and 53), Venosa (see next note), Syracuse (inscription, *Corp. Inscr. Graec*, n. 9895), Palermo, Messina, Agrigentam (*Letters of Gregory the Great*). In Apulia and Calabria the official posts of the different communities could not be regularly filled up, because the Jewish inhabitants refused to undertake them (edict of the Emperors Honorius and Arcadius of the year 398 in the *Codex Theodosianus*, xii 1.158.

[164] The catacomb was discovered as early as 1853, and described in two memoirs (by De Angelis and Smith and by D'Aloe). The MSS. of both memoirs however lay

likewise meet with Jewish communities in various parts of Gaul and Spain in later imperial times. In respect of dates, what has been said with regard to Italy holds good here also.[165]

THE ONGOING DISPERSION

The Diaspora of the Jews since the time of Christ is represented by the following maps. These maps are sketchy at best and don't account for the whereabouts of various Jewish communities identified in Schürer's research.

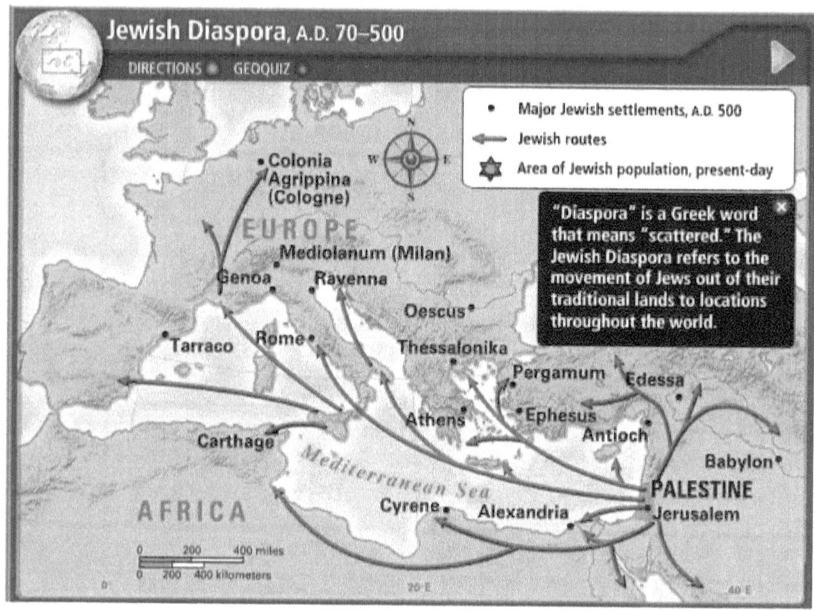

Figure 32 Jewish Diaspora, A.D. 70-500[166]

---

buried in the archives of the museum at Naples, till their contents were recently made known (1) in Ascoli's *Iscrizioni inedite o mal note greche latine ebraiche di antichi sepolchri giudaici del Napolitano*, Torino e Roma, 1880, and (2) in *Corp. Inscr. Lat.* vol. ix. (1883), n. 6195-6214, comp. 647, 648. Hirschfeld had already given a short notice on the catacomb (*Bullettino dell' Instituto di corrisp. archeol.* 1867, pp. 148-152). Comp. also *Theol. Literaturztg.* 1880, pp. 485-488. Grätz, *Monatsschr.* 1880, p. 433 sqq. Lenormant, *La catacombe juive de Venosa* (*Revue des etudes juives*, vol. vi. n. 12, 1883, pp. 200-207). Besides the inscriptions in the catacomb, dated Hebrew epitaphs of Venosa of the ninth century are also known. See Ascoli's above-named work; *Theol. Litztg.* 1880, p. 485.

[165] See the information in Friedländer's above-named work. With respect to Spain, we mention only the inscription *Corp. Inscr. Lat.* vol. ii. n 1982.

[166] https://www.slideshare.net/srgeorgi/judaism-slides.

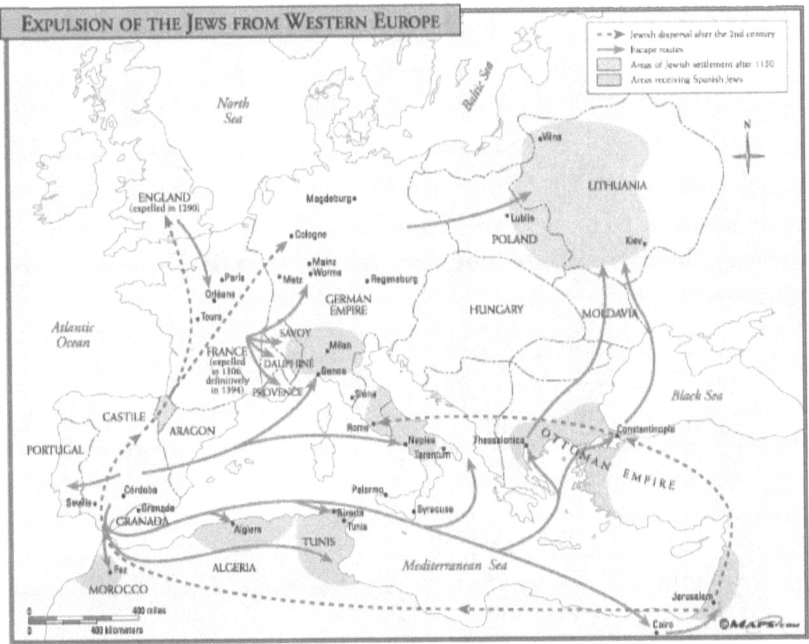

Figure 33 Expulsion of the Jews from Western Europe.[167]

Known to most readers, the Jews were then expelled from Western Europe during the *Fiddler on the Roof* wave of persecution that lasted throughout the span of the Great Wars. Since then, many Jews who survived the U.S.S.R. have, since their release, relocated—many to Israel.

Yes, we have, as in the prior chapter, moved far beyond the Second Temple period in order to bring the present state of the House of Judah up to date. As we see that Day approaching, two things should be remembered:

1. In the Second Commandment, God says: "I, the Lord your God, am a jealous God, punishing the children for the sin of the parents to the third and fourth generation of those who hate me, but showing love **to a thousand generations of those who love me and keep my commandments**" (Exod. 20:5-6). A thousand

---

[167] https://www.pinterest.com/pin/258323728598619421. It has been commented on Pinterest that this map does not show enough influx into Germanic areas and also does not show the expulsion of the Jews from several German cities and states that occurred in the Middle Ages. It was this German Jewish population that formed the bulk of the Polish and Lithuanian Jews.

generations! That should have God's chosen, His elect, His people, covered through the end of this Age.

2. God will never lose track of the plight and whereabouts of the two houses of Israel—the cast away, swallowed up, "**outcast**," House of Israel, nor the "**dispersed**" House of Judah.

We know this to be true from Isaiah's prophecy of the Day of Gathering from the **four corners of the earth** (Isaiah 11:10-12, emphasis added:

10 "And in that day there shall be a Root of Jesse,
Who shall stand as a banner to the people;
For the Gentiles shall seek Him,
And His resting place shall be glorious."

11 It shall come to pass in that day
That the Lord shall set His hand again the second time
To recover the remnant of His people who are left,
From Assyria and Egypt,
From Pathros and Cush,

From Elam and Shinar,
From Hamath and the islands of the sea.

12 He will set up a banner for the nations,
And will assemble the **outcasts of Israel**,
And gather together the **dispersed of Judah**
From the four corners of the earth.

We began our study using the analogy where doctors must first have a proper diagnosis if they are to properly prescribe the remedy. We have indeed seen, through the plethora of evidence, that there has been a forgotten age of Judah and an untold story of grace in the second temple period.

Part of our diagnosis revealed how Mainstream Christianity has overlooked the covenantal good standing of Judah at the time of Christ because it has chosen to ignore God's dealing with the two houses of Israel. The failure to see that a major thrust of Jesus' ministry was repairing the broken relationship with the house of Israel has led to Replacement theology (Supersessionism), which has led to aberrant theologies such as Calvinism (predestination) and its other extreme of Arminianism. It also led to false teachings such as Marcionism, antinomianism, and horrific and unfathomable acts of anti-Judaism, pogroms, the inquisition, and the holocaust. Our diagnosis in a nutshell, is mainstream Christianity has overlooked the covenantal good standing of Judah at the time of Christ because it has chosen to ignore God's dealing with the two houses of Israel.

With the diagnosis in hand, we can now prescribe a treatment, which is, the Church needs to reconsider how it sees the Jews. For our Replacement theology brethren, they need to see that the church has not replaced Israel. For our Dispensational brethren, they need to see that God does not have two different peoples with two different programs, different gospels. We in the church need to see that Judah was in good standing (on the national covenant level) before Jesus came. People like Zachariah and Elizabeth and Simeon were righteous and just. However, when Jesus came, the national leadership in Jerusalem rejected the stone that became the chief cornerstone, which changed their national standing.

We in the church also need to change our views of the Torah (laws) which God spoke through Moses. We need to understand that God has not done away with those, and Jesus did not come to abolish the commandments but to fulfill, that is, to show us how to walk them out in our lives. The laws were not nailed to the cross as some erroneously claim! Jesus died to repair the relationship with the house of Israel, not to free us from His own commandments.

In the end, we in the church need to repent of the attitude that we have corporately had toward the Jews and understand that we are being grafted back into the green olive tree. Those from a Dispensational background should also realize that the Old Testament prophets had a very good idea what they were writing; and that the Jews understood on a heart level what they were reading or hearing read. For instance, when the 23rd Psalm was composed, the psalmist knew the Lord to be his shepherd/provider/protector—he knew the Lord personally. And the same goes for all the Psalms, the Prophets, and the books of the Old Testament. Certainly, believers in Christ see things more clearly, but will as the devout Jews of the Second Temple era, see "as through a mirror dimly" until we are all perfected together ("God having provided something better for us, that they should not be made perfect apart from us" Heb. 11:40).

The Jews returning to the Holy Land after the Babylonian captivity were zealous to keep the Law so that they might please God and thereby continue to abide in the Promised Land without invoking God's anger as in their former disobedience. Seeing the example of the castaway House of Israel, Judah assessed that genetic inheritance alone— claiming Abraham was their father—could not guarantee they would remain "set apart," elect. Not even the Davidic Covenant and looking to "the temple of the Lord, the temple of the Lord" had kept the Jews from being removed from the Land. Therefore, what came to be known as the Traditionalists, or orthodox Jews, believed their election was also tied to keeping God's laws. (Recall, from our discussion of the Passover, Polycrates stated: "All these observed the fourteenth day of the Passover according to the Gospel, deviating in no respect, but following the **rule of faith**. (Faith, in the nascent assembly of Christ, did not stand apart or in opposition to the Law.) The Traditionalists understood, from the time they returned under Ezra's leadership, that they were returning from captivity as an olive tree with only a little "green" left intact.

During the last centuries of the Second Temple period—the Hellenistic period—the Hellenistic Jews saw that their priesthood had been corrupted by political intervention and became disillusioned with the traditional religious system. Historians often blame the appeal of the Greek culture without considering the breakdown in the Jews' own religion. Nevertheless, for however many reasons, the Hellenistic Jews turned away from Jewish customs and tended toward Hellenism. They continued to identify as "set apart" Jews but more or less replaced strict obedience to the Law with a determination to honor the Monotheistic God of Abraham, Isaac, and Jacob; as opposed to the plethora of gods and goddesses of the Greco-Roman pantheon.

Archaeological discoveries have revealed tangible evidence of Hellenistic-era synagogues, which the Bible documents were already existing at the time of Christ. The image below shows a synagogue in Cilicia that may have been one of the many synagogues, built in the Hellenic Age, visited by Paul. A nearby Greek inscription offers solid evidence of a Jewish community with a synagogue at the site. Based on the architecture and weathering of the structure, Mark Fairchild dates it to the Hellenistic period.[168]

Figure 34. Stone door lintel inscribed with a menorah (see lower left in photo.), Catioren, Cilicia.

---

[168]https://www.biblicalarchaeology.org/daily/biblical-sites-places/biblical-archaeology-sites/the-lost-sites-of-ancient-cilicia

As the Second Temple period was coming to a close, the Hellenistic Jews of Antioch would discover through the preaching of Paul and Barnabas that a new, permanent, and incorruptible High Priest had come to replace the, then, disconnected lineages of Aaron and Levi:

And inasmuch as He was not made priest without an oath, for they have become priests without an oath, but He with an oath by Him who said to Him:

"The Lord has sworn
And will not relent,
'You are a priest forever
According to the order of Melchizedek'" (Heb. 7:20-21)

We have such a **High Priest**, who is seated at the right hand of the throne of the Majesty in the heavens, a Minister of the sanctuary and of the true tabernacle which the Lord erected, and not man (Heb. 8:1-2).

Moreover, "you also, as living stones, are being built up a spiritual house, a holy priesthood, to offer up spiritual sacrifices acceptable to God through Jesus Christ" (1 Pet. 2:5).

Furthermore, the Antiochian Hellenists would learn that a new temple for the Holy Spirit to indwell was also being fitted together:

"...do you not know that your **body is the temple of the Holy Spirit** who is in you, whom you have from God..." (1 Cor. 6:19).

Below are Paul's words to the Gentiles of Ephesus, but verses 20-21of Eph. 2:19-22 would have been equally applicable to the Hellenistic Jews:

19 Now, therefore, you are no longer strangers and foreigners, but fellow citizens with the saints and members of the household of God, 20 having been built on the foundation of the apostles and prophets, Jesus Christ Himself being the chief cornerstone, 21 in whom **the whole building, being fitted together, grows into a holy temple** in the Lord, 22 in whom you also are being built together for **a dwelling place of God in the Spirit.**

How is it that the Antiochian Christians, then having a High Priest and a temple, would be reluctant to embrace God's laws? By the second century A.D., the Roman Empire was struggling to deal with the Jews and their peculiar laws. The Empire, for a while, learned to accommodate various religions. But governments, in general, prefer to have only one set of laws, and God's laws were detestable to everyone but the Jews.

As we have seen in the body of this book, even King Hezekiah was influenced by international ideology. It is, then, not hard to imagine the pressures of the Roman Empire that would influence God's followers to reject God's laws. And this is exactly what we have seen in the letters of Ignatius of Antioch.

International pressures have also influenced Christian theologies, which tend toward the reduced requirements of Acts 15: "to lay upon you no greater burden than these necessary things: that you abstain from things offered to idols, from blood, from things strangled, and from sexual immorality" (Acts 15:28b-29). And these same international powers have encouraged the rejection of the Jews; and along with the Jews, they have created and furthered a theology and history—through the Church Fathers—that has contaminated the ongoing relationship between Christians and Jews. But God is able to overturn the counsel of the World-rulers: "The Lord brings the counsel of the nations to nothing; He makes the plans of the peoples of no effect. The counsel of the Lord stands forever, the plans of His heart to all generations" (Ps. 33:10-11).

We trust that telling the untold story of grace in the Second Temple period has had, and will continue to have, a positive impact on a personal level and on Christian theology as a whole. We hope, as well, that the Jewish reader will be pleased that a more truthful and honest account of the Jewish past is now being recognized by a growing contingency of Christians. The forgotten age of Judah's good standing in the Second Temple period should not have been overlooked for the last two millennia; and now it has been remembered!

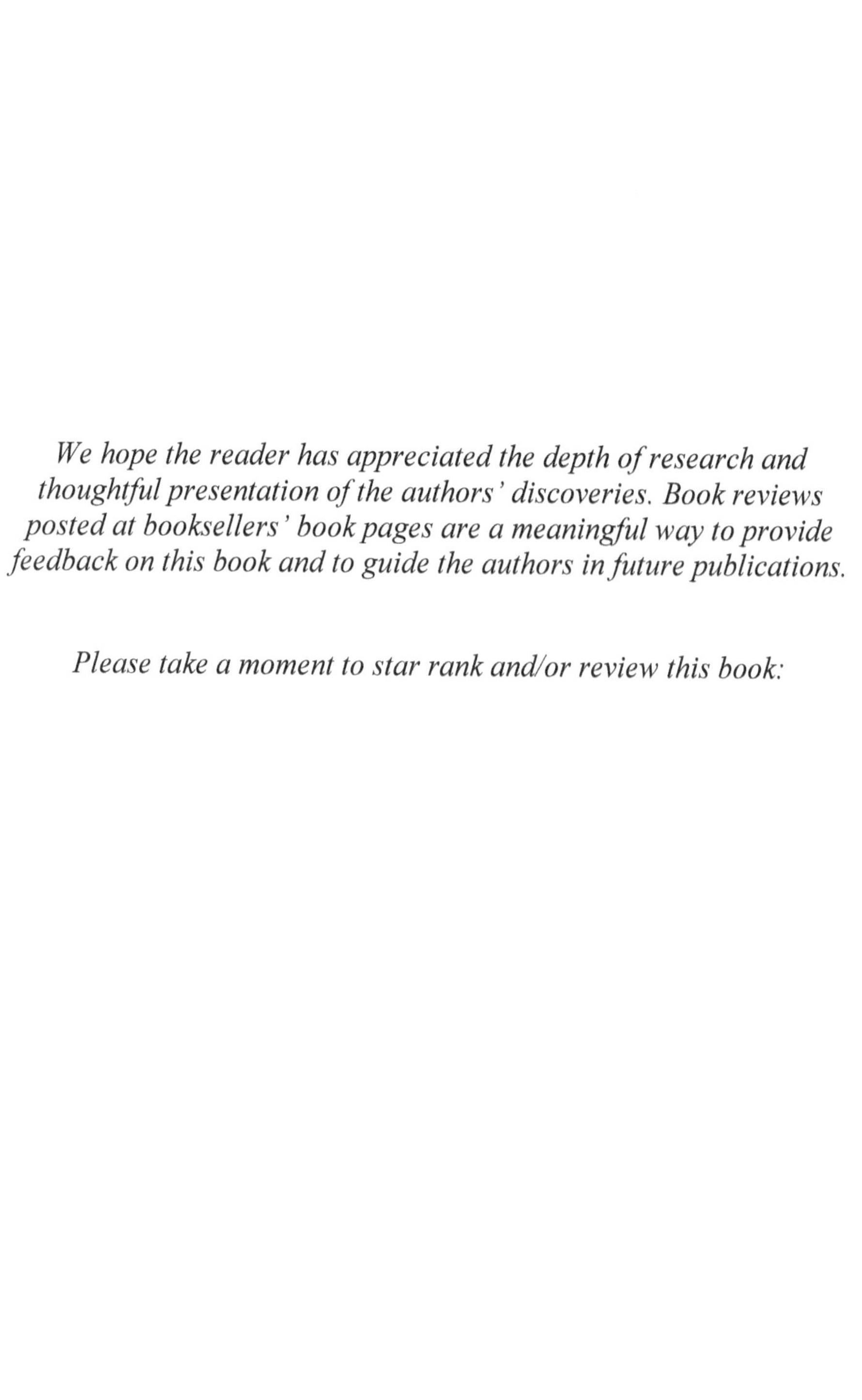

We hope the reader has appreciated the depth of research and thoughtful presentation of the authors' discoveries. Book reviews posted at booksellers' book pages are a meaningful way to provide feedback on this book and to guide the authors in future publications.

Please take a moment to star rank and/or review this book:

About the Authors

Dr. Douglas Hamp, M.A., PhD.

Dr. Hamp earned his M.A. in the Bible and its World from the Hebrew University of Jerusalem and PhD in Biblical Studies from Louisiana Baptist University. He served as a pastor at Calvary Chapel Costa Mesa, CA where he lectured and developed curriculum at the School of Ministry, Spanish School of Ministry and Calvary Chapel Bible College Graduate School. He has authored numerous books, articles, & DVDs and has appeared on TV, radio, and online in English and in Spanish. He pastors the Way Congregation in Lakewood, CO, USA.

Chris Winters Steinle

Author, Christian Philosopher, Former Minister, CPA.

Chris Steinle is a recognized Bible prophecy commentator as a guest and co-host on alternative media as well as the author of more than ten books. (C.W.) Steinle began his professional career as a CPA. The ability to analyze and organized information is crucial in rightly dividing the Word of God. As a layman and ordained minister Steinle has taught thousands of original Bible studies, as well as providing biblical guidance to singles, couples, and families. Chris has taught on location in Israel, Philippi, Thessaloniki, Corinth, Athens, and Egypt. Currently he is intensely vested in the Commonwealth of Israel Foundation and the production of a Commonwealth Reference Bible featuring Commonwealth Theology.

ABOUT THE COMMONWEALTH OF ISRAEL FOUNDATION

The Commonwealth of Israel Foundation is a non-profit religious charitable organization. Please visit CommonwealthOfIsrael.com or .org for details about the Foundation's formation, purpose and goals.

Around the time Douglas Krieger released his book on Commonwealth Theology in early 2018 it became apparent within the burgeoning Commonwealth of Israel Movement that a reference-notes study Bible would be advantageous. Indeed, Protestant/Reformed and Dispensation Theology—the immediate predecessors to Commonwealth Theology—both disseminated their views to the pulpit through the publication of reference Bibles; the Geneva Study Bible and the Scofield Reference Bible, respectively.

Thus, this Foundation was birthed with its primary educational objective being the production of an annotated reference/study-notes Bible. The Bible will present readers with a comprehensive application of Commonwealth Theology to the sixty-six canonical books generally accepted as inspired scriptures.

The Commonwealth of Israel Foundation may also produce, or cause to be produced for the purpose of biblical education, reference or annotated New Testaments, Bible commentaries on individual books of the Bible, commentary sets, original translations of the Bible, and other forms of biblical education which would further our educational and public awareness objectives.

All proceeds from the sale of this publication will be applied toward the purposes of the Commonwealth of Israel Foundation.

Please consider further supporting the Foundation at our website https://commonwealthofisrael.com/donate.html or at the address below. If you have questions or comments please contact us:

info@commonwealthofisrael.org

or write:

Commonwealth of Israel Foundation
P.O. Box 31007
Phoenix, AZ 85046

Also find us on Facebook:

https://www.facebook.com/commonwealthofisraelfoundation